LEARNING POLITENESS

CONTEMPORARY STUDIES IN DESCRIPTIVE LINGUISTICS

VOL. 24

Edited by

DR GRAEME DAVIS & KARL A. BERNHARDT

PETER LANG

Oxford · Bern · Berlin · Bruxelles · Frankfurt am Main · New York · Wien

Ian Walkinshaw

LEARNING POLITENESS

DISAGREEMENT IN A SECOND LANGUAGE

PETER LANG

Oxford · Bern · Berlin · Bruxelles · Frankfurt am Main · New York · Wien

Bibliographic information published by Die Deutsche Bibliothek
Die Deutsche Bibliothek lists this publication in the Deutsche National-
bibliografie; detailed bibliographic data is available on the Internet at ‹http://
dnb.ddb.de›.

A catalogue record for this book is available from The British Library.

Library of Congress Cataloging-in-Publication Data:

Walkinshaw, Ian.
  Learning politeness : disagreement in a second language / Ian Walkinshaw.
     p. cm. – (Contemporary studies in descriptive linguistics)
  Includes bibliographical references and index.
  ISBN 978-3-03911-527-3 (alk. paper)
  1. Japanese language–Honorific. 2. Translating and interpreting. I. Title.
  PL629.H65W35 2008
  495.6'5–dc21

                              2008051288

ISSN 1660-9301
ISBN 978-3-03911-527-3

© Peter Lang AG, International Academic Publishers, Bern 2009
Hochfeldstrasse 32, Postfach 746, CH-3000 Bern 9, Switzerland
info@peterlang.com, www.peterlang.com, www.peterlang.net

Printed in Germany

Acknowledgements

I am indebted to many people and institutions that have assisted me in my research. I am particularly grateful to the Japanese and New Zealand participants who contributed their time and effort to assist me in collecting data for this study. I owe a special debt of gratitude to my two supervisors, Professor Janet Holmes and Dr Jonathan Newton, for their scholarship, guidance and support when I was writing the doctoral thesis upon which this book is based. I would also like to express my thanks to the staff of the School of Linguistics and Applied Language Studies at Victoria University of Wellington, for their support and assistance.

I would like to express my appreciation to the following language schools for their enthusiastic support for this project: Achievement Institute of Language, the University of Canterbury English Language Centre, Christchurch College of English Language, Aspect ILA, Seafield School of English, and also Southern English School. Thanks also to the Audiovisual Services Department and the Department of Linguistics at the University of Canterbury.

I owe a debt of gratitude to the following people who were instrumental in innumerable ways in helping me to complete this project: Glenys Bagnall, Craig Breach and Colleen Biggs, Sally Brown, Carmen Rosa Caldas-Coulthard, Duong Thi Hoang Oanh, Linda Edwards, Ben Fenton-Smith, John Haywood, Meg Harvey, Jonny Grady, Angela Joe, Tony Kan, Kon Kuiper, Meredith Marra, Michael O'Sullivan, Kate Quigley, Tony Quinn, John Read, Stephanie Stadler, Kaye Stewart, Sonia Sonoko Strain, James Stuart, and also Helen Wells.

Thanks very much to my colleagues at the Faculty of Foreign Languages and Asian Studies, Nagoya University of Commerce and Business, and also to those at the Vietnam-USA Society English Training Service Centre.

Additionally, I'd like to thank Graeme Davis, Alexis Kirschbaum, Alan Mauro, Nick Reynolds, Shirley Walker Werrett and the other staff at Peter Lang AG for their assistance in publishing this manuscript in book form.

I am grateful to Juliane House, Cynthia White and Elaine Vine for their detailed and constructive comments on an earlier version of this work when it was submitted for examination as a PhD thesis. Special thanks to Juliane House for allowing me to use an excerpt from her report for promotional purposes.

Finally and most importantly, my sincere gratitude is due to my wife, Yukiko, and to my family, who supported me in so many ways through the various ups and downs of this project. I don't know how I'd have done it without you.

Contents

Preface

Japanese learners of English have generally been a very well-represented ethnic group in New Zealand English language schools. In their daily interactions in New Zealand, the Japanese students are likely to experience sociopragmatic and pragmalinguistic behaviour which may differ significantly from that which is typical in Japanese society. In particular, interpreting negatively affective speech acts such as complaints, refusals and disagreements, and expressing them in a manner that is appropriately polite, is likely to pose problems. At present relatively little is known about the extent to which Japanese learners of English experience pragmatic failure in their interactions with New Zealanders, or the contexts in which such failures most frequently occur.

This book reports on the findings of a research project to understand how Japanese learners of English used a range of disagreement speech act strategies when they were involved in situations of disagreement with native speakers of New Zealand English. The focus was on how well learners could identify and interpret disagreeing utterances, and also on how well they expressed and negotiated them. Three facets of the learners' ability were tested: their capacity to identify and accurately interpret disagreements in conversations between native speakers; to produce disagreement utterances which were sociopragmatically appropriate; and to interpret / produce disagreement utterances in an open role-play situation.

The participants in this study were 14 Japanese learners of English who were studying at several language schools in Christchurch, New Zealand. Their ability to interpret disagreement speech acts was measured through a video judgment task, and their ability to express such speech acts was measured using a discourse completion task and a role-play task.

The study demonstrated that the Japanese learners of English, contrary to stereotype, could be quite direct when disagreeing with a native speaker whom they did not know well, but tended to be less direct when disagreeing with someone whom they knew well. By the same token, the Japanese learners of English often used linguistically complex and pragmatically sophisticated politeness strategies when disagreeing with a native speaker they did not know, but the politeness strategies selected tended to be simple and straightforward when they had an established relationship with their interlocutor. A similar, though less marked, trend was present in situations of equal and unequal power: in power-equal exchanges, the Japanese learners of English were often quite direct and used relatively complex politeness strategies, whereas in power-unequal exchanges they were often less direct and used simple, straightforward politeness strategies.

The Japanese learners of English appeared to perceive power-equal situations and high social-distance situations as having a lower potential for causing loss of face. This in turn may have allowed them to attempt newly-acquired, relatively complex politeness strategies in such situations without obligation to be indirect to their interlocutor. The low threat to face may also have lessened the consequences of using these politeness strategies erroneously.

For ESOL teachers, the findings of this study emphasise the importance of familiarity with form, function and context of a speech act in order for language learners to communicate successfully. This study also stresses the value of understanding a target culture's politeness norms.

List of figures

List of tables

1 Introduction

1.1 Rationale for research

I lived for eight years in Japan, teaching and interacting with Japanese learners of English. My interest in researching negatively affective speech act strategies originates from three aspects of this experience. Firstly, it stems from observing how Japanese learners / speakers of English manage these negative speech acts during conversation with native speakers of English. Secondly, it stems from my own experience as a learner of Japanese as a second language, in which I made countless mistakes through misinterpretation of politeness strategies. Thirdly, it comes from my experience as an ESOL teacher in Japan and New Zealand, where I was conscious of numerous deficiencies in the teaching of politeness strategies, and insufficient understanding of the appropriate use of such strategies in negatively affective interaction. These observations led to concerns that inappropriate use or erroneous interpretation of politeness strategies could propagate misconceptions and stereotypes about Japanese people in general and Japanese learners of English in particular.

Until quite recently, Japanese learners of English were the single largest group in New Zealand language schools. Although there is now quite an eclectic mix of nationalities among second language learners, Japanese learners of English still comprise a high percentage of students at most language schools in New Zealand. Their daily interactions in New Zealand involve conversations with their homestay hosts, interactions with their teachers, with New Zealand friends and acquaintances, and with shop assistants and service personnel. They are also exposed to English through broadcasting and print media. In all these contexts, Japanese students are exposed to sociopragmatic and pragmalinguistic behaviour which can differ markedly from that which is the norm in Japanese society.

One of the areas identified by a great deal of previous research as an area of cross-cultural pragmatic difficulty is that of linguistic politeness (Beebe, Takahashi and Uliss-Weltz 1990; Blum-Kulka 1987; Chen 1993; DuFon 1999; Kasper 1990). Linguistic politeness is concerned with maintaining an interlocutor's *face* during an interaction, i.e.

> the positive social value a person effectively claims for himself by the line others assume he has taken during a particular contact. Face is an image of self delineated in terms of approved social attributes (Goffman 1967: 5).

In particular, acquiring proficiency in appropriately interpreting and expressing speech acts with the potential to damage harmonious relations between interlocutors (referred to as Face-Threatening Acts, or FTAs) frequently poses difficulties, because the sociolinguistic norms of politeness in Japanese are often very different from those of most English-speaking nations. Negatively affective speech acts, such as refusal, complaint and apology, appear to be particularly problematic in cross-cultural contexts. The speech act of disagreement is similar to these in that it carries the potential for error in interpretation or production. Previous research has shown that Japanese learners of English experience difficulties in interpreting and producing such speech acts in interactions with native speakers of English (e.g. Beebe and Takahashi 1989a, 1989b; Hill *et al* 1986; Nakajima 1997).

At present relatively little is known about the extent to which Japanese students experience pragmatic failure in such areas in interaction with New Zealanders, i.e. where they fail to communicate or interpret pragmatic intent appropriately, or the contexts in which these failures are most likely to occur.

1.2 Defining a speech act

What do we mean by 'speech act'? The term refers to possible verbal acts such as making statements, asking questions, issuing commands, giving reports, greeting and warning. The appropriateness of a given speech act varies according to sociocultural rules and norms (Searle 1972). There are, for instance, a number of different ways of performing the speech act of requesting someone to close the door, depending on the speaker's relationship to the hearer:

> Shut the door!
> Could you shut the door?
> Did you forget the door?
> Put the wood in the hole.
> Were you born in a barn?
> What do big boys do when they come into a room, Johnny?
> (Thomas 1995: 51)

The study of speech acts allows researchers to observe human face-to-face interaction, and the speech behaviour through which this interaction is conducted. According to Blum-Kulka, House and Kasper (1989), research on speech acts has three advantages. Firstly, it can enable researchers to conjecture about universality in speech behaviour; secondly, it can identify some of the social implications inferred by differing styles of speech act performance; and thirdly, it can illuminate cultural differences in interactional strategies. In the past 20 years, there has been a great deal of progress in the study of speech acts; numerous investigations have analysed a number of languages, cultures and speech communities. Research has focused on 1) the realisation of a particular speech act within a given language; 2) the realisation of a particular speech act across languages; and 3) the production or interpretation of a particular speech act in a language by non-native speakers of that language (Gass and Houck 1999). The most commonly-employed method of analysis has been to categorise the various strategies and semantic formula of the speech act being analysed. Researchers have also investigated how various social factors may affect the formulation of a speech act, as well as how different linguistic realisations may affect the acceptability of a speech act.

This study, too, identifies strategies used to perform a speech act, in this case the negatively affective speech act of disagreement (the characteristics of which are discussed in section 2.1.1). The goal of the study is to identify how Japanese learners of English (JLEs) use various disagreement speech act strategies – both verbal and paralinguistic – when they are engaged in negatively affective situations of disagreement with native speakers of New Zealand English. There are three major foci in this study. The first focus is on how well the learners are able to identify and interpret disagreement utterances, and also on how well they can express and negotiate them. The second focus is on the degree to which this ability changes over time as a result of the second language learners' immersion in the target culture. The third focus is on some of the key social and cognitive factors which may stimulate progress in attaining pragmatic competence.

1.3 Research questions

This study addresses four central research questions:

> 1. How do JLEs manage politeness when involved in situations of negatively affective disagreement with native speakers of New Zealand English?
> 2. What is the ability of newly-arrived JLEs in accurately expressing the negatively affective speech act of disagreement?
> 3. What is the ability of newly-arrived JLEs in accurately interpreting the negatively affective speech act of disagreement?
> 4. How does their ability to manage politeness alter over a short period of language study and immersion in the host culture?

The first question is concerned with the JLEs' general use of politeness strategies in conversation with native speakers in a target-culture context. The second and third questions focus on the pragmatic ability of JLEs who have only just arrived in New Zealand, have little previous experience of an English-speaking culture and are unlikely to have been explicitly instructed in pragmatic issues. The fourth research question measures the degree of shift in pragmatic competence over a certain period of time in the host culture.

1.4 Methods for operationalising the research questions

Following the methodology employed by Bardovi-Harlig and Dornyei (1998) in their investigation of pragmatic versus grammatical awareness in ESL and EFL learners, data on interpretation of disagreement speech acts was collected by means of a videotaped judgment task observed by participants. Expression-based data was largely compiled through written questionnaire tasks, in line with Blum-Kulka, House and Kasper's (1989) 'written elicitation' method of data collection. JLE participants completed these tasks at the beginning and end of a ten-week period in order to highlight shifts in competence between the initial testing session (pre-testing) and the session ten weeks later (post-testing). A smaller group of JLEs also completed a series of spoken role-plays, which were intended to supplement the written production data elicited through the written task. These tasks were also completed by a reference group of native speakers in order to compare the two groups' speech act behaviour. Chapter 3 discusses these data-collection methods in more detail.

1.5 Contextualising this study

Cross-cultural study, i.e. 'the study of differences in expectations based on cultural schemata' (Yule 1996: 87) has been one of the key areas of interest in pragmatics (Kasper and Rose 2002). Hence, one of the key focal points of this study is cross-cultural pragmatic failure, i.e. 'the inability to understand [or to make understood] "what is meant by what is said"' (Thomas 1983: 91). Pragmatic failure occurs when a hearer (H) perceives the illocutionary strength of a speaker's (S) utterance as other than S intended that H should perceive it. For example, if:

1. H perceives the force of S's utterance as stronger or weaker than S intended;
2. H perceives as an order an utterance which S intended as a request;
3. H perceives S's utterance as ambivalent where S intended no ambivalence; and/or
4. S is relying on a system of knowledge or beliefs which H does not share.

Pragmatic failure may be viewed as a subset of the wider field of *intercultural misunderstanding*, which is defined by House (2000: 145) as 'mismanaged rapport in talk across cultures [in which] speakers fail to successfully manage their interpersonal and interactional relationships' (cf. House 2003). Intercultural misunderstanding may occur for a variety of reasons. Some of those identified by House (2000) are:

– inadequate perception (the listener does not listen or hear properly);
– inappropriate comprehension;
– insufficient knowledge of the world;
– uncooperativeness on the part of one of the interlocutors (who understands but simply wants to be difficult);

– production difficulty (the listener is able to perceive and comprehend sufficiently, but is not yet able to produce an adequate response – particularly in a second language).

Intercultural misunderstanding may have negative consequences both for individual actors, and for larger groups of people. Firstly, such misunderstandings in a face-to-face cross-cultural encounter may be attributed not to cultural differences, but rather to the interlocutor's personality:

> Interactants...may habitually use different, culture-specific communicative styles which are often not recognised as such but rather are ascribed to their interlocutors' personal deficiencies and oddities – an ascription which effectively mars interpersonal relationships and rapport (House 2000: 151).

Secondly, this type of failure has the potential to exacerbate stereotypes, prejudice and discrimination against groups of people, usually minorities (Boxer 2002a). While cultural misperceptions are typically two-way, with each group misperceiving the other, it is typically the minority group that are affected more than the majority group:

> Access to the goods and services inherent in [workplace, social and educational] interaction renders successful [cross-cultural pragmatic communication] critical Without a basis to understand the norms of 'the other', power is wielded in insidious ways. Thus, in a certain sense, the old adage of 'When in Rome, do as the Romans do' does not fit many modern pluralistic societies (Boxer 2002a: 152).

Research into the causes of cross-cultural pragmatic failure is beneficial because it has the potential to ameliorate the consequences of such failure. So there is a particular need for study of this kind.

In spite of this need, however, there have been relatively few studies concerned with this area. 'Despite the richness of the subject for both sociolinguistics and cross-cultural pragmatics, surprisingly few studies have attempted to empirically document requesting [and other negatively affective speech-act behaviour] in one particular society, let alone compare it across different speech communities' (Blum-Kulka and House 1989: 12–13). Fraser (1985) had suggested that strategies for performing speech acts, conveying politeness and mitigating illocutionary strength were essentially alike across cultures and languages. However, Wierzbicka (1985) rejected this claim as English-speaking ethnocentrism, citing the results of her study on differences between Polish and English. An overview of culture-specific studies shows that the linguistic diversity of these studies is limited to a small number of frequently-spoken languages: Wolfson's (1983, 1988) studies of compliments in American English; Holmes' (1986) analysis of complaints and her (1990) investigation into apologies in New Zealand English; Tannen and Kakava's (1992) study comparing American speakers of English with Greek American speakers of English; House's (1979, 2000) and House and Kasper's (1981) studies on German speakers and German English speakers. In recent years, some studies have focused on Asian cultures, e.g. Yu's (1999) analysis of Taiwanese refusals; Mori's (1999) study of Japanese disagreements; and Hill, Ide, Ikuta, Kawasaki and Ogino's (1986) study of Japanese and American English (these studies, and similar ones, are discussed further in section 2.2). Yet the number of languages represented in these studies is only five: English, German, Hebrew, Japanese and Chinese. Even Spencer-Oatey's (2000) collection of empirical studies in managing rapport through talk across cultures largely restricts its scope to these few languages. When compared to the wealth of languages and cultures in the world, these studies simply scratch the surface (Kasper and Rose 2002: 244).

Additionally, there have been relatively few studies of cross-cultural disagreement speech acts. When we consider how thoroughly other speech acts have been studied, there is a clear gap in knowledge. Apology, for instance, has been studied quite extensively (Blum-Kulka and Olshtain 1984; Blum-Kulka, House and Kasper 1989; Cohen and Olshtain 1981; Holmes 1990). Requesting strategies have also received considerable attention (Blum-Kulka 1982; Blum-Kulka and Olshtain 1984; Blum-Kulka, House and Kasper 1989; Tanaka and Kawade 1982). There are a small number of papers which discuss disagreement in a cross-cultural context (e.g. Beebe and Takahashi 1989a, 1989b; Tannen and Kakava 1992), but most studies of disagreement have focused only on one culture (Rees-Miller 2000; Mori 1999; Pomerantz 1984). Thus, the present study, which examines disagreement from a cross-cultural perspective, makes a contribution which extends research in this area.

Specific areas have been identified (Blum-Kulka and House 1989: 12) as being appropriate for research on cross-cultural speech act behaviour:

1. investigation of the similarities and differences in the realisation patterns of given speech acts across different languages, relative to the same social constraints (labelled pragmalinguistic variation by Kasper and Rose 2001: 2);
2. investigation of the effect of social variables on the realisation patterns of given speech acts within specific speech communities (labelled sociopragmatic variation by Kasper and Rose 2001: 2);
3. investigation of the similarities and differences in the realisation patterns of given speech acts between native and non-native speakers of a given language, relative to the same social constraints (interlanguage variation – Bardovi-Harlig and Hartford 2005: 7).

The present study attempts to address these areas. The study investigates pragmalinguistic variation by comparing politeness strategies used by native New Zealand participants with those used by Japanese participants, and it investigates sociopragmatic variation through exploring cross-culturally different perceptions of appropriate linguistic behaviour (Blum-Kulka 1997a; Thomas 1983). The issue of interlanguage variation is examined by obtaining data on the differences in strategy use between native speakers of English and Japanese learners of English.

1.6 The structure of this study

Chapter 1 has outlined the background to this research project, explicated the rationale for conducting the research, and positioned this study in the context of cross-cultural / interlanguage pragmatics. Four research questions have been proposed. A review of the literature on cross-cultural politeness and an outline of the theoretical framework adopted in this research are provided in chapter 2. Chapter 3 describes the aims and objectives of the project, and discusses the methodology by which these objectives are to be met. The first and second research questions, focusing on JLEs' ability to produce disagreement speech acts, are addressed in chapters 4, 5 and 6. Chapter 4 discusses production of written disagreement speech acts, using data elicited from a written discourse completion task (DCT). This chapter also explicates the findings of oral production data elicited through role-play instruments. Chapter 5 discusses utterance length in production, using data from both the DCTs and the role-plays. Chapter 6 shifts the focal point to the third research question, addressing the JLEs' ability to recognise disagreements and to interpret the illocutionary strength of these speech acts. The fourth research question, which addresses increases in production and interpretation ability over a ten-week period of study, is also discussed in chapters 4–6 as appropriate. The findings expounded in these four chapters are summarised and discussed in chapter 7. Finally, chapter 8 summarises the conclusions, including the implications of this research for further study and its possible applicability to the field of English language teaching.

Before considering how the present study addresses the four research questions, it is necessary to review the theoretical tenets of the field of interlanguage pragmatics. This is the focus of chapter 2.

2 Literature Review

2.1 Introduction

This chapter provides background information for the study. It has two specific aims: to place the study in the context of previous relevant studies; and to describe and explain the theoretical frameworks which have been adopted.

Section 2.2 outlines some of the existing literature that is relevant to the current research. It focuses on studies of negatively affective speech acts, in particular the speech act of disagreement. The purpose of this is to place the present research in the context of similar previous studies, and to highlight some of the current trends in speech act research. This section also demonstrates that a gap exists in current knowledge of disagreement speech acts, particularly in an interlanguage context.

One of the likely influences on disagreement strategy selection is the participants' perceptions of what constitutes appropriate politeness (Brown and Levinson 1987). Certain social variables are likely to inform a speaker's perception of what constitutes appropriate politeness – for instance, a person may be more indirect speaking to a boss than a colleague, or when talking about a major issue as opposed to a minor one. Hence, sections 2.3, 2.4 and 2.5 offer a critical review of current theories of politeness, and explicate which theories will be referred to in analysing participants' choices of disagreement strategy.

Section 2.6 presents an outline of strategies for performing disagreement speech acts. At a wider level, it also provides information about *patterns* of disagreement, i.e. disagreements which are formulated over a number of turns at speaking. The goal of this section is to construct a taxonomy of all the disagreement strategies which the participants drew on in constructing their disagreements during the testing sessions. In later chapters, this taxonomy is used for analysis of the disagreement strategies selected by the JLEs in their pre-testing and post-testing responses, as well as the native speaker reference group. This analysis enables identification of which strategies are used most often by each group and which strategies are avoided. It is then possible to extrapolate possible reasons why certain strategies were used by some groups and not by others.

Because this study is concerned with a specific cross-cultural context, that of Japanese English learners in New Zealand, section 2.7 details the cultural dimensions that are central to this study. The primary focus is on individualism-collectivism and power distance, both of which are conceptually related to communication behaviour, and are therefore highly relevant to this kind of cross-cultural speech-act research. Perceptions of appropriate politeness are often based on cultural norms, so they may differ to a great extent between cultures. So, in considering cross-cultural perceptions of politeness, it is important to comprehend some of the specific sociocultural and linguistic differences between the cultures being examined. It is then possible to highlight some of the factors underlying different politeness expectations.

However, this study is not only concerned with cultural differences between JLEs and New Zealanders, but also with how the JLEs' pragmatic ability develops over a period of time, and what social and/or cognitive factors may have influenced (or hindered) this development. In order to provide a contextual framework for the JLEs' acquisition of pragmatic principles of New Zealand English, section 2.8 outlines some of the social and cognitive processes of second language acquisition. These are then referred to as appropriate in later chapters.

The first task is to define what is meant by the speech act of disagreement and to define its main pragmatic components. This is discussed in the following section.

2.1.1 A definition of disagreement

Unlike other speech acts discussed by Searle (1972) (e.g. directives or commissives), disagreement is always reactive, i.e. it is always a reply to a prior utterance from an interlocutor (Sornig 1977: 364). For the purposes of this study, disagreement is defined as follows:

> A speaker *(S)* disagrees when s/he considers untrue some proposition *(P)* uttered or presumed to be espoused by an addressee *(A)*, and reacts with a verbal or paralinguistic response, the propositional content or implicature of which is *not P* (Rees-Miller 2000: 1088).

Disagreements are normally performed with second assessments. In proffering an initial assessment, a speaker formulates the assessment so as to accomplish an action, for example, to make a statement of fact, to praise, complain, compliment, insult, brag, offer an opinion or self-deprecate. In the turn following the initial assessment, the recipient must decide whether to agree with the prior assessment or disagree with it. Hence, in the context of conversation, 'agreement' or 'disagreement' refers to alternative actions that become relevant once an initial assessment has been tendered (Pomerantz 1984: 63).

At this point, it is necessary to explicate the difference between agreement and disagreement speech acts. According to Pomerantz (1984), there are four major differences. Firstly, agreement components normally occupy an entire agreement turn, whereas disagreements are often prefaced with a hesitation, verbal pause etc (see section 2.6.1). Secondly, agreements are normally accomplished with explicitly stated agreement components, whereas disagreements may be accomplished with a variety of forms, ranging from stated (explicit) disagreements to unstated (implied) disagreements (cf. Mori 1999: 93). Stalpers (1995: 278) notes that disagreements are often presented with hedging devices (see section 2.6.1), which are means of softening or mitigating the strength of the disagreement. Such strategies may include pausing before delivering the disagreement, prefacing it with a discourse marker such as 'yes', offering a token agreement, expressing appreciation or apology before disagreeing, or inserting a qualifier such as 'I'm not sure, but'. Additionally, a speaker may displace the disagreement over a number of acts. A disagreement may be accompanied by a supporting / explaining statement, or by modals such as 'maybe'. Thirdly, agreements are performed with as little gap as possible between the completion of the first turn and the beginning of the second, whereas disagreements are frequently delayed within a turn or over a series of turns. Fourthly, disagreements may be unstated, and may be marked only by the absence of forthcoming agreements or by gaps, requests for clarification, and so on. The four distinctions which Pomerantz mentions appear accurate because they correspond with Sacks' (1987) notion that opposing interlocutors will normally attempt to maintain a semblance of cooperation, even when having to disagree. Sacks states that there is a general 'preference for agreement' (1987: 57) and that disagreement is the dispreferred second response. Such a response requires extra interactional effort (Stalpers 1995) in order to prevent negative consequences in the interlocutors' relationship.

Two types of disagreeing utterance, however, are not negatively affective speech acts at all. I will briefly outline these. Firstly, disagreements in certain contexts may be the *preferred* response to a speaker's proposition or evaluation. Such disagreements are often made in reaction to a speaker's negative self-evaluation, in which the speaker is perceived as 'fishing' for a reply from the hearer that is more complimentary than the speaker's statement (Pomerantz 1984). Secondly, disagreement may denote solidarity between two interlocutors who have a close social relationship:

> In sociable argument, speakers repeatedly disagree, remain non-aligned with each other, and compete for interactional goods. Yet they do so in a nonserious way, and in ways which actually display their solidarity and protect their intimacy (Schiffrin 1984: 311).

So a direct and explicit disagreeing response can actually enhance a close relationship by underlining the acceptability of the direct disagreeing response (Holmes 2001; Rees-Miller 2000; Schwebel 1997). These situations are certainly fascinating and worthy of further investigation. Nevertheless, as this study aims to focus on disagreements as a negatively affective speech act (i.e. disagreements that are made when the speaker would clearly prefer an agreement), I do not pursue this type of disagreement here.

The illocutionary strength of a disagreement speech act may be altered through pragmalinguistic devices for conveying indirectness. Indirectness is discussed in the following section.

2.1.2 Indirectness

In making a disagreeing statement, there are many methods by which to convey that an utterance means *not P*, besides stating it explicitly. Indirectness is used frequently on certain occasions, despite the fact that employing an indirect utterance is likely to require greater processing effort than direct speech. Thomas reasons that employing indirectness allows speakers to gain an advantage or avoid a negative consequence:

> They may wish to avoid hurting someone else..., or appearing 'pushy'...or to show how clever they are...Or people may employ indirectness because they are prey to some superstitions or are avoiding a taboo word or topic...But whatever the underlying motivation for using indirectness (even if it is because of an irrational belief) the use of indirectness itself is perfectly rational, if it enables the speaker to achieve his or her goal or to avoid unpleasantness (1995: 121–122).

The type of indirectness mentioned above is consciously adopted by the speaker. However, there are other, non-deliberate, forms of indirectness, such as through linguistic inadequacy, which occurs when the speaker does not know the correct word for some object in his/her own language or a foreign language. Indirectness may also be a result of 'performance error', e.g. when a speaker forgets a word through fear, nervousness or excitement (Thomas 1995: 120). These kinds of indirectness are not considered in this study; only intentional indirectness (i.e. as a mechanism for reducing the strength of a speech act) is discussed.

The disadvantage of indirectly expressing a speech act is that it is costly and risky (Dascal 1983). It is 'costly' in that an indirect utterance takes a long time for a speaker to produce and a hearer to process, and 'risky' in that the hearer may not understand the speaker's intended meaning. Why, then, should the speaker expend so much extra effort and risk so much, even when there is no clear advantage for efficacy of communication? Dascal (1983) mentions four reasons for employing indirectness:

1. There is no other alternative. The speaker can only express him/herself indirectly.
2. The speaker may have a quite precise thought to express, but the circumstances do not allow him/her to convey it directly, e.g. when broaching a topic that is socially taboo; given the circumstances, there is no other option.
3. Indirect speech provides a means for the speaker to convey something, while at the same time avoiding full responsibility for what s/he is attempting to convey.
4. Indirectness is used to save face.

All four of these principles are applicable to JLEs interacting in an interlanguage context. After all, for any hearer to interpret a speech act accurately, an understanding of both the literal and the conveyed meaning of the act is crucial (Searle 1975). Clearly, this understanding is even more critical when the speech act is being delivered in a cross-cultural milieu.

2.2 The literature on speech act research

This section aims to place the present study in the context of the existing literature on speech acts. It reviews some of the relevant current research into negatively affective speech acts, discusses the findings of this research, and highlights some of the gaps that remain in knowledge of negatively affective speech acts.

2.2.1 A general review of negatively affective speech acts

A number of studies have shown how various potentially face-threatening speech acts may be performed by learners of English as a second or foreign language, and how these compare to strategies commonly used by native speakers. These include Cohen and Olshtain 1993, 1994; Gass and Houck 1999 (refusal); Houck and Gass 1996 (refusal); Kasper 1984; Takahashi and Beebe 1987; Takahashi and Roitblat 1994 (requests); Trosborg 1987 (apology); Williams 2005 (requests, rejections and challenges); and Yates 2005 (directives). But Bardovi-Harlig (1999) says that more studies are necessary, and these need to encompass a greater number of issues within interlanguage pragmatics than have so far been addressed. Some of these issues are outlined in this section.

Several investigations into language learners' speech act production have been carried out by Bardovi-Harlig. Bardovi-Harlig and Hartford (1993), for example, studied a group of graduate students from six language backgrounds as they took part in interviews with academic course advisors. The research measured how these students produced suggestions and rejections in conversation, and recorded the changes that took place over the course of a semester. Over time, the students began to perceive when it was appropriate to use suggestions or rejections when speaking to their advisor. However, the form these utterances took was often perceived by non-native speakers (NNSs) as being too direct and strong, suggesting that although the participants were able to perceive appropriate moments for producing negatively affective speech acts, their ability to produce them in a sociopragmatically appropriate manner did not alter over the semester. A similar study by Salsbury and Bardovi-Harlig (2000) focused on second language learners' use of modality (e.g. *maybe, might, could*) when expressing opposing views. The researchers undertook a one-year longitudinal study in which eight low-level ESL learners from a variety of linguistic backgrounds were interviewed once a month. Salsbury and Bardovi-Harlig found that acquisition of linguistic competence did not necessarily mean that the language learners would use their language skills to help them interact appropriately with native speakers. The students learned to use modals more effectively, but they did not use them more frequently. The findings of these two studies by Bardovi-Harlig suggest that although there is some shift in L2 learners' pragmalinguistic ability over a period of time, the shift in sociopragmatic ability may be much less pronounced.

Several studies have discovered a pattern among second-language learners concerning length of utterance in negatively affective speech acts. Olshtain and Weinbach (1993), for example, compared the complaining strategies of British and American university students with those of intermediate and advanced Israeli EFL learners. Olshtain and Weinbach found that these learners commonly produced longer utterances than the NSs did, suggesting that second language learners' utterances are likely to be more lengthy and verbose than those of native speakers when they perform an FTA in their second language. However, there have been few studies of utterance length in L2 learners from other cultures, and this makes it difficult to judge how widely applicable Olshtain and Weinbach's findings are. Are Japanese learners of English likely to be more verbose than their NS counterparts, or less so? This question is addressed in the current study.

A number of researchers (e.g. Eisenstein and Bodman 1993; House 1993, 1996; Rehbein 1987; Wildner-Bassett 1984) have attempted to determine whether pragmatic fluency (i.e. the appropriate use of politeness strategies) can be attained in a language learner's home country, rather than in the target culture. House (1996) studied advanced German learners of English for fourteen weeks while they undertook a course designed to increase their pragmatic fluency. Her aim was to determine whether pragmatic competence stems from input and communicative practice alone, or whether explicit instruction about politeness strategies is more efficient in raising learners' consciousness. Her conclusion was that instruction is essential in helping learners to use speech acts appropriately, but that achieving a measurable result is likely to take considerably longer than fourteen weeks. (House did not speculate on what length of time would be sufficient.) This finding is noteworthy because it implies that immersion in the target culture is the ideal context for learning pragmatic principles, while language classrooms in the local culture may not be adequate. Rose and Ng Kwai-fun (2001) also reported mixed results in

34

their studies of classroom-based pragmatic instruction, as did S. Taka-hashi (2001) and Yoshimi (2001).

A study of how Japanese learners of English produce refusal utterances was undertaken by Robinson (1992). However, Robinson says little about how the JLEs' refusal strategies changed, or whether there was any pattern to the shifts that took place. Further investigation into the speech acts of JLEs would help to illuminate this area.

Requesting strategies by Chinese ESL learners were studied by Yu (1999). Yu's conclusion was that the Chinese learners were generally more direct in their selection of requesting strategies than NSs in the same situational context. A similar conclusion about Chinese speakers was reached by Lee-Wong (2000). Fukushima (2000) noticed the same pattern among Japanese learners of English, but pointed out that the greater the weight of the FTA being performed, the more indirect the JLEs' requesting strategies became. Considering the present study, then, it is possible that the JLEs' negatively affective strategies may also be more direct than those of the New Zealand NSs. If this proved to be the case, it would be interesting to determine a) what effect this directness would have on the potential for pragmatic failure; and b) whether the JLEs' disagreement strategies also became more indirect in accordance with the weight of FTAs.

In sum, a variety of studies have investigated a range of negatively affective speech acts as produced by language learners from a number of different backgrounds. These have shown that shifts in sociopragmatic ability over time are often not marked; that L2 learners ideally require immersion in the target culture in order to develop pragmatic consciousness; and that L2 learners' speech act strategies are often more direct than those of NSs. However, the applicability of these findings for the JLEs in the present study is uncertain. In particular, there is doubt as to whether JLE utterances are likely to be longer or shorter than those of their NS counterparts. There are also questions as to likely shifts in politeness strategies employed by the Japanese participants, and as to which social variables are most likely to influence these. The following section reviews research focusing specifically on disagreement speech acts.

35

2.2.2 Disagreement speech acts

Compared to some other speech acts (e.g. requesting or apology), there has been relatively little study of disagreement. Many of the studies that have been undertaken have employed a discourse analysis approach. This section will review some significant discourse analysis studies in the field of disagreement. Other studies have been concerned with how power variables may affect disagreement-oriented situations. These studies are pertinent to the present study, which also evaluates power as an influencing variable in disagreement speech acts (see section 2.4.3). This section reviews some of these studies.

Disagreement in discourse analysis studies

A number of discourse analysis studies have centred on disagreements (e.g. Gardner 2000; Kotthoff 1993; Mori 1999; Myers 1998; Schiffrin 1984, 1985). Some of these have concentrated on disagreement as a preferred speech act (see section 2.1.1). An example is Schiffrin (1984), who studied disagreement as an expression of co-operation and sociability among Jewish American people. She found that social argument, far from being negative, can in fact be a co-operative enactment of conflict which actually demonstrates the solidarity of the relationship, as the following examples show:

> (1)
> Debby (to husband and wife): Have you travelled very much outside of Philadelphia?
> Wife: No, I think as far as we got was Canada.
> [three turns later]
> Husband (to wife): Um…we just went to Kuch's, what the hell do you mean we don't travel?

> (2)
> Wife: Well, I would like t' travel. But [he doesn't=
> Husband: [You're full of baloney!
> (from Schiffrin 1984: 317)

This phenomenon is what Tannen and Kakava (1992) term 'disagreeing to agree':

36

> Whereas the disagreement pushes interlocutors away, the affectionate term of address brings them closer. Furthermore, it is a means to reinforce involvement, which is potentially threatened by disagreement (1992: 249).

In sum, this kind of disagreement reflects the ability of a relationship to withstand features of talk usually associated with conflict, such as disagreement, insult and interruption (cf. Holmes 2001: 333).

The very opposite case, i.e. dispreferred disagreement, is discussed by Kotthoff (1993). Kotthoff discusses the context of opposition, as opposed to Schiffrin's context of solidarity. She argues that the preference for agreement with assessments (which both Pomerantz 1984 and Sacks 1987 posit) is not universal. Rather, in certain contexts, opponents are expected to defend their positions and stress their disagreement. In such cases, the preference for contiguity and agreement are discarded; the goal is to win the argument (cf. Craig, Tracy and Spisak 1986: 463). Kotthoff's findings suggest that giving up a position that has already been argued for can be a face-threatening act in itself, because it may be interpreted as submissiveness: 'To concede means to give in on the main disputable point' (Kotthoff 1993: 213).

Discourse analysis studies are useful for broad-brush illustration of how a speech act may be performed in a variety of contexts. Nonetheless, discourse analysis studies suffer from some methodological disadvantages. Their value is limited because they normally contain few ethnographic elements, and offer little information about cultural differences in disagreeing strategies. As well, being purely qualitative studies, they lack any quantitative components.

While numerous studies have been conducted on disagreement in American and British English speaking communities, there has been a dearth of discourse analysis dealing with disagreeing strategies in Japanese language. Although a small number of surveys have focused on disagreement in Japanese (e.g. Mori 1994, 1995, 1996, 1999; Takagi 1997), these pale by comparison to the number of studies focusing on English (Mori 1999: 16). In fact, it is partly for this reason that conversation analysis as a methodological tool has been criticised as too closely tied to Western interactional patterns and insensitive to cultural diversity (Gumperz 1982; Duranti 1988). Because of this paucity of Japanese language discourse analysis studies, it is difficult to make a useful comparison with the findings of the present study.

On the other hand, some of the conclusions of these studies are useful for qualitative comparison and contrast with the findings of the present study. These conclusions are referred to in the text as appropriate.

Studies of power in disagreement

A number of research papers have investigated the effect of the variable of power on disagreement strategy selection (e.g. Beebe and Takahashi 1989a, 1989b; Rees-Miller 2000; Tannen 1994; Tannen and Kakava 1992). The conclusions of such studies are highly relevant to the present study, which also applies power as a situational variable. Rees-Miller (2000) analysed some in-class discussions between students and professors at an American university in order to study the effect of power and severity variables on disagreement strategy use. She found that power and severity accounted for some aspects of her data, but that the pedagogical context may also have been an influencing factor because it enabled the interlocutors to employ different disagreement strategies than they might in another context. Professors in the study used a lot of affirmative strategies in disagreeing with lower-status interlocutors so as to keep them involved in the class, while students were often more forceful in their disagreeing strategies than they might have been in different circumstances. Rees-Miller's study was similar to the present study in that it was based on a pedagogical context. However, the study was not cross-cultural, but concerned solely with American culture. Her results are useful for discussing native-speaker disagreement strategies, but they are less applicable to an interlanguage context.

A recent study of power distance and disagreement by Locher (2004) explored how disagreements were enacted in two social situations: a family dinner and an academic meeting. In each case there was relative variation in status between interlocutors. Locher also analysed a number of media extracts from a radio interview with Bill Clinton, another interview with a presidential candidate, and finally a US Supreme Court hearing. Locher found that the ability to exercise power could depend on the interactants' speaking style, cultural background, status, knowledge of frames or gender. It also depended on expertise about the topic being discussed: 'an interactant's involvement with or knowledge about a topic…influenced whether or not and how disagreement was realised and whether this resulted in an exercise of power' (2004: 328). Power was framed as a contestable and dynamic concept which different interactants might hold at different points of a conversation.

Locher's (2004) study is similar to the present study in exploring how the power variable might influence the realisation of disagreement speech acts. It is also similar in structural terms, being primarily a descriptive study which incorporates a certain amount of quantitative analysis to lend depth to the qualitative data. One main point of departure is that there is no cross-cultural aspect to Locher's study, since all the participants shared the same culture (white, educated Americans). Additionally, there is no interlanguage context, since the participants were all native speakers of American English rather than learners of English as a second language. Locher's study is a useful comparison in linguistic terms, but possibly less so in terms of understanding processes of interlanguage pragmatic acquisition.

Two particularly pertinent studies were carried out by Beebe and Takahashi (1989a, 1989b). Similar to the present study, Beebe and Takahashi's study explored how Japanese learners of English performed face-threatening acts in exchanges with status-unequal interlocutors. They then compared these results with those of American English speakers. They came to the following conclusions:

1. Americans are not always more direct or explicit in disagreement than Japanese.
2. Japanese do not always avoid disagreement.
3. Japanese do not always avoid using critical remarks.
4. Japanese and Americans can both use questions as a form of disagreement, but the questions they use can be significantly different in tone and content.
5. Americans tend to use positive remarks more frequently than Japanese (Beebe and Takahashi 1989b: 213–214).

The directness of the disagreeing responses given by the Japanese ESL speakers was shown to vary considerably depending on the relative power inequality between speakers. Japanese participants were often indirect and circumlocutory in their responses to higher-power interlocutors (e.g. employee–employer), but often more direct and succinct when speaking to power-equals (e.g. friend–friend) or those lower in power (e.g. teacher–student). Given the similarity of the participant groups under consideration, it is possible that the results of the present study will correlate with Beebe and Takahashi's findings. It is possible, however, that the variation between these two studies (the NS nationalities are different, as is the second language learning environment) may engender a different set of results. Because of the similarity between Beebe and Takahashi's studies and the present study, their results are referred to and compared/contrasted with the current findings as appropriate.

In conclusion, the discourse analysis studies that have been undertaken on disagreement may be qualitatively comparable to the present study, but are insufficient for any other comparison because, unlike the present study, they do not contain quantitative or ethnographic components. Some quantitative studies of disagreement have been carried out, and have investigated how the variable of power affects disagreement strategy selection. These are useful for comparison, but they are relatively few in number. There is certainly a need for deeper insight into how power affects strategy selection in negatively affective speech acts.

2.3 Politeness

In the last twenty-five years, a great deal of attention has focused on politeness in pragmatics. Unfortunately, politeness is a difficult concept to characterise. According to Watts (2005a: xiii), 'politeness will always be a slippery, ultimately indefinable quality of interaction which is subject to change through time and across cultural space'.

Inevitably, people use the same terms to mean very different things, and therefore researchers are often operating with highly dissimilar definitions of 'politeness' and often at cross-purposes with one another. So it is important to define as clearly as possible what I mean by politeness.

2.3.1 Definitions of politeness

In common, everyday language use, 'politeness' is taken to mean proper social conduct and tactful consideration of others (Kasper 1994: 3206). It can also be confused with related terms such as 'etiquette' and 'manners' (LoCastro 1990). In fact, the *Oxford Advanced Learner's Dictionary*, commonly used by second-language learners, supports the everyday meaning of the term:

> Having or showing that one has good manners and consideration for other people. (Hornby 1995: 893).

However, 'politeness', as a technical term in linguistic pragmatics refers to a broader and more intricate concept than the common meaning cited above. '"Politeness" as a pragmatic notion refers to ways in which linguistic action is carried out – more specifically, ways in which the relational function in linguistic action is expressed' (Kasper 1994: 3206). Politeness may therefore be interpreted as a strategy, or series of strategies, employed by a speaker to achieve the goal of promoting or maintaining harmonious relations with other people.

The present study focuses on politeness from a cross-cultural perspective. Promoting and maintaining politeness calls for displays of appropriate behaviour, but there are many differences between cultures in terms of what constitutes an 'appropriately' polite utterance:

> What is considered to be appropriate varies from situation to situation and culture to culture, while personal values and tastes may also influence judgments of appropriateness (Fukushima 2000: 27).

Clearly, conflicting norms of politeness are inevitably obstacles to smooth intercultural communication.

2.3.2 The conversational-maxim view of politeness

One conceptualisation of politeness is as a series of conversational maxims. This approach requires a speaker to solve the problem: 'Given that I want to bring about such-and-such a result in the hearer's consciousness, what language should I use to accomplish this aim?'. The hearer has another kind of problem to solve: 'Given that the speaker said such-and-such, what did the speaker mean mc to understand by that?'. The speaker is seen as 'trying to achieve his *[sic]* aims within constraints imposed by principles and maxims of "good communicative behaviour"' (Leech 1983: xi).

This section will outline the two prominent theories based upon the conversational-maxim view of politeness.

Grice's (1975) Cooperative Principle

The conversational-maxim view of politeness is based on Grice's (1975) Cooperative Principle. Grice's theory attempts to explain how a hearer gets from what is said to what is meant, from the level of expressed meaning to that of implied meaning. He discusses what he calls 'nonconventional implicatures', which are also known as 'conversational implicatures': i.e. statements that transmit a degree of meaning which is additional to the semantic meaning of the words spoken.

> The notion of conversational implicature…provides some explicit account of how it is possible to mean (in some general sense) more than what is actually 'said' (i.e. more than what is literally expressed by the conventional sense of the linguistic expressions uttered) (Levinson 1983: 97).

Levinson (1983: 97) provides the following example:

> A: Can you tell me the time?
> B: Well, the milkman has come.

The literal meaning of B's response is that the milkman came at some time prior to the time of speaking. But B's likely intent is to be understood as saying 'no, I don't know the exact time, but I can provide some information which may help you to deduce the approximate time'. There is a difference between what is literally said and what the speaker intends to convey. According to Levinson, the gap is too wide to allow for the semantic context to account for the difference; hence, the hearer is able to deduce that the implied meaning is the intended one.

Grice aims to show that, despite its often implied structure, talking is deliberate and rational behaviour:

> Our talk exchanges do not normally consist of a succession of disconnected remarks, and would not be rational if they did. They are characteristically, to some extent at least, cooperative efforts; and each participant recognises in them, to some extent, a common purpose or set of purposes, or at least a mutually accepted direction (Grice 1975: 29).

On this basis, Grice defines his Cooperative Principle: 'Make your conversational contribution such as is required, at the stage at which it occurs, by the accepted purpose or direction of the talk exchange in which you are engaged' (1975: 45). The Cooperative Principle consists of the four maxims of Quantity, Quality, Relation and Manner:

Maxim of Quantity
1) Make your information as informative as is required.
2) Do not make your contribution more informative than is required.

Maxim of Quality
1) Try to make your contribution one that is true.
      a. Do not say what you believe to be false.
      b. Do not say that for which you lack adequate evidence.

Maxim of Relation
1) Be relevant.

Maxim of Manner
1) Be perspicuous.
  a. Avoid obscurity of expression.
  b. Avoid ambiguity.
  c. Be brief.
  d. Be orderly.

A speaker observing all these maxims in conversation says precisely what s/he means, no more and no less. The speaker generates no implicature, i.e. there is no distinction to be made between what is said and what is meant; there is no additional level of meaning. In reality, however, these maxims are violated almost constantly; the vast majority of conversations contain some level of conversational implicature. The most common type of violation is *flouting*, in which a speaker blatantly fails to observe a maxim. This is not usually due to a desire to deceive or mislead, but rather because the speaker wishes to stimulate the hearer to consider whether there is another meaning as well as that being expressed at the utterance level.

However, it is not certain whether these maxims can be viewed as universal. Hymes (1986: 73) argues that all communities will have some understanding of the dimension of quality (truthfulness), of quantity (informativeness), of relevance (significance) and of manner (clarity). However, 'what the orientation will be, and how complexly articulated in relation to kinds of person and context, would be an empirical question'. This argument is supported by Wierzbicka (1985: 175), who suggests that the notion of a universal logic of conversation is ethnocentric. In addition, Fukushima (2000: 31) notes that the very word 'cooperation' is potentially confusing, because what in everyday terms would be considered uncooperative behaviour – such as arguing, lying, or abusing – may yet be perfectly cooperative according to some interpretations of Grice's term (Thomas 1994: 760).

Deficiencies notwithstanding, the Gricean maxims have been acknowledged as important by numerous authors (e.g. Sarangi and Slembrouck 1992; Sifianou 1992; Thomas 1994, 1995). Thomas aptly sums up their value: 'It is this work – sketchy, in many ways problematical, and frequently misunderstood – which has proved to be one of the most influential theories in the development of pragmatics' (1995:

56). Brown and Levinson also reinforce the value of Grice's maxims, stating that the 'theory of conversational implicature and the framework of maxims that give rise to such implicatures is essentially correct' (1987: 3).

Leech's (1983) Politeness Principle

Some of the deficiencies in Grice's work are addressed by Leech (1983), who elaborated on Grice's original concept by conceiving a Politeness Principle as a complement to Grice's Cooperative Principle. Leech claimed that his Politeness Principle 'rescued' the Cooperative Principle by explaining exceptions to and apparent deviations from that principle:

> The CP [Cooperative Principle] enables one participant in a conversation to communicate on the assumption that the other participant is being cooperative. In this the CP has the function of regulating what we say so that it contributes to some assumed illocutionary or discoursal goal(s). It could be argued, however, that the PP [Politeness Principle] has a higher regulative role than this: to maintain the social equilibrium and the friendly relations which enable us to assume that our interlocutors are being cooperative in the first place (1983: 82).

Leech sees politeness (and the related concept of 'tact') as being central to understanding why indirectness is common in the conveying of meaning. This conceptualisation is supported by Thomas (1995), who notes that from a purely grammatical standpoint, it is difficult to politely phrase a negatively affective speech act because such speech acts are, by their nature, likely to cause offence to the hearer. However, 'by employing an utterance which is ambivalent (i.e. one which has more than one potential pragmatic force) it is possible to convey messages which the hearer is liable to find disagreeable without causing undue offence' (Thomas 1995: 158). Leech (1983: 132) presents six maxims in his Politeness Principle:

1) Tact Maxim
a) Minimise cost to other; b) Maximise benefit to other.

2) Generosity Maxim
a) Minimise benefit to self; b) Maximise cost to self.

3) Approbation Maxim
a) Minimise dispraise of other; b) Maximise praise of other.

4) Modesty Maxim
a) Minimise praise of self; b) Maximise dispraise of self.

5) Agreement Maxim
a) Minimise disagreement between self and other; b) Maximise agreement between self and other.

6) Sympathy Maxim
a) Minimise antipathy between self and other; b) Maximise sympathy between self and other.

However, Leech's Politeness Principles have been criticised in their turn. The primary criticism has been that the number of possible maxims is unconstrained (Thomas 1995: 167; Turner 1996: 6; Yeung 1997: 506) and probably unlimited: '[I]f we are permitted to invent a maxim for every regularity in language use, not only will we have an infinite number of maxims, but pragmatic theory will be too unconstrained to permit the recognition of any counter-examples' (Brown and Levinson 1987: 4). It is also difficult to apply Leech's principles to actual language use, or to test them empirically (Fraser 1990; Watts et al 2005: 7; Yeung 1997: 506). In addition, Fukushima (2000) points out that politeness is never explicitly defined (cf. Watts et al 2005: 6).

Both of the major components of the conversational-maxim view of politeness have been shown to contain drawbacks. Because of these limitations, it would not be appropriate to take this framework as a basis for the present study.

2.4 The face-saving view of politeness

The advent of Brown and Levinson's (1978; revised 1987) theory of politeness may be seen as a reaction to the limitations of Grice's theory of conversational-maxims. The basic tenets are a perception of communication as purposeful-rational activity, combined with Goffman's (1967) concept of 'face', i.e. an individual's publicly apparent sense of self-esteem. In the definition proposed by Brown and Levinson (1987), politeness is rooted in people's need to maintain face, their fear of losing it and their reluctance to bring about face-loss in others. People are 'dependent on each other to cooperate in maintaining the fragile balance of respect and consideration necessary for the preservation of face' (Janney and Arndt 2005: 23). According to Brown and Levinson's politeness theory, any kind of linguistic act which has a relational dimension is seen as inherently face-threatening, and needs to be counterbalanced by an appropriate degree of politeness. This is especially true for negatively affective speech acts. Brown and Levinson differentiated a number of strategies for signifying politeness, ranging from avoiding committing an FTA altogether, to carrying it out in a variety of linguistic hedges and guises (discussed in section 2.6.1). The choice of appropriate strategy is made on the basis of a speaker's assessment of the magnitude of the FTA. A speaker makes this assessment based on the parameters of power, social distance, and ranking of imposition (these are discussed in section 2.4.3). These combined values determine the overall 'weightiness' of an FTA, which in turn influences the strategy used.

The sections following this brief introduction to Brown and Levinson's politeness theory describe the major components of the politeness theory in more detail. The first focuses on types of face, while the second discusses strategies for performing an FTA. The third discusses the factors which influence the weight of an FTA.

2.4.1 Aspects of face

Brown and Levinson distinguish two aspects of face: *positive* face and *negative* face. Positive face refers to a person's desire to be respected and approved of by other people, while negative face refers to a person's desire to be free to act as s/he wishes without being imposed upon by others. Brown and Levinson maintain that their notion of face is universal, though they note that there is always a culture-specific context. Thus, the abstract concept of face is subject to cultural elaboration:

> On the one hand this core concept is subject to cultural specifications of many sorts – what kind of acts threaten face, what sorts of persons have special rights to face-protection, and what kinds of personal style (in terms of things like graciousness, ease of social relations, etc) are especially appreciated. On the other hand notions of face naturally link up to some of the most fundamental cultural ideas about the nature of the social persona, honour and virtue, shame and redemption... (Brown and Levinson 1987: 13).

While the concept of face is no doubt widely applicable, some have expressed doubts as to its universality (e.g. Arndt and Janney 1992; Markus and Kitayama 1991), especially with regard to Japanese culture (see section 2.5.2).

2.4.2 Face-threatening acts (FTAs)

What kind of communicative acts can damage or maintain an individual's face? Brown and Levinson (1987) claim that certain communicative acts are inherently face-threatening because such acts 'by their nature run contrary to the face-wants of the addressee and/or the speaker' (Brown and Levinson 1987: 65). Any kind of linguistic act which has a relational function may be seen as inherently face-threatening.

In order to minimise face-loss and maintain the face of both interlocutors, FTAs need to be counterbalanced by appropriate measures of politeness. A number of politeness strategies exist to enable the speaker to either avoid or minimise the potential face-threat (see figure 2.1 below):

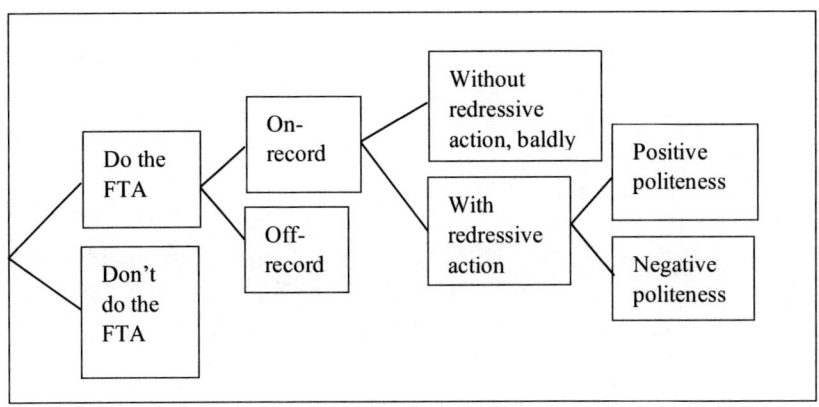

Figure 2.1: Possible strategies for doing FTAs (Brown and Levinson 1987: 69)

A speaker may avoid performing an FTA altogether, or may carry it out using various glossing mechanisms. These may be either 'on-record' or 'off-record'. In an on-record strategy, the communicative intention is clear to both the participants; in an off-record strategy there is more than one possible interpretation, and the speaker cannot be held to have committed him/herself to one particular intent (Brown and Levinson 1987: 68–69). Off-record FTAs (such as hints and meta-phors) have the greatest potential for negotiation, due to their intrinsic ambiguity.

On-record FTAs can be performed without redressive action ('bald on record'), by performing the act 'in the most direct, clear, un-ambiguous and concise way possible' (Brown and Levinson 1987: 69). Alternatively, they might be performed with redressive action, i.e. by including some form of politeness strategy intended to reduce the weight of the FTA being performed. If an FTA is carried out on-record, the speaker has recourse to two modes of redress: positive politeness strategies and negative politeness strategies. Note that these correspond with the disagreement strategies discussed in section 2.6. Positive politeness strategies emphasise closeness between the speaker and the hearer by affirming or establishing common ground, or by citing desirable attributes in the hearer (Scollon and Scollon (1983) label these 'solidarity strategies'). Negative politeness strategies, on the other hand, imply distance by emphasising the hearer's right to territorial claims and freedom from imposition (Scollon and Scollon label these 'deference strategies').

2.4.3 Factors influencing politeness strategies

The choice of which of the above strategies should be adopted is made on the basis of the speaker's assessment of the weight of the FTA. Brown and Levinson (1987: 74) propose three factors which define the seriousness of an FTA:

> 1. The social distance (D) between speaker and hearer (a symmetric relation);
> 2. The relative power (P) disparity between speaker and hearer (an asymmetric relation); and
> 3. The ranking (R), or magnitude, of imposition in the particular culture.

They argue that 'all three dimensions P, D and R contribute to the seriousness of an FTA, and thus to a determination of the level of politeness with which, other things being equal, an FTA will be communicated' (1987: 76). Brown and Levinson present a formula for computing the weightiness of an FTA:

$$Wx = D\,(S, H) + P\,(H, S) + Rx$$

> where Wx is the numerical value that measures the weightiness of the $FTAx$, $D\,(S, H)$ is the value that measures the social distance between S and H, $P\,(H, S)$ is a measure of the power that H has over S, and Rx is a value that measures the degree to which the $FTAx$ is rated an imposition in that culture (Brown and Levinson 1987: 76).

These three dimensions are central to Brown and Levinson's (1987) politeness theory. They are also complex and multifaceted; the terms 'power', 'distance' and 'imposition' have been given an assortment of meanings and interpretations in the literature, in the way the term 'politeness' has. In order to acquire a clear representation of these variables and to understand how they inter-relate, it is necessary to consider each variable in some detail. This is addressed in the following sections.

Defining power

Power is a pervasive entity in human relations, and language is one of the key ways in which it is expressed. Just as languages have evolved as instruments for communication, so they have developed as tools for influence and control (Ng and Bradac 1993). Communication is normally perceived to be authentic and transparent, simply a method for transporting the thoughts and feelings of one person to another. However, the truth of the matter is quite different:

> [T]he use of a human language such as English does more than neutrally inform hearers or readers. It is inevitably an instrument for enacting, recreating, or subverting power (Ng and Bradac 1993: 1).

This is why it is crucial that the conception of power be defined and discussed in this study.

Because the literature contains numerous definitions of power (see below), it is necessary to define what it will mean in this study. According to Brown and Gilman (1972: 255),

> [o]ne person may be said to have power over another in the degree that he is able to control the behaviour of the other. Power is a relationship between at least two persons, and it is nonreciprocal in the sense that both cannot have power in the same area of behaviour.

Brown and Levinson (1987: 77) also emphasise control over another person's behaviour: 'P (H, S) is the degree to which H can impose his own plans and his own self-evaluation (face) at the expense of S's plans and self-evaluation'.

Power is expanded upon in French and Raven's (1959) classic paper, which argues that power can have a number of bases. They claim a 'necessity of distinguishing different types of power in order to account for the different effects found in studies of social influence' (150). The theory on social influence and power is limited to influence on a person, *P*, produced by a social agent, *O*, where *O* can be either another person, a role, a norm, a group or part of a group. French and Raven defined five bases of power:

1. *Reward power* – based on P's perception that O has the ability to negotiate rewards for him/her (e.g. bonus payments or improved job conditions);

2. *Coercive power* – based on P's perception that O has the ability to mediate punishments for him/her (e.g. demotion or allocation of undesirable tasks);

3. *Legitimate power* – based on the perception by P that O has a legitimate right to prescribe behaviour for him/her (e.g. because of his/her role, status or situational circumstances);

4. *Referent power* – based on P's identification with O (i.e. if P admires O and wants to be like him/her in some respect);

5. *Expert power* – based on the perception that O has some special knowledge or expertness that P needs.

Although French and Raven's (1959) paper is not recent, it has been referred to in a number of contemporary studies (e.g. Thomas 1995; Spencer-Oatey 1996, 2000). In fact, the five bases of power incorporate a number of conceptualisations of power which were later put forward by other authors. For example, the Brown and Levinson (1987) / Brown and Gilman (1972) concepts noted earlier may be reformulated as reward power or coercive power in French and Raven's parlance. Cansler and Stiles' (1981) *social ranking* is similar in conception to French and Raven's idea of legitimate power and/or expert power. Leichty and Applegate (1991) referred to power as *the legitimate right to exert influence*, which corresponds to French and Raven's notion of legitimate power.

A range of terms exist for the construct of power. The most common term is simply *power* (used by Baxter 1984; Brown and Gilman 1972; Brown and Levinson 1987; Holmes 1990; Holtgraves and Yang 1990; Lim and Bowers 1991). *Social power* and *status* are also sometimes used (e.g. Beebe and Takahashi 1989a, 1989b; Blum-Kulka and House 1989; Cansler and Stiles 1981; Holtgraves 1986; Olshtain 1989; Vollmer and Olshtain 1989; Wood and Kroger 1991). *Dominance* and *authority* are used only occasionally (e.g. Leech 1983; Trosborg 1987).

For the purposes of this paper, I define power as the ability to influence or control the behaviour of others (Brown and Gilman 1972; Brown and Levinson 1987). I will refer to French and Raven's (1959) five bases of power as appropriate throughout the study.

Defining social distance

The notion of social distance is widely used in linguistics. A great deal of research in the fields of sociolinguistics, pragmatics and discourse analysis has investigated the effect of social distance on how language is both interpreted and produced. In the study of politeness in particular, social distance is an important variable because it affects how interlocutors perceive one another, and consequently how they manipulate politeness strategies in conversation.

Brown and Levinson (1987: 76–77) describe social distance as being 'based on an assessment of the frequency of interaction and the kinds of material or non-material goods (including face) exchanged between [speaker] and [hearer]'. A more detailed definition is postulated by Thomas (1995):

> [Social distance] is best seen as a composite of psychologically real factors (status, age, sex, degree of intimacy etc) which 'together determine the overall degree of respectfulness' within a given speech situation. In other words, if you feel close to someone, because that person is related to you, or you know him or her well or are similar in terms of age, social class, occupation, sex, ethnicity etc, you feel less need to employ indirectness in, say, making a request than you would if you were making the same request of a complete stranger (128).

I will adopt Thomas's definition of social distance for the purposes of this study.

Although the construct is usually labelled as *distance* or *social distance* (e.g. Blum-Kulka and House 1989; Boxer 1993; Brown and Levinson 1987; Holmes 1990; Olshtain 1989; Slugoski and Turnbull 1988; Trosborg 1987), a number of other terms have been used: *solidarity* (e.g. Brown and Gilman 1972; Wood and Kroger 1991), *closeness* (e.g. Holtgraves 1986), *familiarity* (e.g. Leichty and Applegate 1991) and *relational intimacy* (e.g. Lim and Bowers 1991). The term 'social distance' is used here because it is the most widely-accepted definition.

That said, questions have been raised (e.g. Spencer-Oatey 1996) about whether the above terms are all equivalent, or whether different researchers conceptualise this variable in different ways. Brown and Levinson (1987) provide the standard definition of social distance as a symmetric social dimension of similarity / difference between speaker and hearer based on frequency of interaction. By contrast, Wierzbicka (1991) uses the term *intimacy*, which includes both mutual knowledge (which ties in with Brown and Levinson's 'exchange of material or non-material goods') and mutual good feelings (which Brown and Levinson do not mention):

> Intimacy refers to a readiness to reveal to some particular persons some aspects of one's personality and of one's inner world that one conceals from other people; a readiness based on personal trust and on personal 'good feelings' (Wierzbicka 1991: 105).

Wierzbicka's definition evokes both *distance* (the parameter of how well two interlocutors know one another) and *affect* (the parameter of how much they *like* each other) (cf. Slugoski and Turnbull 1988; Holtgraves 1986). Still other authors combine these two factors into one single dimension (e.g. Baxter 1984). Brown and Levinson's (1987) reflections on the concept of affect are not voiced at all in their earlier (1978) work. In their later revision (1987), they concede that 'liking' might be an independent variable affecting strategy choice, but they do not incorporate it because 'complex arithmetical compounding of these factors might be required' (1987: 16) in order to integrate it into their politeness theory. Hence, for the sake of clarity and simplicity, the present study retains the blanket term 'social distance', while also noting the potential importance of the variable of affect for future research.

Defining ranking of imposition

Ranking of imposition is the third of the three social variables noted by Brown and Levinson (1987) as affecting the selection of a politeness strategy.

Ranking of imposition is described as 'a culturally and situationally defined ranking of impositions by the degree to which they are considered to interfere with an agent's wants of self-determination or of approval (his negative- and positive-face wants)' (Brown and Levinson 1987: 42). Imposition, therefore, refers to the magnitude of a negatively affective speech act. Generically speaking, the greater the magnitude of an imposition, the more indirectly a speech act is likely to be phrased. Thomas (1995: 130), discussing requests, uses the following illustration:

> *The speaker was my mother. She made the two following requests to me within the space of a few minutes:*
>
> Shut the window, Jen.
>
> Do you think you could find time to take those invitations to the printers?

Because the first request was a small one, the speaker could deliver it directly without risk of face-damage. The second request required more effort from the hearer, and was thus delivered using a more indirect strategy.

Ranking of imposition is inevitably linked to whether the disagreeing party has the right to make a disagreeing statement, and also whether the other party has an obligation to respond appropriately (Craig, Tracy and Spisak 1986: 463). For example, the weight of imposition would be low if the speaker was an army sergeant offering a disagreeing opinion to a new recruit, but considerably higher if it was the recruit who was disagreeing with the sergeant. Evidently, whether a speaker has a right or not is closely related to the power variable, indicating that these variables are not independent, but are inter-related (Turner 1996: 5). Additionally, rights or obligations may vary culturally (Fukushima 2000). In one culture a teacher may have the right to disagree directly with a student, whereas in another culture the teacher may be constrained to a more indirect approach.

Most studies utilising the variable of imposition provide a similar definition to that of Brown and Levinson. The only differences appear to be 1) the terminology used; and 2) whether rights and obligations are included in the imposition. Brown and Levinson (1987) include them, but Thomas (1995) presents them as being a separate category. In terms of terminology, Baxter (1984) refers to ranking of imposition as 'magnitude of the request'; Brown and Gilman (1989) talk of the 'ranked extremity of a face-threatening act'; Leichty and Applegate (1991) refer to 'magnitude of imposition'; Scollon and Scollon (1995) use the term 'weight of imposition'; and Thomas (1995) uses 'size of imposition'.

This study will use the term 'ranking/magnitude of imposition', approximating Brown and Levinson's (1987) definition of the term. Where appropriate, the rights and obligations of disagreeing inter-locutors will be discussed.

2.4.4 The theoretical position of this study

In this section, I have reviewed two major approaches to politeness: the conversational-maxim view and the face-saving view. The conver-sational-maxim view has some disadvantages and it is not detailed enough to be used as a primary theoretical base, though Grice's work has provided a sound underpinning for Brown and Levinson's polite-ness theory. Leech's (1983) politeness principles are problematic because there is potentially an infinite number of maxims that could be devised, and because it is difficult to apply Leech's theory to actual language use (see section 2.3.2). Leech's politeness principles are referred to only when they are directly relevant.

The face-saving theory of politeness provides a precise and detailed blueprint of politeness and a basis for making cross-cultural comparison. As this is an empirical study concerned with cross-cul-tural pragmatics, a theoretical base is essential, and it is important that it is appropriate for cross-cultural comparison and testability. Brown and Levinson's view is the most appropriate of the two approaches, so theirs will be taken as the theoretical model for the present research.

I have discussed certain other theories concerned with aspects of cross-cultural pragmatics (i.e. those which offer differing conceptualisations of power, social distance and imposition) which will be referred to as appropriate. Rather than contradicting Brown and Levinson's approach to politeness, these theories are presented in order to illuminate and extend it. Yet it would be unwise to ignore the criticisms of this model, since its limitations have been well documented. These are discussed in the next section.

2.5 Critiques of Brown and Levinson's politeness theory

Due to its pervasiveness in politeness literature and the amount of discussion it has generated, a number of criticisms have been made about Brown and Levinson's model of politeness. As I am taking Brown and Levinson's model as the theoretical basis for this study, it is important to consider some of these criticisms.

2.5.1 Polite behaviour only?

One criticism of Brown and Levinson's theory, posited by Eelen (2001), is that the focus is entirely on accounting for the positive thrust of polite behaviour, rather than the negative thrust of *im*polite behaviour. Eelen suggests that this is the case in a number of current politeness theories, including Arndt and Janney (1985) and Watts (1989, 2005b). 'Both the field of study of politeness as well as the conceptual definition of the phenomenon refer to polite behaviour only' (Eelen 2001: 91), and pay scant attention to impoliteness, i.e. the conscious absence of politeness. According to Eelen,

> Commonsensically the two phenomena are closely related. This can be seen not only from the terms' lexical relationship, but also from their dictionary definitions, where impoliteness is usually defined as the inverse or negative of politeness (impolite = not polite). The phenomena are merely two sides of the

same coin, and therefore *any theory that pretends to say something valuable about one side, automatically needs to deal with the other side as well* (2001: 92, my emphasis).

Eelen maintains that while most theories – including that of Brown and Levinson – appear to include some reference to impoliteness, this is seldom discussed in detail.

Eelen's (2001) discussion of politeness and impoliteness, while interesting, seems to be limited to arguing how this deficiency reduces the value of Brown and Levinson's conceptualisation of politeness theory. He does not appear to offer any workable model for analysis of impoliteness, nor does he provide a clear definition of politeness / impoliteness on which future analyses could be based. Hamza (2002) points out that '[Eelen's] model is not clearly identifying its principles and leaves many elements vague and ill-defined, for example the definition of the terms "norm" and "culture"'. Aside from this criticism, however, Eelen's work clearly makes a number of interesting points for further discussion and research in the field of politeness research.

2.5.2 Face and universality: Japanese criticisms of Brown and Levinson

The universality of Brown and Levinson's concept of face has been contested by Matsumoto (1988, 1989) and Ide (1989). These authors argue that the Japanese notion of face differs from that of Brown and Levinson. This section will examine some of their criticisms in detail.

According to Matsumoto (1988), the definition of 'face' in Japanese society is distinct from the supposedly universal constituents of positive face and negative face. 'The sociological and anthropological studies of Japanese...do not support the universality of the two specific aspects of face described by Brown and Levinson' (Matsumoto 1988: 408). Matsumoto argues that the idea of negative face wants as the desire to be unimpeded in one's actions is foreign to Japanese culture. Negative face, she asserts, presupposes that the basic unit of society is the individual, which is not the case in Japanese culture:

A Japanese generally must understand where s/he stands in relation to other members of the group or society, and must acknowledge his/her dependence on the others. Acknowledgement and maintenance of the relative position of others, rather than preservation of an individual's proper territory, governs all social interaction (Matsumoto 1988: 405).

According to Matsumoto, the notion of individuals and their rights is a European / American construct, and is irrelevant to human relations in Japanese culture and society (cf. Nakane 1972; Lebra 1976).

Matsumoto's second claim is that the idea of imposition in Japanese culture is different from that proposed by Brown and Levinson. She states that acknowledgement of interdependence is encouraged in Japanese society: Juniors acknowledge their dependence on their seniors, while these seniors acknowledge their responsibility to take care of their juniors. So imposing on someone, or having been imposed upon by someone else, may actually *enhance* one's face: 'Deferent impositions can enhance the good self-image (that is, the "face") of the addressee' (Matsumoto 1988: 410).

Matsumoto's third point is that the use of honorifics (relation-acknowledging devices such as the deferential prefix *o-*) is obligatory in Japanese language. Brown and Levinson (1987) note the use of honorifics as part of the operation of negative politeness, which 'originate as productive outputs of face-preserving strategies which then become stabilised and change their meaning' (279). Matsumoto disagrees with this statement, suggesting that honorifics in Japanese are simply used to convey differences in rank:

[T]he Japanese morphological and lexical items that [Brown and Levinson] provide as examples (e.g. *masu* 'cause to be, honourably dwell', *watakushi* 'slave, servant') all...convey rank differences. That is, it is not negative politeness, the acknowledgement of the addressee's freedom from imposition that is conveyed by these forms, but a reflection of rank-ordering (Matsumoto 1988: 414).

Matsumoto (1988: 416) points out that the choice of a verb in Japanese depends on the social status of the hearer relative to the speaker. There are, for instance, at least four different verbs that denote the verb 'to eat': *kuu, taberu, meshiagaru* and *itadaku*. These are chosen according to the position which the hearer holds in relation to the speaker – regardless of whether an FTA is being expressed. Matsu-moto's conclusion is that it is not possible to avoid marking the relationship between speaker and hearer, and therefore not possible to construct a sentence that can be used in all situations without honorific forms.

Another Japanese academic, Sachiko Ide (1989) questions Brown and Levinson's claim that their politeness theory is universal. She claims that some aspects of Japanese language and usage are distinctly 'Japanese' and are not concerned with the general concept of face as Brown and Levinson intend it:

> [W]hen examined in the light of languages with honorifics, such as Japanese, none of these frameworks [i.e. Brown and Levinson 1987, Leech 1983, and Lakoff 1973, 1975] appears adequate enough. The major linguistic devices for politeness in Japanese either fall outside of these frameworks or play a minor part in them. The frameworks thus appear to be the product of the Western academic tradition, since even Brown and Levinson...could not avoid an ethno-centric bias toward Western languages and the Western perspective (Ide 1989: 224).

Ide contends that formal forms of language (e.g. honorifics) are not necessarily negative politeness strategies in the case of Japanese language. She maintains that there are fundamental differences be-tween formal forms of language and the use of negative politeness strategies. Ide argues that in Japanese such forms are: i) limited in choice; ii) sociopragmatically obligatory; iii) grammatically obliga-tory; and iv) made in accordance with a person who is not necessarily the addressee, the referent or the speaker him/herself (Ide 1989: 226–230). According to Ide, it is not possible to avoid using these honorifics because they are an innate part of the linguistic structure of Japanese language, and they therefore do not present areas of choice, as face issues do.

Ide's second argument is that Brown and Levinson do not take into account the Japanese idea of discernment,[1] or *wakimae*. She de-

---

1   'Discernment' is defined by Hill et al (1986: 348): '[O]nce certain factors of ad-dressee and situation are noted, the selection of an appropriate linguistic form and/ or appropriate behaviour is essentially automatic'. Ide (1989: 230) considers this definition to be the closest equivalent term to the Japanese *wakimae*.

scribes *wakimae* as '[t]he practice of polite behaviour according to social conventions...to show verbally or non-verbally one's sense of place or role in a given situation according to social conventions' (Ide 1989: 230). Ide contends that discernment, rather than face, is the motivating stimulus behind politeness in Japanese culture. She asserts that the discernment aspect of linguistic politeness in Japanese is oriented toward the requirements of the prescribed positions or roles of the participants, and toward the prescribed norms of the formality of given settings, rather than toward face wants. Ide's perspective appears to resemble that of Matsumoto: both authors claim that in Japanese language 1) the choice of forms is obligatory according to the formality of the setting and the relationship between the participants; and 2) the choice of forms is not always related to FTAs.

However, there are a number of counter-arguments against the claims made by Matsumoto (1988) and Ide (1989). Their assertion that some linguistic choices are obligatory in Japanese language is refuted by Fukushima (2000), who argues that Matsumoto and Ide have simply explained how polite forms work in the Japanese language.

> It is true that the language choice is determined by the relationship between the addresser and the addressee, and one has to be sensitive to the group, as Matsumoto suggests, and one has to *discern* one's place, as Ide claims. However, politeness is not manifested by those obligatory linguistic choices alone (2000: 54).

Kasper (1994: 3207) concurs with this viewpoint. She argues that the features which Matsumoto and Ide describe are *sociolinguistic* aspects of language, and are not the concern of pragmatics at all.

Matsumoto uses the example of the obligatory use of verb forms in Japanese language (from impolite forms to very polite forms) to suggest that it is not possible to avoid marking the politeness between two interlocutors. Thomas (1995), however, counters that this obligatory use of a form of copula is pragmatically insignificant because 'the speaker has no *choice* as to whether to use the deferent form or not – usage is dictated by sociolinguistic norms' (Thomas 1995: 152). So deference has little to do with pragmatic politeness. Rather, it is a distinct phenomenon which refers to the respect shown to other people by virtue of their age or status. Politeness, on the other hand, is con-

61

cerned with showing consideration to others, and is not built into a language. In summary, although Matsumoto (1988) and Ide (1989) do make interesting points, it seems most likely that they are simply demonstrating some sociopragmatic aspects of Japanese language (Fukushima 2000: 55).

Ide's (1989) argument that discernment (*wakimae*), rather than face, is the primary motivator for politeness in Japanese is also disputed by Fukushima (2000). Fukushima doubts Ide's claim that honorifics show discernment and are thus separate from face:

> In fact, speakers who misuse honorifics are regarded as people who do not *wakimaeru* their place, and consequently it is they who lose face (2000: 56).

Fukushima also argues against Ide's claim that face is relevant only in societies which are highly individualistic:

> The loss of face which occurs when an individual displays lack of discernment in the choice of honorifics [i.e. in the Japanese context] suggests that Ide's claim cannot be sustained (2000: 56).

The use of honorifics in Japanese language appears to be tied in with face-maintenance. However, face is associated with acknowledging and maintaining role or status in relation to others, which is no less important in a group-oriented society (such as Japan) than in an individual-oriented society (cf. Mao 1994).

Is the concept of *wakimae* unique to Japanese society, as Ide (1989) implies? Fukushima (2000) doubts that this is the case:

> In every society one is expected, or would like to act according to the norms of that society...[I]n order to act according to the norms of each society, one has to *wakimaeru* his/her own position in society. Therefore I think *wakimae* applies universally (56).

Kasper (1990) concurs with this statement, though she points out that there are differences in the degree to which conformity is required in each culture:

> [W]hile to date no language has been shown to entirely fall short of forms for social indexing, nor to lack contexts where social marking is mandatory, *the*

extent to which social indexing is obligatory varies greatly across languages (1990: 196, my emphasis).

Nevertheless, the necessity for some degree of consciousness of one's position relative to that of others in a society seems to be an inherent part of any society. Ide's argument that *wakimae* is peculiar to Japanese society is questionable.

Matsumoto (1988) and Ide (1989) provide explicit criticisms of Brown and Levinson's (1987) politeness theory. We turn now to a discussion of Japanese politeness norms that does not directly criticise Brown and Levinson, but rather presents a model of social distance that differs significantly from Brown and Levinson's view of this variable.

2.5.3 Doi's concept of 'enryo', and Wolfson's 'bulge' theory

In Brown and Levinson's conception of politeness, the degree of indirectness employed in a speech act is directly related to the degree of social distance between the interlocutors. If two speakers know one another well, indirectness is not necessary; otherwise, a degree of indirectness is required in order to minimise the potential face-threat of a negative speech act. However, there are two theories of social interaction which contrast with that of Brown and Levinson (1987). The first of these is Takeo Doi's (1981) notion of *enryo*, and the second is Nessa Wolfson's 'bulge' theory of interaction (1988). These two conceptions of indirectness are in many ways very similar; their principal difference lies in their intended area of application. Doi's concept was formulated specifically for Japanese culture, while Wolfson's concept was intended to apply to middle-class American culture.

Enryo

Enryo is a Japanese concept which roughly means 'restraint' or 'holding back' (Doi 1981). The two *kanji* (Japanese characters) of which the word is comprised – *en* and *ryo* – mean literally, 'distant consideration'. *Enryo* describes a pattern of behaviour towards others which is delineated by the closeness of the relationship, and of which conversation is one aspect. In terms of speech behaviour, *enryo* is roughly synonymous with indirectness.

Enryo is used primarily as a negative benchmark for measuring degrees of intimacy in interpersonal relationships. Some relationships, as between family members, contain no *enryo*, i.e. there is no need for 'restraint' or 'holding back'. Relationships that are close, but not as close as family, call for a degree of *enryo*. Work-based or socially-based relationships require a greater degree of *enryo*. One might surmise that in interactions between strangers a great deal of *enryo* would be necessary, but in fact the opposite is the case. According to Doi (1981), an encounter in which no relationship has been established does not require any *enryo* at all. The reason for this peculiarity is that Japanese divide their lives into inner sectors (family and close relatives) and outer sectors (friends, colleagues, acquaintances), as well as a third sector, that of strangers. Each sector prescribes its own, distinctive standards of behaviour. Doi explains that

> [i]f one takes relationships in which *enryo* is at work as a kind of middle zone, one has on the inner side of it members of one's family with whom there is no *enryo*, and on the other side strangers…with whom the need for *enryo* does not occur (Doi 1981: 41).

Figure 2.2, below, illustrates this precept. Note that the middle circle is considerably wider than the inner and outer circles, reflecting that the majority of interactions require *enryo*, while only a relatively small number do not.

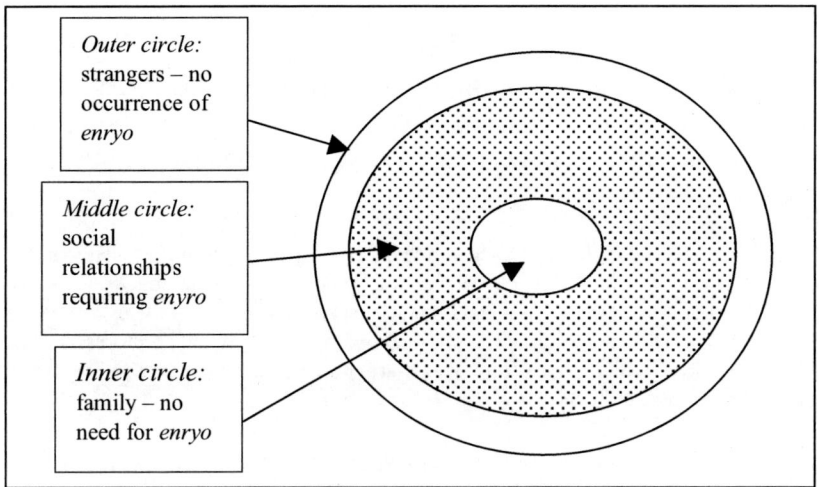

Figure 2.2: Types of interpersonal relationships (stratified by degree of intimacy) and required *enryo* (based on Doi 1981: 41)

Doi clarifies *enryo* by describing what he sees as generic attributes of Japanese people. There are those who are 'good outside but bad inside'; in other words, they are selfish and difficult in dealing with family members, but present a pleasant and considerate front to friends and acquaintances. Also mentioned are the *uchi-benkei*, or 'indoor heroes' who are the lords in their own home but are weak once they step outside the door. Additionally, Doi makes mention of people who are pleasant in personal contacts yet behave with complete indifference to people whom they do not know: '[This is the] type of man – familiar from the proverb 'the traveller discards his sense of shame' – who is diffident and circumspect in the place where he lives, yet in strange surroundings behaves just as the fancy takes him' (Doi 1981: 40).

Although Doi refers only to Japanese culture and does not discuss whether *enryo* or similar forms of speech behaviour exist in other cultures, there is evidence that the concept may be applicable in other cultural contexts: Wolfson's 'bulge' theory, which is discussed next, reports a very similar phenomenon in a middle-class American speech community.

'Bulge' theory

Wolfson (1988) claims that in certain speech communities, the most linguistically polite speech behaviour occurs between acquaintances, colleagues or friends, rather than between close relatives or strangers. She notes that

> When we examine the ways in which different speech acts are realised in actual everyday speech, and when we compare these behaviours in terms of the social relationships of the interlocutors, we find again and again that the two extremes of social distance – minimum and maximum – seem to call forth very similar behaviour, while relationships which are more toward the centre show marked differences (Wolfson 1988: 32).

According to Wolfson, people within these speech communities may not utilise explicit linguistic politeness strategies when interacting with people at either end of the social-distance continuum, i.e. intimate relations and strangers. It is people in between these extremes – acquaintances, colleagues and friends – who are the recipients of the most linguistically polite speech act strategies. As figure 2.3 illustrates, there is a bulge in the degree of linguistic politeness that is used in interaction with people who are neither complete strangers nor intimate friends and family.

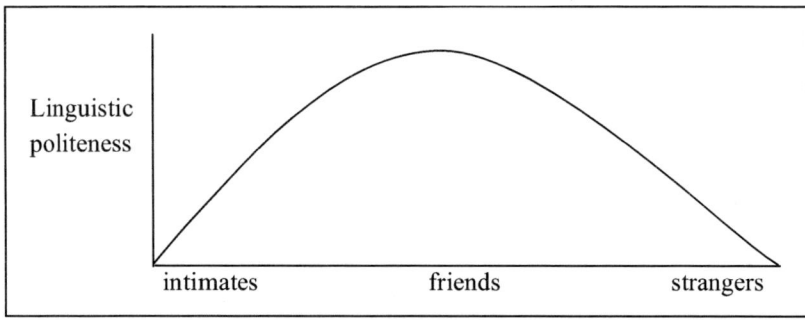

Figure 2.3: Wolfson's 'bulge' model (Wolfson 1988)

Why does this phenomenon occur? What do close relatives and strangers have in common that friends, co-workers and acquaintances do not share? And what do the latter group have that is not shared by the former group? In basic terms, it is the relative *certainty* of the former relationships in contrast with the *instability* of the latter ones. The more a relationship is seen as fixed, the more straightforward it is for speakers to know what to expect of each other. Strangers know where they stand with one another, as do intimates (Holmes 1995: 13). Because there is little uncertainty in such clear-cut relationships, there is little call for ambiguity in speech behaviour. It is the arena of *social* relationships which is most affected by uncertainty and ambiguity:

> In a complex urban society in which speakers may belong to a variety of non-overlapping networks, relationships among speakers are often uncertain. On the other hand, these relationships are dynamic, and open to negotiation. There is freedom here but not security. The emergent and relatively uncertain nature of such relationships is reflected in the care people take to signal solidarity (Brown and Gilman 1972) and to avoid confrontation (Wolfson 1988: 33).

In sum, both Doi's (1981) notion of *enryo* and Wolfson's (1988) 'bulge' theory of social interaction stand in contrast to the model proposed by Brown and Levinson (1987). While Brown and Levinson posit that indirectness and degree of politeness increase as social distance becomes more pronounced, both Doi and Wolfson have suggested that the two extremes of social distance appear to require only the most basic politeness strategies, and that it is the relationships which are grouped in the centre of the social-distance continuum that are the most marked in terms of politeness and indirectness.

Wolfson reinforced the validity of her hypothesis by pointing to similar results in previous studies of speech behaviour. Firstly, she mentioned a study by Beebe (1985) of refusals among native speakers of American English. Beebe reached the same conclusion as Wolfson regarding how social distance affects speech act production:

> Strangers are brief. If they want to say 'no', they do so. Real intimates are also brief. It is friends and other acquaintances who are most likely to get involved in long negotiations with multiple repetitions, extensive elaborations, and a wide variety of semantic formulae (Beebe 1985: 4).

Secondly, Wolfson noted that D'Amico-Reisner (1983, 1985) had reached a similar conclusion in her study of disapproval expressions. D'Amico-Reisner had found that, among native speakers of American

English, direct disapproval was expressed almost exclusively to intimates or to strangers in service encounters. Conversely, '[w]hen exchange types are considered with respect to social distance, the data reveal generally low non-intimate participation in disapproval exchanges'. When disapproval was expressed to interlocutors who were neither intimates nor strangers (i.e. those near the centre of the bulge), only indirect forms were used. A similar pattern exists in Blum-Kulka's (2005) study of politeness in Israeli society. In discussing the public and private domains, Blum-Kulka says that 'you have to be more polite to people who are less close, in the family there is less formality' (2005: 259). In the public domain, however, considerations of politeness carry less weight: 'street behaviour is found lacking in restraint (loud voice, bad language) and consideration (not queuing, pushing and shoving)' (259). Though Blum-Kulka does not explicitly refer to the 'bulge' model, it is possible to infer from her conclusions that Israeli society correlates with Wolfson's pattern.

Boxer (1993) takes Wolfson's theory to task in her analysis of complaining behaviour. Boxer argues that indirect complaining, or griping about circumstances (e.g. the weather, the bus being crowded, work being very busy, long queues at the bank), is often done in an attempt to increase solidarity with an interlocutor, and that the preferred response is commiseration. Boxer found that 'even total strangers engaged in this type of conversational exchange, and agreement of commiseration abounded as responses among strangers' (2002b: 58). It was among intimates that responses differed: there were more contradictions, and higher instances of advice being given. Strangers were amenable to establishing a temporary solidarity, while intimates did not need to do so. Does this finding reduce the validity of the 'bulge' theory for the current project? It is true that Boxer's findings run counter to Wolfson's hypothesis, in which neither strangers nor intimates needed make an effort to establish rapport. However, Boxer refers to complaint as a positive, *preferred* response, i.e. solidarity through commiseration, rather than a negatively affective, dispreferred speech act. The present research, conversely, deals with disagreement solely as a *negatively affective* speech act and not as a means of positively denoting solidarity (see section 2.1.1). So Boxer's criticism does not appear to be relevant to the applicability of Wolfson's 'bulge' theory in the context of this study.

68

Oddly, Brown and Levinson (1987) mention neither Doi's notion of *enryo*, nor Wolfson's 'bulge' theory, despite the fact that these two theories contrast with the Brown and Levinsonian conceptualisation of social distance and politeness. Brown and Levinson do refer to several of Wolfson's earlier pertinent studies (Manes and Wolfson 1981; Wolfson, D'Amico-Reisner and Huber 1983). They refer to D'Amico-Reisner's (1983) study, which showed that speakers in the 'bulge' almost never voiced their disapproval of one another overtly. However, even though all three studies reported findings that contrasted with Brown and Levinson's politeness theory, they make no mention of this discrepancy.

In general, the 'bulge' theory seems to present a useful treatise of speech behaviour. Wolfson (1988) notes that the phenomenon has been documented in other research. Doi's (1981) notion of *enryo* is similar in conception to the 'bulge' theory; his theory is useful because it pertains directly to Japanese culture.

2.5.4 Evaluation of criticisms

I have argued that Brown and Levinson's (1987) framework is a valuable instrument for assessing, comparing and contrasting the different variables which can be utilised in the selection of politeness strategies. In spite of some limitations, their politeness theory is evidently widely applicable among different cultures. Because of this, I will adopt this theory for my research into cross-cultural pragmatics.

However, questions have been raised about the accuracy of the politeness theory for the JLEs in the present study. Doi (1981) implies that Japanese people 'do' politeness differently from the manner proposed in Brown and Levinson's model. Wolfson's (1988) 'bulge' theory reinforces Doi's claim. So which theory is most applicable for Japanese learners of English in New Zealand? Do they follow Brown and Levinson's model, and become more indirect as social distance increases? Or do they follow the pattern proposed by Doi and by Wolfson, and use indirect strategies in the social sphere of interaction but not with intimates or strangers? Because of this uncertainty, I will apply Brown and Levinson's model to the JLE findings with some caution. I will consider the results in relation to both theoretical models, and will account for findings on the basis of whichever provides the most satisfactory explanation.

2.6 Strategies for performing disagreement speech acts

As Stalpers (1995: 276) points out, there are numerous strategies for performing the speech act of disagreement: 'They can be explicit negations of the previous speaker's statement, but they can also be highly mitigated indirect expressions, such as a support of the speaker's own position'. In fact, a disagreement might well be delivered paralinguistically, without recourse to linguistic communication at all. The degree of mitigation required depends on the extent of the speaker's desire to minimise the magnitude of the FTA. As disagreement speech acts are often conducted over a number of turns, it is also possible to discern *patterns* of disagreement strategies conducted over the course of an extended period of talk. These patterns may show that the interlocutors ultimately aim to agree with one another; alternatively, they may show that one interlocutor is determined to verbally discredit the other. This section will discuss the various strategies of disagreement and describe the contexts in which these strategies are likely to be selected. This section also describes patterns which may be formed by combinations of disagreement utterances.

2.6.1 Types of disagreement

Certain illocutionary acts have the potential to damage another person's face. Disagreements, due to their negatively affective nature, fall into this category.

> Disagreement is asymmetrical: it says 'We are different' and it is a short – maybe an inevitable – step from 'We're different' to 'I'm right, so you're wrong' or 'I know and you don't' (Tannen and Kakava 1992: 249).

Consequently, in the context of the mutual vulnerability of face, an individual will normally attempt to either avoid performing this face-threatening act, or to employ certain strategies to minimise the threat to the other's face (Brown and Levinson 1987: 68). In doing this, the speaker will take into consideration three desires:

1. the desire to communicate the content of the FTA;
2. the desire to be efficient and economic; and
3. the desire to preserve the hearer's face to any degree.

In section 2.1.2, I noted that a speech act may be delivered with varying degrees of indirectness, ranging from stating the speech act explicitly to implying it. As there are numerous strategies for performing disagreement speech acts, normally based on the degree of indirectness with which the speaker wants to deliver the speech act, it is useful and expedient to be able to separate these into a set of categories.

A useful discussion of indirectness comes from Searle (1969, 1975). Searle proposes a distinction between direct speech acts, where speakers say what they mean, and indirect speech acts, where speakers mean more than, or something other than, what they explicitly state. Searle argues that there are two types of indirectness in speech acts: conventional and nonconventional. The first type of utterance is indirect because it is conventionally meant to perform an act that is not suggested by its literal meaning: for example, a request such as 'Could you give me a hand?' is polite in that the speaker does not presume to know about the hearer's ability, and also because the hearer has the right to refuse. The second type of utterance is not conventionally associated with any pattern, and so must be calculated. For example, when one speaker says 'Lets go to a movie tonight' and the respondent says 'I have to study for an exam' (Searle 1975: 61), the speaker then has to calculate whether the respondent's answer is intended to reject the speaker's proposal, or whether s/he indeed has to study. These rankings of indirectness might form a useful base for a taxonomy of disagreement speech acts. However, as Thomas (1995: 106–7) points out, Searle's rules seem suited only to the most typical or central instances of a speech act, and fail to delineate effectively between one speech act and another:

> In reality...the reasons for classifying a speech act in a particular way are complex and it is often impossible to assign a speech act to a clear-cut category.

Thomas (1995: 99) charges that, although Searle claims to be setting down rules for speech acts, in fact he is merely describing the semantics of speech act verbs. Also, Searle does not account for face-threat, even though contemporary pragmatic theory accepts that maintenance of face is central to speech act delivery. Clearly, there is a need for a more up-to-date and comprehensive taxonomy, with face-maintenance as a theoretical underpinning.

A more useful template for a taxonomy is described by Brown and Levinson (1987). As noted in section 2.4.2, a speaker may adopt certain strategies in order to lessen the potential damage to the interlocutor's face: the FTA may be delivered bald-on-record, hedged with positive politeness, hedged with negative politeness, or off-record. These categories are more applicable to this study than those of Searle because they are more extensive, and because they are concerned not simply with semantic properties but with the effect of a speech act on an interlocutor's face. Based on Brown and Levinson's (1987) classification for performing speech acts, a taxonomy of four categories is set out below. In the italicised fictional examples, the speaker has been asked if s/he agrees with an interlocutor's assessment of a second-hand couch:

1. Explicit / direct disagreement, e.g. 'I don't like this couch at all.'
2. Disagreement hedged with positive politeness, e.g. 'It's a nice couch, but I don't like it.'
3. Disagreement hedged with negative politeness, e.g. 'You've obviously set your heart on it, but I don't like it.'
4. Implied disagreement, e.g. 'Um, well, it's certainly an interesting colour...'

These categories are utilised in the analysis of data collected by the various methodological instruments used in this study. The four categories are discussed in the following sections, and listed in table 2.1, below.

Explicit strategies

Explicit strategies for performing FTAs are those that have only one literal meaning. An FTA will usually only be performed in this way if the speaker is not concerned about retaliation from the hearer. Such circumstances may include a) when hearer and speaker both tacitly agree that the relevance of face requirements may be suspended in the interests of efficiency, e.g. during an emergency; b) when the threat to the hearer's face is negligible; and c) where the speaker is vastly superior in power to the hearer, or is able to enlist the support of others to destroy the hearer's face without damaging his or her own (Brown and Levinson 1987: 69).

This category was formulated to identify and classify any explicit disagreements produced by JLEs. There is evidence that second language learners from an Asian cultural environment might, in certain circumstances, be more direct than NSs in using negatively affective strategies (Fukushima 2000; Lee-Wong 2000; Yu 1999) (see section 2.2.1). Hence, this category is valuable for determining the extent to which the JLE participants in the present study use explicit disagreeing strategies as opposed to other, less direct strategies.

Mitigating strategies (positive politeness)

According to Brown and Levinson, it is common for a speaker to orient him/herself toward the hearer's positive face, i.e. the hearer's desire to be liked and approved of. Such strategies '[enhance] the face of the addressee by indicating that in some respects, S wants H's wants (e.g. by treating him as a member of an ingroup, a friend, a person whose wants and personality traits are known and liked)' (Brown and Levinson 1987: 75). Mitigating strategies of this kind are likely to be adopted to some degree by both NS and JLE participants, due to a desire for contiguity in communicative interaction (Sacks 1987). So it

73

is useful to gather information about precisely which mitigating strategies are most likely to be utilised by each participant group, and which are least likely to be employed.

Note that in table 2.1, the category of positive politeness strategies has been sub-divided into two groupings: simple and complex. This was done because some of the positive politeness strategies are likely to require a greater degree of sociopragmatic and pragmalinguistic fluency than others, and it is useful for analytical purposes to be able to delineate broadly between two distinct levels of complexity. Examples of the positive politeness strategies incorporated into the 'complex' category are in-group jargon and slang, which require specific lexical knowledge, and joking, which necessitates a degree of ability to use humour appropriately in the target culture.

Mitigating strategies (negative politeness)

Negative politeness strategies are oriented toward the hearer's negative face, i.e. his/her desire not to be impeded or put upon, to be free to act as s/he chooses. 'Negative politeness manifests itself in the use of conventional politeness markers, deference markers, minimising imposition etc' (Thomas 1995: 172). Just as speakers may hedge their disagreements using positive politeness strategies, so they may use negative politeness strategies such as questioning or stating the disagreement as a personal opinion. Analysis of the data will reveal which of these negative politeness strategies are most likely to be used by JLEs, and also whether they use these strategies more than positive politeness strategies.

Implied strategies

Implied disagreement strategies are performed 'in such a way that it is impossible to attribute only one clear communicative intention to the act' (Brown and Levinson 1987: 211), such as through hinting or through vague, unfinished sentences. This approach roughly corresponds with Brown and Levinson's category of 'off-record' strategies. In performing an implied disagreement strategy, the speaker is able to avoid responsibility for the FTA, because it is left to the addressee to interpret it. The form of such strategies may be linguistic, pragmatic, or a combination of both.

74

Many implied disagreements are expressed using paralinguistic cues, i.e. those that are separate from the explicitly-stated utterance but are still intended to convey meaning. In speech behaviour, a variety of paralinguistic channels are used for this purpose; these include gaze direction, facial expression, head or body movement, gesture or posture (Gass and Houck 1999: 109), as well as verbalised channels such as tone of voice, verbal pauses or hesitations. Disagreement strategies frequently involve some of these channels; in fact, implied disagreements may rely on them entirely, since 'nonverbal behaviour can express a message on its own' (Gass and Houck 1999: 108). As Hall (1976) notes, paralinguistic cues are culturally determined and must be read against a cultural backdrop. Accordingly, there is greater propensity for misreading of such cues in a cross-cultural context:

> In new and unknown situations, in which one is likely to be most dependent on reading non-verbal cues (NVC), *the chances of one's being correct decrease as cultural distances increase* (Hall 1976: 76, italics original).

Because the meaning of paralinguistic cues often alters in a cross-cultural context, it was crucial that both native and non-native speaker perceptions of these cues be elicited as part of the data-collection. Obtaining information about participants' sensitivity to paralinguistic cues was one function of the judgment task used to elicit interpretation of disagreement speech acts (see section 3.4.2).

2.6.2 A table of disagreement strategies

The strategies subsumed under the four categories above are presented in table 2.1, below (the examples are non-authentic and were created for illustrative purposes):

Strategy	Example
Explicit, i.e. Direct disagreement Criticism / negative evaluation	I'm afraid I don't agree. That's not practical.

Hedged with simple positive politeness, i.e.	
Exaggerate sympathy with hearer	It's certainly an excellent attempt, but...
In-group address forms or slang	Hey mate, that was my seat.
Use safe topics	Your car is beautiful! It's parked in my spot though.
Token agreement	I agree with you, but...
Hedge opinions	It's beautiful, in a way.
Alternative suggestion	How about trying...?
Hedged with complex positive politeness, i.e.	
Positive remark	You've certainly put a lot of work into this.
Raise common ground	I know you've had a hard time lately...
Compromise	Let's try a lighter colour as well as this one.
Joke	The green curtains look like a pile of lawn clippings.
Offer / promise	I'll help you redo it.
Be optimistic	If I listen to the song some more I may get used to it
Give reasons	We should turn the heater off, so we don't have a fire.
Hedged with negative politeness, i.e.	
Conventional indirectness	A: Shall I turn the heater on? B: We're going out.
Question	Do you think that would work smoothly?
Minimise imposition	There's just one thing I'm not sure about.
Give deference	You know more about this than I do, but...
State disagreement as a personal opinion	This is just my opinion, but...
Admit the impingement	I'm sure you must be very busy, but...

Implied, i.e.	
Hint	I suppose if you like it, you could wear it at home…
Understate	I suppose it's not too bad.
Be vague	I think someone might be missing the point.
Over-generalise	Everybody has to obey the law, you know
Be incomplete, use ellipsis	Well, if you're going to split hairs about it…

Table 2.1: Strategies for performing disagreement speech acts

The disagreement strategies presented in table 2.1 are based for the most part on the strategies expounded by Brown and Levinson (1987). Since Brown and Levinson published their original work in 1978, there has been much commentary about, and re-evaluation of, their conception of politeness theory (see section 2.5). Consequently, various additional politeness strategies have been suggested by other authors. Pomerantz (1984: 70), for instance, mentions that a 'delaying device' such as pausing or requesting clarification may be utilised before making a disagreeing statement. Beebe and Takahashi (1989a) also propose a number of semantic formulae for power-unequal disagreements, including criticism, questioning, offering an alternative suggestion or making a positive remark. These have been integrated into the table above as appropriate.

Some researchers have considered disagreement from the perspective of *patterns* of strategies. These patterns provide a larger and more comprehensive representation of disagreement delivery, and complement the discussion of strategies with which the present study is primarily concerned. They are outlined in the following section.

2.6.3 Patterns of foregrounded disagreement

Three primary types of disagreement were proposed by Scott (2002). These appear to exist on a continuum of increasing explicitness and escalating hostility. The three types consist of *backgrounded*, *mixed* and *foregrounded* disagreement. The characteristics of these are presented in table 2.2, below:

Disagreement type	Characteristics
Backgrounded Mixed Foregrounded	Implicit, solidarity-oriented Ambivalent (possibly defensive or aggressive) Explicit, hostile

Table 2.2: Scott's (2002) taxonomy of disagreement types

Within the framework of foregrounded disagreement, there are three disagreement patterns: *collegial* disagreements, *personal challenge* disagreements, and *personal attack* disagreements. These three patterns are comprised of different linguistic features, taking place over a number of turns, which Scott identified within the category of foregrounded disagreement. Such features include flow of conversation, use of questioning, use of the second person, negation, repetition, use of modals, and bids for the floor (Scott 2002: 311). These patterns provide a means for considering and describing the *overall* conceptualisation of the disagreement speech act, rather than discussing each individual strategy. Each pattern will be elucidated in the next three sections, and will be used as appropriate in discussing and interpreting the findings of this research.

Collegial disagreement

Patterns of collegial disagreement are usually found in mild disagreement sequences. These patterns emphasise the flow of turn-taking and the use of questions. There is frequent overlapping and latching, repetition, negation, modality and many short turns. These elements give collegial disagreement patterns a 'chaotic, fast-paced air, as multiple voices compete simultaneously for the floor' (Scott 2002: 318). In line

78

with the relatively mild tone of collegial disagreement patterns, questions used tend to be relatively innocuous. For example:

> *Rhetorical questions*, e.g. 'Why are we having this silly argument about people who are in the country illegally?'
> (from Scott 2002: 317)
>
> *Wh-questions*, e.g. 'What do you think?'; 'Where's the decency here?'.
> (from Scott 1998: 222).

Although patterns of collegial disagreement tend to be relatively mild, this is not the case for the other two patterns, personal challenge disagreement and personal attack disagreement.

Personal challenge disagreement

Personal challenge disagreements attack the individual, questioning his/her integrity or the reliability of his/her argument. The aim is often to discredit the individual (Scott 1998). Patterns of personal challenge disagreements are particularly strong on the use of questioning and negation:

> The large number of overtly confrontational questions in [personal challenge disagreements], combined with a tendency towards accusatory second-person pronoun use, contributes to negation playing a prominent role..., as interlocutors deny and rebut comments (Scott 2002: 320).

An example of negation is below:

> A: 'It's because of the conservative politics. [You don't want to hear Justice Scalia
> B: [*No no no no.*
> (from Scott 1998: 252)

Speakers in this type of disagreement pattern tend to use questions in order to personally challenge their interlocutors. In the example below, the speaker is drawing a seemingly unfavourable comparison between the hearer's opposition to a conservative judge giving speeches, and the hearer's presumed absence of comment when a former liberal Justice participated in environmental marches:

[William O. Douglas was] constantly involved in environmental issues. He made marches on the CNO Canal that took days, not mere hours as a speech would. He was one of the most outspoken justices we ever had. *Where were you then, Bill Press?*
(from Scott 1998: 264, emphasis original)

By personally attacking the hearer's purportedly incongruent behaviour, the speaker is attempting to discount the hearer's argument. The next level of disagreement takes the focus away from the interlocutor's argument, and attacks the interlocutor *as a person*.

Personal attack disagreement

This type of disagreement pattern is characterised by confrontational use of the second person, negation used to deny allegations, repetition, frequent overlapping and a tendency towards short turns. 'Competition for the floor is fierce' (Scott 2002: 322). Much of the negation used in this pattern of disagreement directly follows accusational uses of the second person. For example:

A: Isn't that just patently, absolutely, totally ridiculous?
B: To you it may be, given - given your limited knowledge on the subject...
(from Scott 1998: 268)

Repetition is also a common feature of this type of pattern, reflecting the fast-moving, overlapped talk: 'Not surprisingly, the use of repetition to have one's voice heard dominates' (Scott 2002: 322). Repetition has three purposes in personal attack disagreements:

1. to emphasise or elaborate on a point already made, e.g.

A: [You don't want to hear Justice Scalia.
B: [No, no, no, no.
(from Scott 1998: 264)

2. to refocus talk onto a topic which has previously been raised and ignored, or to refocus talk onto a contradiction of a previous point, e.g.

A: It's a bogus number.
B: It is not a bogus number.
A: It's a bogus number.
(from Scott 1998: 234)

3. to ensure that one's voice has been heard after a period of overlapping speech, e.g.

A: We just don't want it written [into law.
B: [And maybe on that-
C: [?] don't want it written into the   [law.
B: [Maybe on that point of agreement, we've
got to=
(from Scott 1998: 219)

Personal attack seems to be the most explicit and hostile form of disagreement pattern.

This section has outlined three patterns of foregrounded disagreement. Scott regards these three patterns as separate entities which
nonetheless have overlapping features. She points out that the three
patterns have a number of linguistic features which are common to
more than one pattern of disagreement (1998: 216). This seems to be a
weakness in Scott's discussion of patterns of disagreement. The types
of disagreement share so many of the same characteristics (albeit to
different degrees) that they tend to meld into one another. There appears to be a blur in the distinction between what features constitute,
for example, a personal challenge disagreement as opposed to a personal attack disagreement. In order to prevent any confusion in this
study, I will refer to Scott's patterns of foregrounded disagreement
only when the patterns I am referring to in my data are clear and un-
ambiguous examples of these disagreement patterns.

2.6.4 Summary

This section has explained the various strategies of disagreement, and described the contexts in which these strategies are most likely to be selected. It has also described patterns which may be formed by combinations of these disagreements.

It seems that, unless an utterance is intended to be offensive (e.g. regard when insulting someone or denigrating their argument), speakers generally need to consider how to phrase their disagreement so that the weight of the FTA is minimised, but the point is still made. The overwhelming factor in selecting appropriate disagreement strategies is the speaker's perception of how *polite* s/he needs to be in that situation. This is discussed in the next section.

2.7 Cultural dimensions of this study

There are numerous pragmatic differences between Japanese culture and New Zealand culture. The sociopragmatic and pragmalinguistic politeness norms in each culture invariably influence how its members select politeness strategies in talk, as well as how they interpret strategies produced by their interlocutor. In cross-cultural interaction, the differences between these two sets of cultural norms are a major cause of pragmatic failure. In order to gain a clearer understanding of how cross-cultural pragmatic failure occurs, it is important to understand some of these differences. Hence, this section outlines an approach for identifying and quantifying some of the points of divergence between cultures. It then applies this approach as a theoretical underpinning to the cultural milieus of Japan and New Zealand.

2.7.1 Defining culture

Just as 'politeness' has been defined in various ways, so there are numerous interpretations of 'culture'. Scollon and Scollon (1995) have identified the two most common definitions of the word:

1. high culture, which refers to intellectual and artistic achievements; and
2. anthropological culture, meaning 'any of the customs, worldview, language, kinship system, social organisation and other taken-for-granted day-to-day practices of a people which set that group apart as a distinctive group' (Scollon and Scollon 1995: 126).

Because the focus of this research is on intercultural communication, I am concerned not with high culture, but with anthropological culture, which Adler (1997: 15) defines as being:

1. something that is shared by all or almost all members of some social group;
2. something that the older members of the group try to pass on to the younger members; and
3. something (as in the case of morals, laws and customs) that shapes behaviour, or structures one's perception of a society and his/her place within it.

According to Adler, individuals articulate culture and its normative qualities through the principles that they embrace about life and the way they perceive the world. In turn, these principles affect their attitudes about the form of behaviour considered most appropriate in any particular situation. Barnouw (1982: 4) offers a similar definition:

A culture is the way of life of a group of people, the complex of shared concepts and patterns of learned behaviour that are handed down from one generation to the next through the means of language and imitation. A person is destined to learn the patterns of behaviour prevalent in the society in which [s/he] grows up.

Robinson (1988) notes the danger of adhering too closely to one particular definition of culture, and stresses the merits of combining cultural conceptualisations. With this in mind, the present study does not adopt any one view of culture, but uses the more general conceptualisation of anthropological culture proposed by Adler (1997) and Barnouw (1982) above.

Sperber (1996) proposes a naturalistic approach to culture. In his conceptualisation, culture refers to the causes and effects of thought processes spreading continuously among people, social groups and environments. He says that the 'mental modularity' of these processes serves as the basis for not only the universal aspects of culture but also for cultural diversity. Sperber's approach is useful from an anthropological and cognitive standpoint, but the present study requires a perspective that is socioculturally and linguistically informed. Also, Sperber favours a holistic view of culture, whereas I intend to analyse specific components of culture such as power and social distance. For these reasons, Sperber's 'natural approach' is not used for analytical purposes in this study.

2.7.2 Dimensions for measuring culture

A frequently cited instrument for analysing culture is Hofstede's (1991; 2001) cultural framework, which discusses culture in terms of the mental programming of cultural groups. Hofstede (1991) outlines four dimensions by which the value systems of different cultures may be ordered: individualism–collectivism; uncertainty avoidance; power distance; and masculinity–femininity. I will briefly explain each of these.

Individualism–collectivism
In individualistic cultures, people tend to look after only themselves and their immediate family. Such societies are likely to encourage behaviour that brings merit to specific people. Conversely, in collectivist cultures people belong to in-groups or collectives which look after them in exchange for loyalty. This kind of society places a high value on harmony and good interpersonal relationships (Hofstede and

Bond 1984; Yoshida 1994; Triandis 1994). Table 2.3 below summarises some of the most important differences between collectivist and individualist societies.

Collectivist	Individualist
People are born into extended families or other in-groups which protect them in exchange for loyalty	Everyone grows up to look after him/herself and his/her immediate family only
Identity is based on one's social network	Identity is based in the individual
Harmony should be maintained and direct confrontations avoided	Speaking one's mind is a characteristic of an honest person
Employer-employee relationships are perceived in moral terms, like a family link	Employer-employee relationships are based on mutual advantage
Hiring and promotion decisions take employees' in-group into account	Hiring and promotion decisions are based on skills and rules only

Table 2.3: Key differences between collectivist and individualist societies
(from Hofstede 1991: 67)

One of the primary differences between individualistic and collectivistic cultures is that the latter tend to focus on an *in-group*, rather than an *out-group*. Collectivist cultures emphasise the goals, needs and views of the in-group over those of the individual. The social norms of the in-group are more important than an individual's preferences; mutually-held in-group beliefs carry greater weight than unique individual beliefs; cooperation with members of the in-group is more important than individual outcomes (Triandis 1986). Also, members of collectivistic cultures make a sharper distinction between people who are members of in-groups (e.g. those with whom they work) and out-groups (e.g. interaction with strangers), and tend to perceive in-group relationships as being more intimate than members of individualistic cultures (Gudykunst, Yoon and Nishida 1987: 296). The larger the number of in-groups, the narrower and less pervasive the influence each in-group has on the individual. 'Since individualistic cultures have many specific in-groups, they exert less influence on individuals than in-groups do in collectivistic cultures where there are few general in-groups' (Gudykunst, Yoon and Nishida 1987: 296).

In short, individualism pertains to societies in which the ties between individuals are relatively loose. Conversely, collectivism pertains to societies in which people are from birth integrated into strong and cohesive in-groups which often last through the lifetimes of the in-group's members.

Uncertainty avoidance

Uncertainty avoidance refers to the degree to which a culture feels threatened by ambiguous situations and tries to avoid uncertainty by establishing more structure. In comparison to members of cultures low in uncertainty avoidance, members of cultures high in this dimension have a lower tolerance for uncertainty and ambiguity. This expresses itself through higher levels of anxiety, greater need for formal rules, and less tolerance for people or groups with deviant ideas or behaviour.

Power distance

Power distance is 'the extent to which the less powerful members of institutions and organisations accept that power is distributed unequally' (Hofstede and Bond 1984: 419). Members of high power distance societies tend to accept power inequality as being an inherent part of the society, whereas people from low power distance societies do not.

Table 2.4 below outlines some of the major differences between societies with a low degree of institutional inequality (known as *small* power distance societies), and those with a higher degree of inequality (*large* power distance societies). Note that tables 2.3 and 2.4 deliberately polarise the two types of society in order to stress the differences between them. In reality, most cultures will fall somewhere between the two extremes presented in these examples.

Small power distance	Large power distance
There is interdependence between less and more powerful people	Less powerful people depend on more powerful people
Parents and children treat one another as equals	Parents teach children obedience; children treat parents with respect
Teachers expect initiative from students in class	Teachers take all initiatives in class
Narrow salary range between top and bottom of organisation	Wide salary range between top and bottom of organisation
Subordinates expect to be consulted	Subordinates expect to be told what to do
Privileges and status symbols are frowned upon	Privileges and status symbols for managers are expected and popular

Table 2.4: Key differences between small and large power distance societies
(from Hofstede 1991: 37)

The dimension of power distance conveys information about *dependence* relationships in a country (Hofstede 1991). In small power distance countries there is only limited dependence of subordinates on bosses, and a preference for consultation. Conversely, in large power distance countries there is considerable dependence of subordinates on bosses, and consultation is rare. 'Power distance can therefore be defined as the extent to which the less powerful members of institutions and organisations within a country expect and accept that power is distributed unequally' (Hofstede 1991: 28).

Masculinity–femininity
Masculinity refers to societies in which social gender roles are clearly separate (i.e. in which men are expected to be confident, tough and focused on material success whereas women are expected to be more modest, caring and concerned with the quality of life). Femininity pertains to societies in which these gender roles overlap (i.e. both men and women are expected to be modest, tender and concerned with the quality of life) (Hofstede 1991: 82–3).

2.7.3 Relevant cultural dimensions for this study

Two of Hofstede's dimensions are particularly pertinent to the present study: individualism–collectivism, and power distance. The dimension of individualism–collectivism is applicable because it is concerned with the relationship between the self and the group. Differing orientations of individualism–collectivism can frequently influence how interlocutors select communication strategies in cross-cultural talk. The dimension of power distance is important because an individual's perception of power inequality is likely to influence his or her selection of politeness strategies. As power distance varies according to each culture, individuals with differing cultural backgrounds are likely to have differing ideas about power inequality in a given situation, and are therefore likely to choose different politeness strategies. Note that this dimension is linked to Brown and Levinson's (1987) variable of power, one of the key factors influencing the selection of politeness strategies (see section 2.4.3). Hofstede's remaining two dimensions, uncertainty avoidance and masculinity–femininity are less likely to be applicable in this kind of study because they are not conceptually related to perceptions of communication behaviour (Gudykunst, Yoon and Nishida 1987: 303). Consequently, these two dimensions are only referred to in circumstances where they seem particularly relevant. Thus, in order to explain some of the cross-cultural differences between politeness strategies chosen by JLEs and those chosen by New Zealand NSs, I will primarily use the dimensions of individualism–collectivism and power distance.

In doing this, there is a danger of presuming that all members of a cultural group have the same – or even similar – perspectives. This perception is condemned by Trompenaars (1993: 25): 'People within a culture do not all have identical sets of artefacts, norms, values and assumptions. Within each culture there is a wide spread of these'. Trompenaars warns that there is a risk of cultural stereotyping if one presumes that all members of a culture subscribe to the same patterns of behaviour. However, for the purposes of quantification, a cultural 'average' may exist:

This spread [i.e. that of artefacts, norms, values and assumptions in a society] does have a pattern around an average. So, in a sense, the variation around the norm can be seen as a normal distribution. Distinguishing one culture from another depends on the limits we want to make on each side of the distribution (1993: 25).

I will refer to this 'normal distribution' in discussing the dimensions of individualism–collectivism and power distance among Japanese learners of English and native speakers of New Zealand English.

This section has outlined what is meant by the dimensions of individualism–collectivism and power distance, and described some of the generic characteristics of exemplar cultures. The next section will apply these two dimensions to the cultures of Japan and New Zealand in order to quantify some of the primary distinctions between these two cultures.

2.7.4 Collectivism / power distance in Japanese and New Zealand culture

In terms of individualism, Japan's culture differs to some extent from that of New Zealand. According to Hofstede's individualism index, Japan is ranked 22/23rd out of 53 countries and regions and has a score of 46 out of a possible 91 (which is the score attained by the USA, deemed the most individualist culture). So Japan is only a moderately collectivist culture. However, New Zealand is positioned 6th out of 53 countries and regions and has a score of 79, and is consequently considered a highly individualistic society. Comparatively speaking, Japan is considerably more collectivist than New Zealand.

Japan's ranking of power distance is also different from that of New Zealand. Japan is ranked 33rd out of the 53 countries and regions, with a score of 54 (the highest score was that of Malaysia, with 104). Japan could therefore be said to have a moderate tolerance of inequality. New Zealand, however, is ranked 50th, and has a very low score of 22, indicating that New Zealand as a society has a low tolerance of inequality. When it is weighed against egalitarian New Zealand, Japan's tolerance of power distance is very high.

89

Japan is by no means an extreme example of either the collectivism dimension or the power distance dimension, but when juxtaposed with New Zealand's culture the differences between the two societies are considerable. Japan is moderately collectivistic and tolerant of inequality, while New Zealand is highly individualistic and egalitarian. These cultural differences lay the groundwork for cross-cultural pragmatic failure.

2.8 Approaches to pragmatic development in a second language

This research project considers possible theoretical explanations for the JLE participants' shifts in pragmatic development during their period of residence in New Zealand. Specifically, it aims to illuminate some of the social and cognitive forces that may have helped the participants to increase their ability as second-language learners. In order to provide an appropriate theoretical underpinning for explaining the findings and placing them in the proper theoretical context, this section will delineate two complementary approaches to second language acquisition. The first part is a discussion of cognitive processing of pragmalinguistic items and sociopragmatic features of the L2, and it comprises three models: Bialystok's (1993) two-dimensional model of pragmatic development, Faerch and Kasper's (1987) notion of interlingual transfer, and McLaughlin's (1990) attention-processing model. The second part describes Ochs' (1986) language socialisation approach. The application of each model to second language learners' pragmatic development is explained. I also discuss how each model may be employed in analysing the results of this study. The discussion of these theories is necessarily limited in scope. More extensive discussions are provided by Kasper and Rose (2002), and by Kasper and Blum-Kulka (1993).

2.8.1 Cognitive processing

The first model to be discussed is the two-dimensional model of pragmatic development proposed by Bialystok (1993). Bialystok's model contends that children learning a language have the task of developing new pragmatic knowledge, while adult L2 learners mainly have to acquire processing control over representations that are already fully formed in their L1. Of course, adults need to acquire some new representations as well. European learners of Japanese, for instance, need to learn sociopragmatic categories such as *uchi* (in-group) and *soto* (out-group), as well as sociolinguistic distinctions such as using appropriate degrees of polite speech with different interlocutors. But adults have the advantage of being able to adapt a currently-existing store of available pragmatic knowledge when learning the pragmatic norms of another language. Rose and Kasper (2001) believe that Bialystok's model is an underestimation of the complexity of second language pragmatic learning. Nonetheless, her model 'underscores the significant role that existing pragmatic knowledge plays in L2 learning and suggests that language instruction purposefully build on it' (2001: 6). Bialystok's model is discussed here because it may be applicable to the adult JLEs in this study. Several other relevant studies (Hassall 1997; Kasper and Rose 1999; Kasper and Schmidt 1996; Koike 1989) have produced findings which support Bialystok's two-dimensional model. It will be useful to determine the extent to which the current study supports this model.

The second cognitive strategy which may be applicable to this study's findings is interlingual transfer (Faerch and Kasper 1987). I will briefly explain what this means. According to O'Malley and Chamot (1999), interlingual transfer occurs when an L2 learner projects linguistic features of the L1 onto the target language to assist comprehension or production. There are two kinds of transfer: positive (if the L1 feature is also appropriate in the L2 and is used correctly), or negative (if the L1 feature is not applicable and is used erroneously). Negative transfer is seen as 'a significant source of error for all learners' (Brown 2000: 224), since it can interfere in the processing of a linguistic item, and may also lead to fossilisation, whereby the incorrectly-processed item becomes internalised and is thereafter used erroneously.

Although discussions of transfer have most commonly applied the term to grammatical and lexical items, transfer can equally be applied to the learning of pragmatic principles in the L2. Kasper (1997: 119) defines pragmatic transfer as 'use of L1 pragmatic knowledge to understand or carry out linguistic action in the L2'. As with linguistic transfer, pragmatic transfer may have a positive or a negative outcome. Positive pragmatic transfer results in successful exchanges, whereas negative pragmatic transfer, resulting from an assumption that the L1 and L2 are similar where, in fact, they are not, may result in inappropriate use of speech acts or linguistic forms (Rose and Kasper 2001: 29).

There has been a certain amount of research into the relationship between pragmatic transfer and L2 development. Takahashi and Beebe's (1987) study of refusals by Japanese learners of English at both intermediate and advanced proficiency levels revealed that the intermediate-level learners employed pragmatic transfer as often as advanced learners, despite limited second language knowledge. Hill's (1997) study of requests by advanced Japanese learners of English indicated that these learners transferred requesting forms from Japanese to English as soon as they had the necessary linguistic skills to do so. However, the transfer was not necessarily appropriate: Hill found that the pragmalinguistic features of the JLEs' utterances often deviated from those of native speakers and showed clear evidence of negative transfer, such as overuse of apology moves as external modifiers (e.g. 'So I'm sorry very much', 'I'm feel bad but' and 'Sorry to interrupt you but'). Negative pragmatic transfer also occurred in S. Takahashi's (1996) investigation of how L2 proficiency influenced learners' perceptions of the transferability of requesting strategies from their first language. She found that the Japanese learners of English in her study could not identify English requests that were the real functional equivalent of Japanese request strategies. For example, participants at all levels of proficiency were unaware that the Japanese requesting form *V –tte itadakitai n desu kedo* (I would like you to *V*) would have the functional equivalent 'I was wondering if you could *V'*, which carries less illocutionary force than the literal translation.

92

Takahashi concluded that the learners, no matter what their level of proficiency, continued to rely on their first language request conventions in second language requesting. The findings of the studies by Takahashi and Beebe (1987), Hill (1997) and S. Takahashi (1996) suggest that Japanese learners of English are likely to transfer pragmatic information from their first language to situations in the second language, sometimes inappropriately.

The third model to be discussed is McLaughlin's attention-processing model (McLaughlin 1990; McLaughlin et al 1983; McLaughlin and Heredia 1996; Skehan 1998). According to this model, people store and categorise information by means of two types of cognitive processing: controlled and automatic processing. Controlled processing is defined as a 'capacity limited and temporary' (McLaughlin et al 1983: 142) form of cognitive learning. It is not a learned response, but rather a short-term activation of nodes in a sequence. This activation is consciously controlled by the learner and, because conscious attention is required, only one such sequence can normally be controlled at one time. Automatic processing, by contrast, involves the activation of certain nodes in memory each time the subject is exposed to the appropriate stimuli. This activation is a learned response that has been built up through the repeated mapping of the same stimuli to the same pattern of activation over many trials. Language skills are learned and routinised only after the earlier use of controlled processes:

> Controlled processing requires attention and takes time, but through practice, sub-skills become automatic and controlled processes are free to be allocated to higher levels of processing. Thus controlled processing can be said to lay down the 'stepping stones' for automatic processing as the learner moves to more and more difficult levels (McLaughlin 1990: 115).

The need to increase in cognitive skill requires a language learner to develop a set of well-learned, effective cognitive procedures for dealing with linguistic information so that the more attention-demanding processes are freed up for fresh tasks. When one part of a task – such as the use of a certain grammatical form – becomes automatic, consideration can be given to other, more complex parts of the task and what was previously a difficult task becomes achievable (McLaughlin and Heredia 1996). Automaticity is achieved through a process of 'restructuring' in which 'the components of a task are coordinated, integrated, or reorganised into new units, thereby allowing the old components to be replaced by a more efficient procedure' (McLaughlin 1990: 118).

The present study employs McLaughlin's model in two distinct ways. The model is used in its conventional role, i.e. to illuminate how lexical–grammatical items may be automatised in order to reduce L2 learners' cognitive loads so that pragmatic items can be considered. The model is also extended as necessary to apply to acquisition of pragmatic knowledge as well as linguistic knowledge. Although the information processing model was conceived with purely linguistic processes in mind, it seems reasonable to propose that the model could be extended in this manner since linguistic and pragmalinguistic processes are so closely interconnected.

A caveat is necessary, however: the relevance of the information processing model may be limited to the internalising of pragmalinguistic items, rather than sociopragmatic information. Sociopragmatic knowledge is more complex than pragmalinguistic knowledge, as well as being more nebulous: a speaker constantly has to weigh up the relative status of the interlocutor, the social distance, and the severity of the disagreement, with little recourse to any preset formula for use. Continual conscious processing is often required, and speakers are less likely to reach a point where processing happens automatically. For these reasons, the information processing model is applied to the present study in order to illuminate stages of pragmalinguistic acquisition, rather than acquisition of sociopragmatic information.

2.8.2 Language socialisation

Language socialisation is an interdisciplinary approach, drawing from aspects of sociocultural theory, phenomenology, ethnography of communication, and symbolic interactionism. It refers to the process by which novices in society acquire knowledge of principles of social order and systems of belief through participation in social interaction with experts. These 'novices' may be children, but the term also connotes any newcomer to a community, including second and foreign language learners of any age group (Kasper and Rose 2002: 43). Experts, in the case of second language learners, might include native-speakers, host-family members or teachers, or any other knowledgeable person with whom the learners have language-based interaction. Experts can, through repeated interaction with novices, set out the prototypical structure of given genres that are in use in the L2 community, and demonstrate 'prototypical choices made in exemplars of the genre' (Tarone 2005: 162).

Language socialisation has been described as 'an interactional display (covert or overt) to a novice of expected ways of thinking, feeling, and acting....through their participation in social interactions, children come to internalise and gain performance competence in these sociocultural defined contexts' (Ochs 1986: 2). Sociocultural information is generally encoded in conversational discourse. Many linguistic structures are socially and culturally informed, and carry information concerning social order, local conceptions and theories about the world: 'formal and functional features of discourse carry sociocultural information, including phonological and morpho-syntactic constructions, the lexicon, speech-act types, conversational sequencing, genres, interruptions, overlaps, gaps, and turn length' (Ochs 1986: 2).

A language socialisation model is readily applicable to acquisition of pragmatic knowledge. Blum-Kulka (1997b: 3) delineates the subcategory of *pragmatic socialisation*, which she describes as 'the ways in which children [and also second language learners] are socialised to use language in context in socially and culturally appropriate ways'. So pragmatic novices have an incomplete awareness of the pragmalinguistic forms by which to express a disagreement, or they might have incomplete or inaccurate sociopragmatic understanding of what kinds of disagreement are appropriate in a given context (Yates 2005: 69), and they are reliant upon NSs of the L2 to gradually expose them to these things. Language learners thus acquire 'the local cultural rules regulating conversation, such as the choice of topics, rules of turn-taking, modes of storytelling, and rules of politeness' (Blum-Kulka 1997b: 12).

The participants in this study will undergo a process of language socialisation during their ten weeks of immersion in the target culture, through language-mediated interaction with teachers, host family members, friends and acquaintances who are native speakers. The study will investigate the JLEs' ability to acquire sociopragmatic and sociocultural principles and to learn pragmalinguistic aspects of the L2 through their participation in social interaction.

I said earlier that the language socialisation approach draws on sociocultural theory. In that case, why not simply use sociocultural theory as a theoretical basis for this analysis? The problem is that although sociocultural theory describes how language and cognition are shaped through interpersonal interaction, it focuses solely upon cognitive development rather than on the relationship between language acquisition and culture. Conversely, 'language socialisation research subscribes to a broader, more holistic, culturally contextualised and interpreted view' (Kasper and Rose 2002: 44).

2.8.3 Summary

Two complementary approaches to second language acquisition – cognitive processing and language socialisation – have been extended to provide a theoretical underpinning for the pragmatic development process of the JLE participants. The first is valuable for illuminating some of the cognitive processes which may underpin the JLEs' shifts in pragmatic competence. The second offers a useful construct for identifying ways in which the JLEs may have been socialised through interaction with teachers, host family members and other native-speaker 'experts'. These two approaches to pragmatic acquisition are referred to as appropriate in accounting for the findings of this study.

2.9 Conclusion

Although there has been a considerable amount of previous investigation into speech acts, there has been relatively little study of the speech act of disagreement. Furthermore, disagreement speech acts that are delivered in a cross-cultural milieu have rarely been studied. There appears to be a gap in current research on speech act awareness. Specifically, there are questions as to whether JLEs' negatively affective strategies would be more direct than those of NSs (as Fukushima (2000) found with Japanese requests, and Yu (1999) found with Chinese requests). If so, then this raises issues as to a) what effect this directness would have on the potential for pragmatic failure; and b) whether the JLEs' disagreement strategies would also become more indirect in accordance with the weight of FTAs. In addition, it is uncertain whether Japanese learners of English would be more or less verbose than their NS counterparts.

One of the key tenets of this study is that perceptions of acceptable politeness are often based on culture-specific principles, which may vary widely from one culture to another. It is therefore necessary to understand the cultural dimensions of this study as they pertain to the Japanese context and the New Zealand context. New Zealand is a relatively individualistic, egalitarian culture, while Japan is a relatively collectivistic, stratified culture. In cross-cultural communication, these differences are likely to result in pragmatic failure.

Now that the relevant literature has been reviewed, the next point to be discussed is the design, intention and application of the data-collecting instruments employed in this study.

3 Methodology

3.1 Introduction

The present study takes a multi-method approach to data collection, combining several data-gathering procedures. Each of these provides a unique perspective on the phenomenon under investigation. The methodological framework merges commonly-used procedures with those that are less often utilised. This is advocated by Cohen (1996):

> The complexity of speech act realisation and of strategy selection requires careful development of research methodology in this area. Rather than choosing between ethnographic and elicited data methods, *the combining of different approaches to studying the same speech act* may best enable the researcher to reach useful and reliable descriptions of speech act behaviour (23, my emphasis).

The current project does not utilise any ethnographic data-collecting instruments, but it does employ a combination of data-elicitation techniques which will be discussed in this chapter.

Some previous empirical studies into areas of cross-cultural pragmatics have been shown to suffer from methodological deficiencies. This in turn raises questions about the reliability of their data. Planken (1997: 15) criticises researchers who '[take] the easy way out by complaining about the disadvantages of traditional [methods for collecting data] but [use] them to collect data anyway'. Several data-collecting instruments were utilised in the present study in order to provide multi-faceted data, which would add to the robustness of the conclusions which could be drawn. This chapter describes the aims and objectives of the project and discusses the methods by which these objectives were met.

3.2 Data collection instruments

The data collection instruments utilised in this study were designed to obtain two kinds of data: production data, i.e. data which participants produced when performing the speech act of disagreement; and interpretation data, i.e. data which illuminated how participants construed and translated disagreement speech acts which they were exposed to. Four data-gathering methods were developed:

1. A judgment task, which gathered data about how participants *interpreted* a sequence of disagreements which they observed in a series of short video clips (see section 3.5).
2. A discourse completion task (DCT), which elicited data about how participants *produced* disagreement speech acts. Subjects reported on how they believed they would express disagreement in certain situations (Beebe and Cummings 1996; Kasper 1999) (see section 3.6).
3. A role-play instrument (see section 3.7), which provided information on how subjects might interpret and express disagreement strategies in contexts which were similar to naturally occurring speech (Cohen and Olshtain 1994; DiPietro 1987).
4. A personal information form (PIF) (see section 3.8), which elicited information about the JLE participants' age, previous language learning experience, educational background and other things.

Each of these tasks is discussed in more depth in later sections of this chapter.

3.3 Data collection procedure

3.3.1 Pre- and post-testing of tasks

The DCT and the judgment task were administered to the JLE participants twice: first, as a pre-test at the beginning of a ten-week period of intensive English language instruction in New Zealand; and then as a post-test after this period had concluded. The role-play tasks were also completed twice over the ten-week period, by 2 JLEs (participants are discussed in section 3.4). A ten-week period was decided upon because it is representative of the length of time which many Japanese learners of English spend in New Zealand language schools.

The ten-week interval between pre-testing and post-testing lends a longitudinal aspect to the present study. A longitudinal study 'allows for the direct observation of developmental patterns over time' (Kasper and Rose 2002: 75). The present study is roughly comparable in length with Bardovi-Harlig and Hartford's (1993) 14-week study of NS/NNS student advisory sessions, which they considered longitudinal. However, the ten-week testing duration is very short compared to many other prominent longitudinal studies such as Ohta's (2001) one-year study, or Schmidt's (1983) three-year study. So the conclusions which this study makes about pragmatic development are restricted to the findings from the ten-week period surveyed, and may be less applicable to pragmatic development over longer periods of time.

The same materials were used for both pre- and post-tests. Although this clearly raises the problem of practice effects, these were minimised by a number of features of the experimental design. Firstly, there was a considerable length of time (i.e. ten weeks) between the two testing periods. Secondly, the participants were not aware that they would receive the same testing materials in the post-tests. Thirdly, they were not given feedback on their pre-testing responses, and finally, they had no access to the data-eliciting materials between pre- and post-testing.

3.3.2 Sequence of tasks

The data-collecting sessions, as completed by all 3 groups of participants, took the form presented in table 3.1, below:

JLE Group (n=12)	JLE Role-Play Group (n=2)	NS Group (n=10)
PIF DCT Judgment task	PIF DCT Judgment task Role-plays 1–6	PIF DCT Judgment task Role-plays 1–6
10-week interval	10-week interval	
DCT Judgment task	DCT Judgment task Role-plays 1–6	

Table 3.1: Format of tasks completed by each group

As the first column of table 3.1 indicates, 12 JLEs completed the generic tasks: the personal information form, the DCT and the judgment task. The total length of time taken for each session was roughly 2 hours. As the judgment task and the DCT were administered to the JLE group in both the pre-testing and post-testing sessions, each JLE participant committed a total of approximately four hours to the project.

The administering of the DCT task was always carried out prior to the administering of the judgment task, because the DCT was designed to elicit responses that were based on the participants' current store of pragmatic knowledge. As the judgment task exposed the participants to a number of verbalised and paralinguistic disagreement sequences, their responses to the DCT scenarios may have been influenced if they had seen the judgment task scenarios beforehand.

Therefore, it was necessary to administer the DCT before the judgment task.

The group who participated in the role-play task as well as the three generic tasks always completed this task last. This enabled participants to readily understand the structure and the requirements of the role-play task as a result of their exposure to the previous tasks. Unfortunately, it also raised the possibility that exposure to the previous tasks influenced their responses in the role-play scenarios. However, this problem was mitigated because the data from the spoken role-plays was intended primarily to supplement the data from the written production tasks, rather than to present a separate set of findings.

3.3.3 Compensation

All participants (both NSs and JLEs) received compensation for volunteering their time. They were given a free movie voucher after completing the first testing session, and a second movie voucher after completing the second one. Snacks and drinks were supplied at each testing session.

3.4 Participants

A number of criteria were taken into consideration when selecting participants for the various parts of this study. Too many dissimilarities within the JLE sample would undermine the validity of any claims made about their pragmatic ability. In order to ensure a degree of uniformity, factors such as age and level of language ability were controlled. The criteria for participation, and the various ways in which participants were employed, are described in this section.

There appear to be no firm guidelines for selecting participants for a study of this kind. Bardovi-Harlig and Hartford (1993) chose non-native speakers (JLE) with a TOEFL score of 573 or higher. Conversely, Bardovi-Harlig and Dornyei (1998) chose students who were in levels 4 to 7 of a seven-level programme. Olshtain and Weinbach (1993) and Fukushima (2000) simply used students in an undergraduate university English programme. In such studies, the requirements for participant selection were dictated by the specific phenomena under investigation. The same principle is applied to the present study.

This study involves intermediate-level rather than advanced-level learners. This is partly through necessity, since there were relatively few Japanese learners of English studying at an advanced level when the research was being carried out. However, it also contributes to a research gap. Until now, interlanguage pragmatics research has largely concentrated on advanced level learners, partly because controlled tasks such as role-plays and stimulated recall instruments tend to favour learners with high proficiency. But as research into interlanguage pragmatics increases its emphasis on acquisition, it is becoming necessary to involve learners at different levels of proficiency (Bardovi-Harlig and Hartford 2005: 25). It is important to learn more about the various stages of pragmatic acquisition and to establish which stages are the most productive in terms of L2 pragmatic development.

A total of 14 JLEs took part in this study. The requirements for eligibility in the participant sample called for 1) JLEs of the average age at language schools; and 2) students of a high enough ability to ensure that they might be able to differentiate pragmatic errors from grammatical errors. The participants in this study were selected on the basis of the following criteria:

– they were between the ages of 18 and 25;
– they had reached at least an intermediate level of English language ability (this was determined independently by each of the participating language schools);
– they were Japanese nationals studying ESL on a full-time basis at a language school in Christchurch, New Zealand.

3.4.1 Participant sub-groups

The JLE group of 14 participants was divided into two sub-groups based on their length of residence in New Zealand and their English ability. These are summarised in table 3.2, below:

Group (# of people)	Requirements	Tasks
New-arrival (12)	Less than 3 months in NZ; no exposure to other Anglophone cultures	Personal information form DCT Judgment task
Role-play (2)	Intermediate-level language-learners	Role-plays

Table 3.2: Participant sub-groups, stipulations for participation, and set tasks

New-arrival group: 12 people

The new-arrival group was comprised of twelve JLEs who had been in New Zealand for less than three months. This group participated in the completion of the two primary data-gathering tasks.

Role-Play group: 2 people

This sub-group participated in a series of role-play tasks, acting out disagreement-oriented situations with native-speaker 'interlocutors' – characters acted out by the researcher. The two participants had been in New Zealand for longer than three months. They had gained an intermediate score on a Nelson Assessment Test, which measured lexico-grammatical ability: one had scored 54/100; the other had scored 57/100. These two participants are separated from the new-arrival group because they had been in New Zealand for longer than 3 months (the maximum time period for pre-testing) at the time their pragmatic ability was tested. They were part of a larger number of students who completed the role-plays, but this group's data was not useful since they were advanced students who had been studying in New Zealand for longer than the three-month cut-off period. The role-play data from two students whose ability matched that of the main JLE group was eventually added; however, their DCT and judgment task data was not used.

3.4.2 Enlisting participants

The original plan had been that all the participants in the study should be students at one language school, and that they would all undergo the testing together. This proved unfeasible because no Christchurch language school had such a large number of JLEs who were a) of a sufficient level of ability and b) studying at the language school for ten weeks or longer. Participants were enlisted from six language institutions; in most of these schools, about three or four students were eligible.

3.4.3 Attrition of participants between pre-testing and post-testing

All participants received both verbal and written notification that they would be tested a second time after ten weeks. Nonetheless, there were problems with attrition. Of the original group of Japanese learners of English who volunteered to assist in the study, almost half had left their language schools by the time post-testing sessions began. Consequently, new Japanese participants had to be sought.

3.4.4 Native speakers of New Zealand English

Ten native speakers of New Zealand English participated in the study. These participants acted as a reference group whose data could be compared with that of the JLEs. They were similar in age and education to the Japanese participants in that they were undergraduate university students who were aged between 18 and 25. All of the native-speaker participants completed the DCT, the judgment task and the role-play task.

3.4.5 Participant sample size

The general applicability of this data is somewhat limited by the relatively small sample size. For this reason, statistical analysis is only used for indicative and descriptive purposes. The quantitative elements in this study are chiefly intended to complement the qualitative discussion.

Nonetheless, a considerable number of recent pragmatics-related studies have used samples of a similar size to the one in the current study. Knapp-Potthoff's (2005) study of politeness in mediated telephone calls used 5 participants. Locher's (2004) study of disagreement between guests at a dinner table drew on data from 7 participants, while her analysis of disagreement at a business meeting used 11 participants. Ranney (1992) made a study of the difference between NS–NNS doctor-patient interviews. There were 9 native speaker participants and 9 non-native speakers. Rose and Ng Kwai-fun's (2001) study of complimenting strategies used several groups of 12 to 16 subjects each. Tateyama (2001) investigated explicit and implicit methods of teaching pragmatic routines using two groups of L2 learners. One group had 13 participants, the other 14. Williams' (2005) analysis of teacher-student interaction at a university writing centre used 9 participants. Yates' (2005) study of how non-native speakers established an institutional identity as teachers at a high school comprised 9 native speakers of English and 9 NNSs who were Chinese. A study of interactional discourse markers by Yoshimi (2001) used a sample of 17 people. So the current study is not atypical in terms of sample size for a study of interlanguage pragmatics.

3.5 Judgment Task

3.5.1 Introduction

A judgment task was designed in order to identify the proficiency of JLEs in recognising and accurately interpreting disagreement speech acts in English. This task was based on Bardovi-Harlig and Dornyei (1998), who tested L2 learners' awareness of differences between the production of learners and that of native speakers. They used video-taped, scripted role-plays because '...the richness of the contextual information provided by the video recording allowed the learners to view the type of interaction that best captures the sense of pragmatic infelicities' (1998: 242). As one of the aims in the present study was to gain an 'objective' determination of how participants interpreted disagreement situations, a judgment task was deemed to be the most appropriate method of collecting this type of data.

Four specific areas of comprehension and interpretative ability were weighed up:

1. Could JLEs identify a disagreement speech act?
2. Could they interpret the pragmatic devices used by native speakers of English?
3. Could they accurately interpret how serious a disagreement was?
4. Given the differences between the cultural context of New Zealand and that of their own culture, could they accurately interpret how polite or impolite these interlocutors were being?

These were presented in each of the 18 judgment task situations.

3.5.2 The format of the judgment task

The judgment task was designed to be as comprehensible as possible, and to be completed in a minimal amount of time, in order to reduce participant fatigue (section 3.5.3 has more detail on this). However, it also needed to be efficacious in eliciting meaningful data. This section describes how these two aims were met.

In each section of the judgment task, participants were asked to watch a 5–10 second segment of a New Zealand TV programme. New Zealand TV programmes were selected because the judgment task was designed to measure New Zealand norms of politeness. The original intention had been to present examples of *authentic* New Zealand language and politeness norms, so the most useful programmes would have been unscripted, e.g. news, current affairs, and family-oriented reality shows. However, due to the relatively small number of such shows on New Zealand TV, it was necessary to include numerous segments of scripted drama programmes. Although efforts were made to ensure that the situations depicted in the judgment task were as 'authentic' as possible, many of the situations used cannot be considered strictly 'authentic'. To be sure, both Salzmann (1989) and Washburn (2000) argue that scripted TV programmes such as dramas and situation comedies are quite similar to authentic speech, and that speech acts and pragmatic routines are performed much as they would be in naturally occurring situations. But in a later article, Washburn is less positive:

> In accepting the pragmatic language use offered on television dramas and sitcoms, we must also keep in mind the skewed picture of society that television presents: It is more male, more affluent, more violent and more Caucasian (Comstock 1980). This skewing will affect the kind and quality of pragmatic language use (Washburn 2001: 22).

So there is some doubt about the extent to which the judgment task situations can be construed as containing 'authentic' New Zealand English. Consequently, caution is exercised in drawing conclusions about the authenticity of the situations represented in the judgment task.

Twelve of the eighteen segments portrayed interlocutors enacting a disagreement-oriented exchange, i.e. one of the speakers was using a disagreement strategy that was either explicit, hedged or implied in nature (see section 2.6.1). The remaining six segments were not disagreements. They contained either:

1. other negatively affective speech acts which were linguistically similar to disagreement, e.g. refusal or complaint; or
2. paralinguistic cues which would suggest a negatively-oriented exchange, such as an angry facial expression, or a raised voice.

The objective in presenting these non-disagreement situations was to determine whether the JLEs could accurately identify a disagreement speech act and distinguish it from other negative speech acts. Although the participants were made aware that some of the judgment task situations did not present a disagreement, they were not told how many, nor which speech acts the non-disagreement situations represented.

As Brown and Levinson (1987) stated, the weight of an FTA is influenced by power, social distance and ranking of imposition (see section 2.4.3). Therefore, it was crucial to the effectiveness of the judgment task that participants understood the power and social distance between the TV characters in each segment, and that they could comprehend the situational context well enough to be able to estimate the severity of the disagreement. Accordingly, a short and concise introduction was placed at the beginning of each segment. The aim of this was to contextualise the segment, i.e. to provide the participants with information about the scenario that may not have been obvious from the segment itself. The introduction stated i) the differences in power between the interlocutors; ii) the social distance between them; and iii) a brief outline of the information needed to enable the participants to make a determination about the severity of the situation.

The format which the participants adhered to in completing the judgment task was as follows: The participants were given a written transcript of the segment. They watched the segment three times, with a 30-second break between each viewing to allow them to reread and reconsider the transcript. Once they sufficiently understood the seg-

110

ment, they then indicated in the questionnaire whether they thought the segment contained any form of disagreement:

Is there a disagreement in this section? ❏ Yes   ❏ No

If the participants considered that the situation *did* contain a disagreement speech act, they were asked to consider the disagreement's severity, i.e. the disagreement's ranking of imposition (Brown and Levinson 1987: 42). They then ranked their perception on a 5-point Likert scale:

How <u>serious</u> do you think this disagreement is? Circle a number below.

very serious   1   2   3   4   5   not serious at all
serious

Next they decided whether the character who had made the disagreeing statement was acting with politeness appropriate to the situation. This was also ranked on a 5-point Likert scale:

Is the student being appropriately polite for this situation? Circle a number below.

1	2	3	4	5
Too polite		Appropriately polite		Not polite at all

In the tasks above, participants were asked to highlight any words, phrases or paralinguistic cues in the text that indicated the presence of disagreement, its severity, and the politeness or impoliteness of the characters involved.

If the participants considered that there was *no* disagreement speech act in the segment they had viewed, they were instructed to simply indicate whether they believed the character making the negatively affective statement was being appropriately polite for the situational context. This was to ensure that all participants were actively writing in the questionnaire, regardless of whether they thought the segment contained a disagreement. This would offset the problem of participants being influenced in their assessments by other members of the group who were or were not writing.

111

Because this study was intended to consider both spoken and paralinguistic speech act data, it was necessary for the judgment task questionnaire to contain some means of eliciting the participants' perceptions of NSs' paralinguistic cues (see section 2.6.1). This was presented as follows:

Tick any of the items below that helped you decide how serious (or not) it is (you may tick more than one):

a) face expression b) sound or loudness of voice
c) hand or body movements d) other: _____

This method was the most efficient way of collecting data on paralinguistic cues. It was quicker than having the participants write in long-hand; it was simpler to categorise; and it outlined some paralinguistic cues which participants needed to be aware of as they viewed the segments. However, it may also have created a bias, causing participants to focus their attention on these cues only, and neglect others.

In summary, the judgment task was required to be concise and easily understood, but also effective for collecting quality data. These requirements were met by selecting and editing a series of brief TV disagreement scenarios which presented various combinations of P, D and R variables. These scenarios were delivered to participants in a succinct and comprehensible form, allowing them to complete the task in a reasonable period of time.

3.5.3 Piloting the judgment task

The judgment task was piloted on four occasions. The first occasion was with staff members and postgraduate students from the School of Linguistics and Applied Language Studies at Victoria University of Wellington. The second occasion was with a group of eight native speakers of New Zealand English. The third was with a group of ESL learners who were non-native speakers of English. The fourth was with a group of Japanese university students who were ESL learners, and who were similar in age and English ability to those who would participate in the study proper. Four piloting sessions were required because the judgment task was complex in a number of ways. Clear instances of disagreement had to be found and ambiguous scenarios removed. Extraneous language also had to be eliminated. The most efficient methods of completing the questionnaires needed to be explored, and strict time constraints had to be adhered to in order to minimise participant fatigue. Hence, these four testing sessions were required in order to make the instrument as concise, coherent and effective as possible in collecting relevant data.

The judgment task was designed to draw attention to pragmatic deficiencies among non-native speakers of English. However, the primary methodological pitfall was that the participants' responses to the questionnaire could be construed as simply being due to a grammatical deficiency rather than to a deficit of pragmatic competence. If advanced vocabulary or grammar was used, it would be difficult to distinguish whether errors were due to inappropriate pragmatic interpretation, or simply lexico-grammatical deficiency. It was necessary to make this distinction because '[lack of] grammatical competence may…limit the value of the pragmatic input to the learner' (Bardovi-Harlig 1999: 696). So it was important to reduce this possibility as much as possible in order for the linguistic competence of the JLEs to be emphasised.

Accordingly, one of the aims of piloting was to ensure that the judgment task was grammatically understandable to intermediate-level JLEs. Piloting focused on the following:

1. Ensuring the understandability of the language used in the TV segments and the judgment task questionnaire. There were some concerns about complex vocabulary, colloquial language, and the speed at which native-speaker TV characters spoke.
2. Reducing participant fatigue.
3. Minimising ambiguity about the disagreements presented in the judgment task, i.e. uncertainty about whether they were actually disagreements or another similar speech act.

The potential areas of concern are discussed below.

Vocabulary, colloquial language and speed of speaking

The entire text of the judgment task fell within Nation's (1996) list of the 2,000 most frequently-used words for English language learners. Words which could not be simplified were clarified by 'glossing', i.e. adding the Japanese translation of the word in question. This appeared next to the problematic word, in italicised brackets (see appendix 1).

Piloting revealed that some TV segments contained idioms, colloquial language or potentially complex grammar. These segments were deleted and replaced with segments which were less problematic. Where potentially problematic language still remained, it was supplemented with an explanation in Japanese in order to increase the clarity of the text.

Pilot-testing also revealed that the speed at which the characters in the TV segments spoke was a potential obstacle to understanding the segments. Participants were thus given the opportunity to watch each segment three times (as discussed in section 3.5.2), and were also provided with a written transcript of the utterances in each segment. Additionally, each segment was shortened to the minimum amount of speech required for participants to identify disagreement speech acts.

Reducing participant fatigue

An early version of the judgment task required participants to write all their responses in longhand, but this increased the length of time needed to complete each section. Participants quickly became fatigued, and this affected the quality and quantity of information in their answers.

To solve this problem, a more efficient method of responding was conceived. Each section of the judgment task required participants to:

a. circle words or phrases in the transcript which indicated the *existence* of a disagreement;
b. underline words that suggested the *severity* of the disagreement; and
c. draw a box around words or phrases that denoted the *politeness* of the central character.

114

Subsequent piloting showed that it was much simpler, faster and less tiring for participants to simply mark pertinent speech, rather than to write everything in longhand.

Ambiguity

Piloting revealed that certain TV segments in the judgment task were ambiguous, i.e. it was uncertain whether they presented a disagreement or another speech act, such as qualified agreement. An example from the New Zealand programme *Changing Rooms* illustrates this:

> A: I'm thinking of keeping these chairs.
> B: Yeah, you should keep them, but I think maybe changing the colour would be good.

These segments were eliminated from the instrument and replaced with segments that were more obviously disagreement speech acts. These new segments, in their turn, were piloted with other groups of participants. The final piloting session with a group of JLEs (who were not involved in the actual data collection) established that the segments that were finally decided upon were most certainly unambiguous disagreements.

As mentioned earlier, some of the TV segments were *intended* to present a negatively affective speech act apart from disagreement, such as refusal or complaint. These were piloted along with the disagreement-oriented segments. As with the piloting of disagreements, the piloting of the remaining segments ensured that they presented the speech act which they were intended to present.

3.5.4 Explaining and demonstrating the judgment task to participants

The judgment task was a complex instrument. Participants were asked to view TV segments in an L2 medium, listen to a series of L2 dialogues, and interpret L2 politeness norms. They were also required to follow some quite complicated instructions (detailed in section 3.5.2). So it was imperative that the judgment task be explained clearly and

115

succinctly to the participants. Without sufficient explanation, the data gathered during the first two or three scenarios – before the participants had become familiar with the format of the task – could well be inaccurate. To counteract this problem a three-step plan for explanation was devised, as follows:

i) demonstration;
ii) participant practice, with a disagreement situation;
iii) participant practice, with a non-disagreement situation.

These are briefly discussed one at a time.

Demonstration
An example of a disagreement sequence was screened for the participants. They were shown an example of a questionnaire response page, which was laminated, so that it could be marked or written on with an erasable water-based marker. The participants then watched the example segment three times, and the researcher demonstrated how to respond by writing the appropriate symbols on the laminated questionnaire page.

Participant practice – with disagreement situation
A second example TV segment was screened. This time the participants were instructed to fill out the example response section of their questionnaires by themselves. Once this had been completed, discussion and questions were encouraged. The example segment which was screened for the participants contained an explicit disagreement situation, which was intended to be simple for them to identify.

Participant practice – with non-disagreement situation
Before watching the third example segment, participants were told that not all the segments in the judgment task contained disagreement. They then watched the third segment, which contained an example of a refusal. They were then asked verbally whether they thought there was a disagreement in the segment, and were encouraged to discuss it and to ask questions.

Hence, by the time the participants began to complete the actual judgment task, they should have had a clear understanding of the format for doing so. They had been introduced to the process of filling in the questionnaire and had practiced doing it; they had viewed a TV segment containing a disagreement; and they had viewed a segment which contained no disagreement. Consequently, when they came to complete the task itself, their responses were more likely to be accurate representations of their interpretive ability.

3.5.5 Summary

The judgment task was conceived as a tool for eliciting JLEs' ability to recognise disagreement strategies in face-to-face speech, and to accurately interpret a) the politeness of native speaker interlocutors, and b) the severity of the disagreement situations portrayed. The format for presenting the judgment task was intended to be as time-efficient as possible, while eliciting the maximum amount and quality of data. This format was piloted repeatedly to ensure that it was concise and effective, and that faults were minimised.

The judgment task inevitably has some limitations as a data-collecting tool. Although these have been minimised through piloting, it is impossible to control all the variables that can affect participants' responses. Fortunately, the judgment task data is reinforced by a number of other tools which collect varying types of supplementary data. One of these is the discourse completion task, which is discussed next.

3.6 Discourse Completion Task (DCT)

3.6.1 Introduction

A written DCT consists of a questionnaire containing a number of descriptions of hypothetical scenarios. In each question, a social context is presented. There is a brief scripted dialogue by the imaginary interlocutor. A blank space is left for the participant to complete. An example is below:

> At the university:
> Ann missed a lecture yesterday and would like to borrow Judith's notes.
> Ann: _____
> Judith: Sure, but let me have them back before the lecture next week.
> (from Blum-Kulka, House and Kasper, 1989: 14).

The participant writes what s/he considers an appropriate response in the blank space. For the example above, such a phrase might be: 'Hey, could I borrow your notes from yesterday? I missed the class'. The response depends on the power and social distance variables at play between the two interlocutors.

DCTs have been used as data-collection instruments in a number of studies (Kasper and Dahl, 1991). One of the most notable DCT-based studies has been the Cross-Cultural Speech Act Realisation Project (CCSARP) (Blum-Kulka, House and Kasper, 1989). Other studies employing this technique include Beebe, Takahashi and Uliss-Weltz (1990); Bergman and Kasper (1993); Blum-Kulka (1982); Blum-Kulka and Olshtain (1984, 1986); Eisenstein and Bodman (1986); Faerch and Kasper (1989); Lee-Wong (2000); Olshtain and Weinbach (1993); Robinson (1992); Rose and Ng Kwai-fun (2001); S. Takahashi (2001); Takahashi and Beebe (1987) and Yu (1999). The number of studies that have utilised DCT questionnaires is testament to their expediency and their usefulness as a data-collection method. This will be examined in greater detail in the following section.

3.6.2 Advantages / disadvantages of DCTs

The principal reason for the prevalence of DCTs in speech act research is their numerous advantages. Beebe and Cummings (1996: 80) outline some of these:

– gathering a large amount of data quickly;
– creating a basic taxonomy of semantic formulae and strategies that are likely to occur in natural speech;
– studying the stereotypical, perceived requirements for a socially appropriate response;
– gaining insight into social and psychological factors that are likely to affect speech and performance; and
– ascertaining the canonical shape of speech acts in the minds of speakers of that language.

However, the use of DCTs has not been without reservation. As Beebe and Cummings note, DCTs 'are not intended to give us natural speech and they do not accurately reflect natural speech or even unselfconscious, elicited speech' (1996: 80). DCT data does not reflect:

– actual wording used in real interaction;
– the range of formulae and strategies used;
– the length of response or the number of turns it takes to fulfil the function;
– the depth of emotion that affects the tone, content and form of linguistic performance;
– the number of repetitions and elaborations that occur; or
– the actual rate of occurrence of a speech act

Also, as Tarone (2005: 159) points out, DCTs provide insufficient contextualisation, so that participants are asked to make idealised responses to idealised situations. Nonetheless, a DCT questionnaire is suitable as one of the methods for collecting production data in the present study. There are four reasons: firstly, as Eisenstein and Bodman (1986) argued, the use of a DCT gives informants time to plan their responses, reduces the anxiety of face-to-face encounters, and permits the collection of large amounts of data. It is an activity which 'involve[s] slow and controlled processing...[which] opens the possibility for introspecting on procedural knowledge' (Faerch and Kasper, 1987: 12). Secondly, it is possible to control Brown and Levinson's (1987) variables of power, social distance and imposition, thus enabling exploration of how these variables affect response strategies. Thirdly, the DCT data can be used in conjunction with the spoken production data, which is closer to 'naturally-occurring' speech act data (see section 3.7), thus providing a more comprehensive picture of JLE speech act production. Fourthly, because DCTs are a commonly-used method for collecting speech-act production data, it is possible to compare and contrast the data from this study with data from numerous other studies which employed the same method. For these reasons, a DCT was designed for the purpose of identifying the proficiency of JLEs in accurately expressing disagreement in English.

3.6.3 Format of the DCT questionnaire

The DCT contained eight situations (see appendix 2) which aimed to elicit a disagreeing statement. In order to avoid 'leading' participants (i.e. to ensure that only their independent thoughts were being elicited), the DCT situations gave only the details necessary to describe the situations clearly (see figure 3.1, below).

You are in town with your friend, who is a student. You walk past a shop that sells second-hand (*chuko*) furniture. Your friend sees a big, purple and pink sofa (*nagaisu*) in the window. 'Oh, that's nice,' she says. You look at the sofa. You do not like it at all. If you tell her you don't like it, she may be a little upset that you disagree with her opinion.
Your friend says: '*Pink and purple are good colours. Don't you think it's beautiful?*'

You say:

_____

_____

_____

How serious is this situation for you (not your friend)? Circle one:
> *1: Not very serious*
> *2: Quite serious*
> *3: Very serious*

Figure 3.1: Example DCT situation

The DCT was designed to present a binary variation of two social factors: i) relative *power* of one speaker over the other; and ii) *social distance* between the pair of interactants (Brown and Levinson, 1987; Blum-Kulka, House and Kasper, 1989). In the cases where social distance was low, JLE participants were to imagine they were interacting with native speakers of New Zealand English with whom they had a social relationship. Following the approach of Yu (1999), two scenarios were formulated for each of the four combinations of variables, in order to educe a fuller and more reliable picture of learners' speech behaviour. The combination of power and social distance variables resulted in eight DCT situations:

> 1. two in which the speakers knew one another and were power-equal (-P-D);
> 2. two in which the speakers knew each other, but were unequal in power (+P-D);
> 3. two in which the speakers were power-equal but did not know one another (-P+D); and
> 4. two in which the speakers did not know each other, and were unequal in power (+P+D).

A third variable is incorporated into each DCT situation: serious-ness. 'Seriousness' refers to the potential negative consequences of a disagreement, and how severe they are likely to be. This is in accord-ance with Brown and Levinson's (1987) ranking of imposition (see section 2.4.3). Note that the word 'serious' was used in the text of the DCT questionnaire because 'ranking of imposition' was potentially confusing for second-language learners. For the sake of clarity, I con-tinue to use the term 'seriousness' in explaining the DCT format.

Originally, there was a binary value of seriousness in each situ-ation, as with relative power and social distance. As the designer of the DCT questionnaire, I made a decision as to whether a situation was high or low on the seriousness scale. However, piloting of the in-strument revealed several contentious points concerning seriousness. The first of these was that the seriousness of a situation depended very much on the perspective of the speakers in the situation. For example, in situation 6, 'Footpath,' two people collided with one another on a footpath, causing one to drop his/her laptop computer. The situation was clearly more serious for the person who owned the computer than it was for the other interlocutor. Secondly, seriousness is culturally informed (Brown and Levinson 1987: 77). Piloting revealed that a situation may not have been considered serious in one culture or com-munity, but may have been considered more serious in another. Third-ly, the fact that there were consequences did not necessarily mean that a situation was serious. All the DCT situations had consequences of one kind or another, whether these were paying for a broken computer or offending a friend. My judgment of the seriousness of these con-sequences would be very subjective. In order to extract more objective data, I amended the DCT questionnaire so that the participants them-selves could rank each situation on a three-point scale of seriousness:

How serious is this situation for you (not the interlocutor)? Circle one:
1. not very serious
2. quite serious
3. very serious

The initial sentence stressed that the participant him/herself was to decide the seriousness of the situation, and not his/her interlocutor.

The three-point scale allowed participants to indicate their perceptions of the seriousness of the situation.

In sum, the eight DCT situations were designed to demonstrate how the JLE participants perceived they would respond to varying degrees of power and social distance in disagreeing with native speakers of English in New Zealand. The DCT also provided data on how the participants perceived the seriousness (i.e. ranking of imposition) of these situations.

3.6.4 Piloting and modifications

The testing process for the DCT was conducted concurrently with the four testing sessions that were carried out for the judgment task (see section 3.5.3). Piloting of the DCT questionnaire raised several methodological issues. Specifically, there were concerns about:

1. whether the level of English used in the DCT situations was appropriate for intermediate-level JLEs;
2. whether the fictional situations depicted in the DCT questionnaire could conceivably happen, or conversely, were difficult to visualise;
3. whether the length and/or intensity of the DCT was likely to induce fatigue in the participants.

The modifications that were made to the DCT in response to these issues are outlined below.

Understandability of English used

If the DCT questionnaire contained language that was potentially too complex for the participants to understand, it would be difficult to judge whether responses were due to pragmatic infelicities or purely lexico-grammatical deficiency. As in the judgment task, all words and expressions were limited to those used most frequently in the English language. Additionally, for potentially problematic words or phrases, Japanese translations were included in brackets (see figure 3.1). Piloting with Japanese university students indicated that the language used in the DCT questionnaire was understandable.

Conceivability of fictional situations

If the DCT situations were easy for the participants to imagine (i.e. language students interacting within an educational domain), their responses were more likely to be an accurate representation of their speech behaviour in those situations (Robinson 1992; Yu 1999) than if they were presented with a situation that was difficult to envisage (e.g. on board a sinking ship). Hence, all the situations were set in domains that were likely to be familiar to the participants. Pilot-testing demonstrated that the situations presented in the final version of the DCT instrument were plausible to both New Zealand and JLE participants.

Dealing with fatigue

Participant fatigue is a problem in written production tests that last longer than 20–30 minutes (Boxer 2002b; Robinson, 1992), since participants may write shorter and less considered responses. In order to offset this potential shortcoming, the length of the DCT questionnaire was limited to eight situations. Pilot-testing revealed that a questionnaire with eight situations would take an average of twenty minutes for a JLE participant to complete. Participants reported that they considered this a reasonable length of time.

In sum, piloting of the DCT questionnaire was intended to ensure that it was understandable to the JLE participants, that it presented situations which they found plausible, and that it was as time-efficient as possible, in order to minimise participant fatigue. The results of the final piloting session, with a group of JLEs, indicated that these goals were met.

3.6.5 Summary

The DCT has been shown to be valuable for eliciting production data, despite certain limitations. The piloting process has illuminated ways to maximise the task's efficacy.

As I mentioned earlier, the DCT questionnaire was not intended to be the only method of eliciting speech-act production data, but it was to be used in tandem with a series of role-plays which elicited spoken production data. These role-plays are the focus of the next section.

3.7 Role-Plays

3.7.1 Introduction

A role-play task was designed for the purpose of identifying the proficiency of JLEs in accurately producing spoken disagreement in English (see appendix 3). This data collection technique was based on Gass and Houck (1999), who employed role-plays to test the spoken ability of Japanese learners of English to produce refusals in an interlanguage context. The role-play data in this study provides a descriptive supplement to the written production data elicited through the DCT questionnaire.

3.7.2 Format

This method of data collection required participants to play a specific role in a speech situation, acting out their parts *ad lib* while they were audiotaped and/or videotaped. Theoretically at least, participants who acted out their responses would provide a closer approximation of natural language data than written responses would (Boxer 2002b). This is because in role-plays, it is possible to simulate conversational turns and to have the interlocutor apply conversational / paralinguistic pressure in ways that are not possible in a DCT, e.g. through vocal intonation, body language or pausing. Also, as DiPietro (1987) pointed out, performing scenarios in real-time stimulates an intuitive reaction to strategic interactions. Studies which investigated a variety of speech acts such as requesting, refusing, apologising and inviting have often employed role-plays as a means of collecting data (Cohen and Olshtain 1981, 1993, 1994; Eisenstein and Bodman 1993; Gass and Houck 1999; Houck and Gass 1996; Hudson 2001; Liddicoat and Crozet 2001; Rintell and Mitchell 1989; Trosborg 1987).

The literature specifies two types of role-play: closed and open. Closed role-plays may best be described as an oral version of a DCT, in which participants are asked to give a one-turn disagreeing response to a proposition or opinion put forward by a native speaker interlocutor. Open role-plays permit participants to make an open, multi-turn response to a given situation, allowing 'full operation of the turn-taking mechanism, impromptu planning decisions contingent on interlocutor input, and hence, negotiation of global and local goals' (Kasper and Dahl 1991: 228).

The present study employed an open role-play instrument, comprising six scenarios which were acted out by both the NS and JLE participants. In each case the part of the interlocutor was taken by the researcher, but the participants were asked to respond as though they were talking to the person depicted on their role-play card. Figure 3.2, below, is an example of a role-play (see appendix 3 for all six role-play scenarios):

Native Speaker of English:

You are: a New Zealand university student.
The other person is: a Japanese student of English. You don't know him/her at all.

You are a member of the international students' club. You are making a big paper poster with the other student, and you plan to hang it outside to advertise your club. You have a good photo for the poster, and you show it to the other student. You tell him/her that you think it will look good on the poster.

Japanese Learner of English:

You are: a Japanese student, studying English at university.
The other person is: a New Zealand university student. You don't know him/her at all.

You are in the international students' club at university. You are making a big paper poster (*posuta*) with the other student, to advertise your club. Your partner shows you a photo. S/he wants to put it on the poster. You do not like it, because it's very dark and not there are not many colours. You don't want to put it on the poster.

Figure 3.2: Example of open role-play scenario

    The role-plays were recorded on audio-tape in order to ensure that the recordings were of high quality. The role-play performances were also video-taped in order to record the paralinguistic aspects of the participants' disagreement strategies. As Gass and Houck (1999: 110) point out, paralinguistic communication may differ across cultures in terms of its degree of importance and the functions it serves. So it was useful in the present study to be able to compare and contrast the differences between NS paralinguistic communication and that of JLEs.

3.7.3 Advantages and Disadvantages

Like all data-elicitation methods, role-plays have both advantages and disadvantages. The major advantages noted in the literature are summarised here, followed by some of the main disadvantages.

The value of role-plays lies in their facility for extracting spoken data, which is thought by many (e.g. Rintell and Mitchell 1989) to be a reasonable indication of subjects' 'natural' way of speaking. More specifically:

> they allow examination of speech act performance in its full discourse context and sequential organisation in terms of negotiation of meaning, the strategy choice, and politeness investment, all of which are strong characteristics of authentic conversation (Yamashita 1996: 26).

So one of the key advantages of role-plays is that the data they elicit may be closer to naturally-occurring speech than that elicited through written questionnaires.

> [Role-play] is the closest one can get to spontaneous speech in a non-natural situation. It shows that [participants] do try to portray the speech situation as close to real-life situations as possible. That being so, data from [role-plays] would be a step closer to natural speech and therefore provide some shades and nuances of speech behaviour and language use which the researcher can cue into in the course of his/her field study (Lee-Wong 2000: 54–55).

However, role-play data cannot be considered equivalent to naturally occurring speech data. Role-plays have few, if any, genuine real life consequences (Gass and Houck 1999), so the situation in which the participants are performing is artificial. This artificiality is compounded by the fact that the performance is being videotaped and/or audio-recorded. Additionally, role-play scenarios present a rather simplified, simplistic scenario which invariably fails to explore context fully (Bardovi-Harlig and Hartford 2005: 21). This means that 'we do not know to what extent the subjects' responses are representative of what the subject would say if he or she encountered the situation in real life' (Rintell and Mitchell 1989: 251). Likewise, Boxer (2002b: 16) suggests that role-plays, while closer to natural spoken data than DCTs, 'remain contrived insofar as participants are asked to indicate

128

what they think they would say and do in a particular situation'. Boxer points out that role-plays are difficult to set up, conduct and transcribe; it may also be difficult to find participants who are willing to be videotaped. Clearly, role-plays are not the perfect methodological tool.

Despite the disadvantages noted above, the role-play instrument was a useful data-collection tool in the present study. As mentioned in section 3.7.2, its primary function was as a supplement to the written production data provided by the DCT questionnaire. The role-plays provided qualitative data which illuminated the more quantitative data from the DCT questionnaire.

The combining of written and spoken production data does not appear to be a common feature of speech act studies. Until now, most studies which utilised both written DCTs and spoken role-plays did so in order to contrast the value of the data which each produced (Beebe and Cummings 1996; Hudson 2001; Sasaki 1998; see Brown 2001 for a comparison of DCTs and role-plays as data-collecting instruments). To my knowledge, few studies in interlanguage pragmatics have used data from these two instruments in concert with one another. Nonetheless, a combination of the two types of data appears to be most useful in providing a descriptive view of the more quantitative DCT data.

3.7.4 The aim of the role-plays

The role-plays were developed in order to establish, as closely as possible, how JLE participants would perform when they were required to simultaneously interpret an interlocutor's talk and to produce talk of their own. While both interpretation and production of disagreement speech acts were analysed in other instruments, each was gauged in isolation, without any of the immediacy of instantaneous conversation; the participants had the opportunity to think, self-correct, re-read anything not understood and alter their responses. By contrast, the role-play instrument's methodological focus on an immediate and intuitive response (DiPietro 1987) greatly reduced the opportunities for deliberation and reflection. Thus, rather than eliciting what participants believed they would say in any given situation, the role-plays came somewhat closer to eliciting what they actually would say.

3.7.5 Piloting and modifications

The role-play instrument was developed at a later stage than the DCT and judgment task instruments, so the piloting of the role-plays was not conducted over the four sessions which had been the locus of piloting for the other two data-gathering devices (see sections 3.5.3 and 3.6.4). Instead, the six role-play scenarios were piloted on two occasions with a group of ESL learners from a language institution in Christchurch. The students were from Switzerland, China, Korea and Japan, were aged between 18 and 25 years, and were all in an upper-intermediate class. The session was intended to determine:

- whether the role-play scenarios were confusing or difficult to understand;
- whether anything could be done to encourage a greater degree of similarity to 'natural' speech; and
- whether the participants were properly aware of, and taking into account, the power / social distance variables integrated in each scenario.

The results of the piloting gave no indications that any language used in the role-play task was difficult to understand. This may have been partly because the role-plays were designed after the DCT task had been designed and piloted, so that it was relatively simple to replicate the format of the written production task when designing the spoken task.

The next section outlines how the role-play instrument was administered to the NS and JLE participants.

3.7.6 Administering the role-plays to participants

The role-plays were less complex than the judgment task. The main concerns were to minimise participants' self-consciousness, to ensure their comprehension of the situations and the social variables embedded within them, and to enable them to relate to their interlocutor as a character in a role-play scenario.

In order to minimise self-consciousness among participants, only the researcher and an individual participant were present when the role-play task was being carried out. Each session began with an initial explanation period during which participants could ask questions. They were told how many role-plays there were and how long the exercise would take. They were also informed that the performances would be recorded on videotape and audiotape.

At the beginning of each role-play performance, the participants were given a card outlining the situation which they were to imagine (see the example in figure 3.2). They were then given 60 seconds to read the card and to ask questions if they did not understand something. This ensured that the participants had a clear idea of what was required. Once they had read the card, participants were asked to state aloud:

- the type of character they were to play (for the JLEs this was normally a Japanese learner of English at a New Zealand language school, while for NSs it was a university student);
- their relationship (in terms of both power and social distance) to their interlocutor.

The intention of this explicit description of the imaginary interlocutor's character (e.g. 'a teacher I don't know'; 'a close friend') was to assist the participants to imagine they were interacting with that character, rather than with the researcher. The goal was to prevent them from simply relating to the researcher as himself, with the same P and D variables in all the scenarios. While it was impossible to eliminate the problem entirely, this strategy did help to raise the participants' consciousness about how to act, and may therefore have ensured that the role-play data was a somewhat more precise indicator of their

131

actual speech behaviour. In fact, this may have had the unintentional side-effect of causing participants to consciously *over*-focus on the P and D variables of a given situation. Consequently, participants may have used disagreeing strategies that in reality they would be less likely to use because they would be less mindful of these variables. This may restrict the 'authenticity' of the role-play data.

Realia (such as a photo, or a piece of fabric, or some cash) was used in the role-plays as required. The objective of this was to reduce the sense of artificiality which is common to such instruments (Gass and Houck 1999; Rintell and Mitchell 1989). This was in line with Hudson, Detmer and Brown (1995), who stressed that role-play instruments should not place too much burden in terms of conceptualisation, and drama should not be overused. They advocated the use of realia in order to overcome these problems (1995: 59–60).

In sum, the role-play format was designed to minimise the sense of artificiality and self-consciousness. This was achieved by ensuring that the participants were not under any unnecessary scrutiny, and were working with realia. Steps were taken to ensure that participants were relating to their fictional interlocutor appropriately, and were not simply talking to the researcher. All these things were done to ensure that the role-play data was as similar as possible to naturally-occurring speech behaviour.

3.7.7 Summary

The role-play instrument was designed in order to extract oral production data, which supplemented the written production data obtained through the DCT. The role-play data also supplemented the interpretation data acquired through the judgment task.

3.8 Personal information forms

The personal information forms (see appendix 6.1) were designed to extract background information about the 14 JLE participants. Specifically, they elicited participants' nationality, first language, age group and employment. The forms also solicited information about the participants' language-learning history, their experience of English-speaking countries, and how long they had been studying in New Zealand. Finally, the participants indicated their level of English language ability and whether they had scores from relevant English language tests such as TOEFL or IELTS.

The personal information form was not devised as a comprehensive tool for collecting information about factors that may contribute to pragmatic knowledge. Its aim was simply to gain information about the participants' gender, ethnicity, age and language learning background.

3.9 Conclusion

The data collection methods used in this study were selected and developed as appropriate procedures to address the research questions. These procedures have focused on identifying aspects of JLEs' ability to extract recognise, interpret and produce disagreement speech acts in an interlanguage interactional context.

Inevitably, each data-collecting method is limited in terms of effectiveness and in 'authenticity' of collected data. Nonetheless, the triangulation of data through the three inter-related instruments is likely to reinforce the findings. The judgment task provides information about how the JLE participants might interpret situational severity and politeness utterances, while the DCT indicates their likely strategies for producing disagreements. The role-plays offer a descriptive

representation of the JLEs' likely speech behaviour if they were producing and perceiving disagreements simultaneously.

As mentioned earlier, the primary method for collecting written
data about the JLEs' production of disagreements is a DCT. The next
chapter is concerned with analysing the written production data recorded with this instrument.

4 Examining Shifts in Production

4.1 Introduction

This chapter deals with how the JLEs considered they would produce disagreement speech acts, and how their production compares with that of native speakers of New Zealand English in similar situational contexts. It analyses changes in the JLEs' selection of disagreement strategies between the beginning of their ten-week period of study and the end. Additionally, this chapter explores the extent to which the patterns found in the written production data are supported by the spoken data.

This chapter addresses the following research questions, as set out in section 1.3:

– How do JLEs manage politeness when involved in situations of negatively affective disagreement with native speakers of New Zealand English?
– What is the ability of newly-arrived JLEs in accurately expressing the negatively affective speech act of disagreement?
– How does their ability to manage politeness alter over a short period of language study and immersion in the host culture?

Two hypotheses were proposed, based on previous research findings in interlanguage pragmatics (as indicated below). This chapter investigates the validity of the previous findings for JLEs studying in New Zealand. The first hypothesis is that at the beginning of the ten-week period the JLE group would use less explicit speaking strategies when disagreeing than the NS group. This hypothesis is based on Stalpers' (1995) study, which found that NNSs interacting with NSs normally used more mitigation strategies than NSs interacting with one another. A similar result was reached by Olshtain and Weinbach (1993), who argued that newcomers to a culture would try to avoid any interactions that could cause loss of face. When engaged in this kind of interaction, they would attempt to minimise the impact through avoidance of explicit strategies. The second hypothesis is that after ten weeks of living and studying in New Zealand, the JLE group's reported use of disagreement strategies would become more similar to those of native speakers of New Zealand English in terms of appropriateness.

4.2 Methodology

This chapter utilises both written and spoken production data. Written data was collected through a DCT questionnaire (see appendix 2). Section 3.6 provides a detailed discussion of this method of gathering data. The participants in this portion of the study consisted of 12 JLEs who had recently arrived in New Zealand. This group is referred to as the *new arrival group* (as outlined in section 3.4.1). Spoken production data was collected by means of role-plays (see appendix 3), a detailed description of which is provided in section 3.7. Data was extracted from two JLE participants, known as the *role-play group* (as outlined in section 3.4.1). These two participants were intermediate-level language learners who had been studying in New Zealand for three months at the time of pre-testing. They performed the role-plays at both the pre-testing and post-testing stages. Although two JLE participants is a small sample, it is important to remember that the role-play instrument is intended primarily as a supplement to the written DCT data, illuminating and adding depth to those findings. For this purpose a small sample is sufficient. The NS group also completed the role-plays, and their data is used as appropriate.

4.3 Changes in strategy selection

4.3.1 Defining strategy selection

'Strategy selection' refers to politeness strategies which the participants chose to apply in accordance with the variables of power, social distance and ranking of imposition (Brown and Levinson 1987) in order to deliver a disagreement with the minimum risk of face-loss. As noted in section 2.6.1, a strategy may be explicit (e.g. 'No it was not my fault!'), or hedged (e.g. 'I think it might be best to turn left'), or implied (e.g. 'Um, are you sure we can't print in colour?'). There is also a strategy of avoidance, in which the speaker does not disagree at all (e.g. 'You're right, it's my fault. I'm sorry').

4.3.2 Eliciting strategy selection data

The participants in this study reported on their likely selection of disagreement strategy by writing what they believed they would say in response to the situations depicted in the DCT questionnaire. The strategies which the participants used in responding to each situation were divided into four categories:

1 = Explicit disagreement
2 = Hedged disagreement
3 = Implied disagreement
4 = Avoidance, i.e. no disagreement

For each of the eight situations in the DCT, a score was calculated. This consisted of the mean of all the strategies – 1, 2, 3 or 4 – which the participants in each group (JLE and NS) elected to use. This score will be referred to as a *Strategy* score. A score close to 1 would indicate that in general the participants were likely to employ explicit disagreement strategies, whereas a score close to 3 would indicate that they chose very indirect strategies. A score close to 4 would imply that in general the participants believed they would opt out of the disagreement. For each of the eight Strategy scores, a standard deviation (SD) was calculated. A low SD would indicate that the majority of the responses were close to the Strategy score, while a high SD would mean that there was a wide variation of responses.

4.3.3 Strategy selection: findings

The mean Strategy scores for each group in each of the eight DCT situations are presented in table 4.1, below:

	NS:	SD	JLE pre:	SD	JLE post:	SD
Car (+P+D)	2.3	1.06	1.8	1.14	1.5	0.52
Coffee (-P+D)	2.2	1.03	1.8	1.11	1.7	1.07
Computer (+P-D)	1.5	0.67	1.8	0.62	2.3	0.78
Sofa (-P-D)	2.4	0.84	2.6	0.90	2.6	0.79
Airport (+P+D)	1.7	0.48	1.8	0.39	2.6	1.88
Footpath (-P+D)	2.2	1.14	2.7	1.30	1.9	0.90
Meeting (+P-D)	2.1	0.99	1.9	0.79	2.0	0.95
Cake (-P-D)	2.1	0.99	2.1	0.79	2.1	0.67
Group mean:	*2.06*	*0.9*	*2.06*	*0.88*	*2.09*	*0.95*

Table 4.1: Comparison of NS and JLE (pre and post) Strategy scores

Table 4.1 suggests that in most of the situations the disagreement strategies employed by the JLE new arrival group did not become similar in indirectness to the NS group. Initially, the JLE group's mean score (2.06) was the same as that of the native-speaker participants (2.06), but the post-testing mean score rose to 2.09, suggesting that the JLE group were more *indirect* after ten weeks of study than they were initially.

Upon further analysis, however, a trend does become apparent. *Car*, *Coffee* and *Footpath* are all situations in which the participants were asked to imagine they did not know the person they were disagreeing with (i.e. they are +D situations). In all three of these situations the JLE group's Strategy scores were lower after ten weeks than they had been in the initial test. This indicates that the JLE new arrival group may have been selecting more explicit disagreement strategies after ten weeks than they were originally, although this characteristic only seemed to be prominent when they were speaking to people whom they did not know (see figure 4.1, below).

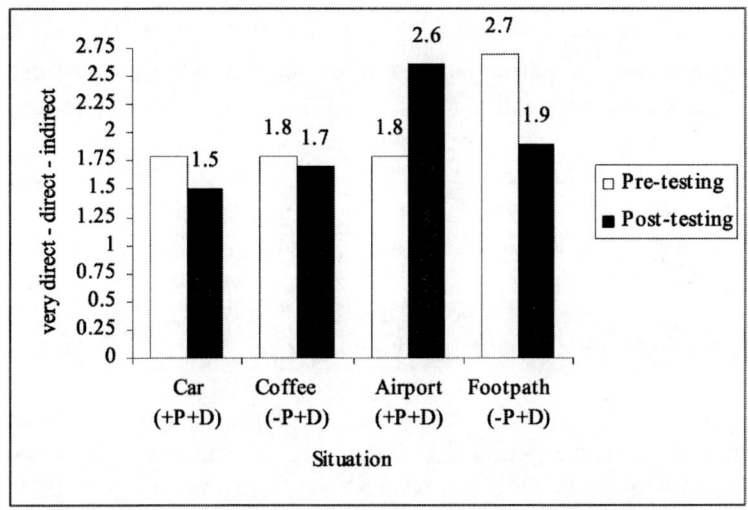

Figure 4.1: Changes in Strategy scores between pre- and post-testing in high social-distance situations

The three situations which demonstrated a shift toward directness are worth discussing in more detail.

Car (+P+D):
The disagreement in this situation is between the participant and a 50-year old male teacher whom s/he does not know. The teacher's car has hit the participant's car from behind, and the teacher is claiming that the accident is the participant's fault for stopping too quickly. The pre-testing Strategy score for this situation was 1.8, but this decreased to 1.5 in post-testing, a shift of 0.3 along the four-point indirectness scale

which is shown in figure 4.1 (vertical axis). Put another way, the JLEs appeared to become 8.3% more direct in disagreeing with a person they had not spoken to before. The standard deviation (SD) of the JLEs' Strategy score also became lower: the pre-testing SD was 1.14, but the post-testing SD was 0.52, suggesting that the post-testing data is highly uniform in choice of disagreeing strategy. In sum, a number of the JLE participants reported in their post-testing responses that they would use more explicit disagreeing strategies.

Coffee (-P+D):
In this situation the participant is in a coffee shop with a friend called Tom and a classmate called Rick, whom the participant has not talked to before. When Tom says that he is considering taking an essay-writing class, Rick laughs at him and says that only stupid people need to take that kind of class. Rick then asks the participant if s/he agrees. The pre-testing Strategy score for this situation was 1.8, and the post-testing Strategy score was 1.7, a shift of 0.1 along the scale of directness. The JLEs therefore reported a minor shift of 2.8% towards direct disagreement with a person they did not know.

Footpath (-P+D):
In this situation, the participant is walking on a footpath and is accidentally hit by a woman cycling past on the path. The participant is carrying a laptop computer, which is damaged in the collision. The woman, whom the participant does not know, retorts that the accident is the participant's fault because s/he should have gotten out of the way. Figure 4.1 shows that the newly-arrived JLEs' mean Strategy score was 2.7. Their mean Strategy score ten weeks later was 1.9, a shift of 0.8 along the indirectness scale. Their reported disagreement utterances appeared to become 22.4% more explicit in this context. The SD of the JLEs' Strategy score also became lower: the pre-testing SD was 1.30, but the post-testing SD was 0.90. This suggests that the post-testing data is reasonably uniform, i.e. a considerable number of the non-native participants believed that they would choose a more explicit disagreement strategy.

Airport (+P+D):

In this situation, the participant is being driven to the airport by the director of his/her school. The director, who is not familiar with the city, is about to make a wrong turn. The participant, who does not know the director, must correct him. Although there was an increase in direct disagreement strategies in three of the +D situations, it was not proven in this one: the JLE pre-testing Strategy score was 1.8 but the post-testing score was 2.6, i.e. more indirect than previously. It seems likely that the high power inequality in this situation overrode all other factors, discouraging participants from making a direct reply.

In summary, the 12 JLEs indicated that they would produce more direct statements of disagreement after ten weeks of intensive study in New Zealand than they had initially; however, this was only demonstrated in situations where the interlocutors did not know each other. In considering these findings, there are two caveats to be addressed. The first is that the shifts that occur in the above situations are relatively minor. If only one of these situations manifested this move toward explicitness, the change might be due to chance. However, the pattern is noted in three situations, all of which present a high degree of social distance between the participants and their interlocutor. Secondly, as noted at the beginning of this section, the JLEs' competence in production did not become similar to that of the native speaker group after ten weeks. Their tendency toward more direct disagreement did not follow the original hypothesis that the JLEs would begin to become more native-like in terms of their disagreement strategy selection.

Nonetheless, it is possible that the pattern of increased directness in +D situations may be a precursor: the trend towards explicitness of response may in itself be indicative of a nascent improvement in pragmatic competence in situations of high social distance. According to table 4.1, the JLEs appeared to become increasingly confident in their ability to interact with people they did not know. Figure 4.1 indicates that in 3 out of 4 high-social-distance situations (*Car, Coffee* and *Footpath*) the JLEs reported that they would use more explicit disagreeing strategies after ten weeks of study in New Zealand. This trend is also evident in other sections of this chapter. It will be noted where appropriate, and then expounded further in the discussion of findings in section 4.6.

4.4 Pragmatic sophistication in expressing disagreements

4.4.1 Defining pragmatic sophistication

I use the term 'pragmatic sophistication' to refer to the pragmalinguistic complexity of the strategies which the participants are able to use in order to alter the illocutionary strength of their disagreeing statements. This term was also used by Yates (2005: 85) in her study of mitigating devices by NS and NNS secondary-school teachers in Australia:

> One factor that seems to be important in understanding the variation among the [NNS respondents] is their *level of pragmatic sophistication in English*, which I characterise here in terms of the size of their repertoire of mitigating devices and the way in which it was used (emphasis in original).

To demonstrate the varying degrees of pragmatic sophistication with which these strategies may be expressed, let us examine these two responses (from two different participants) to the DCT situation *Car*:

> A) JLE (pre): This is not my fault. Because you are too close behind my car. You have to make an interval. So you didn't hit my car.

> B) JLE (post): Oh. Excuse me, teacher. Did you look carefully when you were driving? Can you see this part of broken car? I stopped because you run into just behind me. So it's not only my fault.

The disagreement utterance made by A (a JLE who had recently arrived in New Zealand) is adequate but mechanical. By comparison, the disagreement strategy formulated by B (a JLE who had completed ten weeks of language study) is considerably more sophisticated. The participant commences by saying 'excuse me', a formulaic politeness phrase signalling her intended imposition. She implies her disagreement by asking several questions, before explicitly stating her belief that the fault is not only hers. Arguably, the second utterance is more appropriate than the first because it is less abrupt, more circumspect, and less likely to be construed as rude or overly-direct by the higher-power native-speaker interlocutor. The second participant exhibits a greater degree of pragmatic sophistication in her strategy selection.

Note that this term is only concerned with a learner's ability to manipulate pragmalinguistic items of speech, and is not intended to provide an indication of sociopragmatic competence. Sociopragmatic ability was measured through the judgment task, the findings of which are discussed in chapter 7.

4.4.2 JLE increases in pragmatic sophistication over ten weeks

Both the JLE new arrival group and the NS reference group wrote disagreeing statements for each of the eight situations depicted in the DCT questionnaire. The JLE group completed the DCT a second time ten weeks later. The pragmatic sophistication of the participants' utterances was then calculated by relating them to the disagreement strategies presented in table 2.1. This table presented five categories of strategy, generally increasing in pragmalinguistic complexity:

1. explicit
2. hedged with simple positive politeness
3. hedged with complex positive politeness
4. hedged with negative politeness
5. implied

Accordingly, the participants' responses to each DCT situation were given a ranking from 1 to 5. An explicit disagreement strategy (requiring little pragmalinguistic skill to produce) would be given a score of 1, a disagreement hedged with a simple positive politeness strategy (requiring a slightly higher degree of pragmalinguistic skill) would be given a score of 2, and so on.

The mean of all scores in each group (NS, JLE pre-testing and JLE post-testing) for each situation was calculated. These were then

143

labelled *Sophistication* scores. If a group's Sophistication score was high, i.e. 4 or higher, the participant group was thought to be able to produce pragmatically sophisticated disagreement strategies. If the score was low, i.e. 2 or 1, then the participant group was generally considered to be lacking in ability to produce sophisticated utterances.

The Sophistication scores of the three groups for each of the eight DCT situations are presented in table 4.2, below.

DCT situation	NS	SD	JLE (pre)	SD	JLE (post)	SD
Car (+P+D)	4.2	0.8	2.6	0.9	3.2	0.7
Coffee (-P+D)	4.8	0.6	2.4	0.7	3.1	0.7
Computer (+P-D)	4.7	0.7	2.7	1.2	3.0	0.7
Sofa (-P-D)	4.5	0.7	3.3	0.9	3.5	0.5
Airport (+P+D)	4.5	0.5	2.9	0.9	3.3	0.6
Footpath (-P+D)	4.4	0.7	2.6	0.7	3.4	0.7
Meeting (+P-D)	4.3	0.7	2.8	0.7	3.3	0.5
Cake (-P-D)	4.8	0.4	3.3	0.9	3.4	0.5
Group mean:	*4.5*	*0.6*	*2.8*	*0.9*	*3.3*	*0.6*

Table 4.2: Sophistication scores of NS compared with JLE pre-testing and
JLE post-testing

The native speakers' Sophistication scores are very high, as one might predict. For each situation the mean Sophistication score is 4 or higher; the mean for the NS group is 4.5. The JLE group also formulated more sophisticated strategies at the end of the ten weeks. The mean JLE (pre) Sophistication score across all eight situations is 2.8, while the mean JLE (post) Sophistication score is 3.3. Note also that the mean standard deviations for the JLE group reduce from 0.9 to 0.6, indicating that a higher number of the participants were able to employ more sophisticated disagreement strategies than during the initial stages of testing.

In sum, there is an overall mean shift of 0.5 points in the JLEs' pragmatic sophistication after ten weeks of immersion in New Zealand's culture. However, the small sample size and the relatively high standard deviations limit the strength of conclusions that can be drawn based on this finding.

4.4.3 Increases in sophistication: analysing margins of shift over ten weeks

For each DCT situation, the JLE participants exhibited a *margin of shift* in pragmatic sophistication over ten weeks. This margin of shift is calculated by determining the difference between the participants' pre-testing Sophistication scores and their post-testing scores. The margins of shift are presented in table 4.3, below.

DCT Situation	Margin of shift	Percentage (%) of shift
Car (+P+D)	0.6	12
Coffee (-P+D)	0.7	14
Computer (+P-D)	0.3	6
Sofa (-P-D)	0.2	4
Airport (+P+D)	0.4	8
Footpath (-P+D)	0.8	16
Meeting (+P-D)	0.5	10
Cake (-P-D)	0.1	2

Table 4.3: JLE margins of shift in pragmatic sophistication from pre-testing to post-testing

All the DCT situations reveal some degree of overall shift in pragmatic sophistication. Two particularly interesting patterns are revealed: firstly, the most prominent margins of shift are found in the responses to +D situations, in which the participants were to imagine that they did not know their interlocutor. Secondly, the *lowest* margins of shift are manifested in -D situations, in which the participants were to as-

145

sume they *did* know their interlocutor. Figure 4.2 (below) illustrates this pattern. In this figure, the DCT situations in which the margins altered the most are coloured white, while the situations in which they changed only nominally are coloured black:

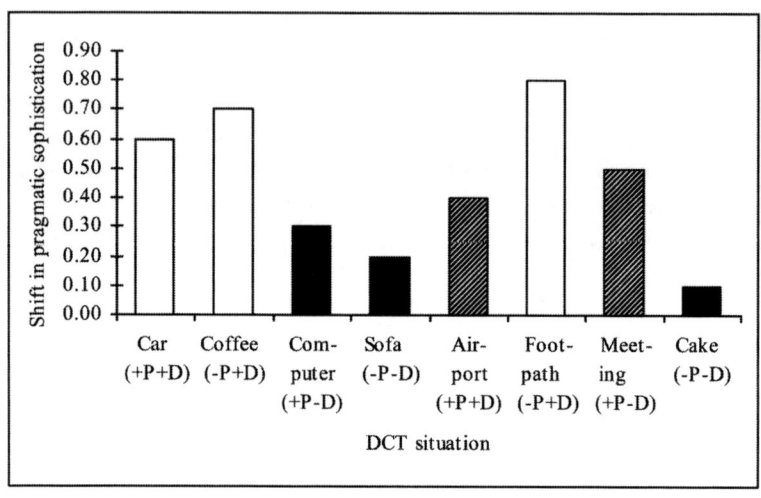

Figure 4.2: JLE margins of shift in pragmatic sophistication
from pre-testing to post-testing

The situations manifesting the highest rate of shift are *Footpath* (0.8), *Coffee* (0.7) and *Car* (0.6). All three situations present high social distance variables. Those situations exhibiting the lowest rate of shift are *Cake* (0.1), *Sofa* (0.2) and *Computer* (0.3), all of which present low social distance scenarios. So the JLE group's ability to use pragmatically sophisticated disagreement strategies in high social distance situations appears to have increased by an average of 0.7, or 14%. By contrast, the same group's ability to use sophisticated strategies in *low* social distance situations increases by an average of only 0.2, or 4%.

Another point of interest is that the two situations that present the highest margin of shift (*Coffee* at 0.7 and *Footpath* at 0.8) depict a power-equal relationship. These suggest the possibility that JLEs were most likely to attempt new and more sophisticated strategies when

146

they held a position of equal power to their interlocutor, and were less inclined to do so when they were lower in power.

The findings presented in this section suggest that over a period of ten weeks, the JLEs became considerably more confident in managing politeness strategies in disagreement situations, but they only exhibited this in situations of high social distance. Furthermore, the same pattern is present in the JLE group's Strategy scores (presented in table 4.1) after ten weeks have passed. In both sets of data – Sophistication scores and Strategy scores – there is a pattern toward confidence (suggested in the Strategy scores by the explicitness of the responses chosen) in the JLEs' reported disagreements with interlocutors who were not known to them. The next section explores this trend in further detail, examining what strategies were most commonly employed and what situations they were used in.

4.4.4 Increases in sophistication: Strategies commonly employed by JLEs

This section will examine in detail some of the more sophisticated strategies (as set out in table 4.2) employed by the JLE participants in their responses to the DCT questionnaire. The objective in presenting these strategies is to demonstrate how the participants' reported pre-testing strategy selection differed from their post-testing selection.

Analysis of both the JLEs' pre-testing and post-testing results reveals five strategies which the participants reported they would use only rarely in the former but with considerable frequency in the latter. The five strategies are:

– Stressing that one's disagreement is merely one's own opinion (not simply 'I think', but 'It's just my opinion' or a similar statement that reduces the force of the utterance)
– Offering an alternative suggestion ('But some of our friends could not like alcohol in their food, shall we try it next time?')
– Hinting
– Offering a token agreement ('I think the colour is beautiful, but it doesn't suit your room')

147

– Questioning ('Are you sure you told me to come here at 3 o'clock?')

Table 4.4, below, presents the total number of times each of these five strategies was used by the twelve JLEs in their responses to each of the eight scenarios in the DCT questionnaire.

	Total Pre	Total Post
Opinion	2	5
Alt. Sug.	2	5
Hint	2	4
Token Ag.	9	11
Question	17	8

Table 4.4: Total selection of JLE disagreement
strategies in pre-testing and post-testing

Table 4.4 demonstrates that during the pre-testing phase the participants often utilised relatively familiar and straightforward disagreeing strategies. The most frequently-employed strategy was questioning, a common method for conveying indirect disagreement among Japanese ESL learners (Beebe and Takahashi 1989a: 107). This strategy was employed 17 times by the JLEs in the present study. The second most frequently-used strategy was token agreement, which has been noted (Beebe and Takahashi 1989b: 207; Mori 1999) as a common preface to a disagreeing statement among Japanese learners of English. In the responses to the DCT scenarios it was applied 9 times. Of the remaining strategies, which are arguably more complex than token agreement and questioning, the combined number used is only 6. This suggests an initial reliance among the JLEs upon strategies that are linguistically uncomplicated. There are three possible reasons for this:

1. The JLE group initially lacked the linguistic (i.e. lexico-grammatical) confidence to use more sophisticated strategies;

148

2. They lacked understanding of the sociopragmatic appropriateness of these more sophisticated strategies, and so opted to use 'safe' strategies that were grammatically simple and which were used often in their first language; and/or
3. They were transferring the strategies directly from their first language.

It is necessary to point out, however, that token agreement by JLEs often followed the *'Yes, but'* + *immediate criticism* formula, which may reflect lack of fluency and/or proficiency in the social rules of speaking used in the target culture (Beebe and Takahashi 1989b: 207). Use of token agreements does not necessarily equate with pragmatic fluency.

In the post-testing data, a considerably wider range of strategies was reported. As table 4.4 shows, the frequency of stating disagreement as one's own opinion increased from two instances to five. Alternative suggestions and hints were employed more frequently than previously. Token agreements remained a commonly-reported strategy; the number of token agreements used in the post-testing data increased from 9 to 11. However, the number of questions asked as part of a disagreement utterance declined dramatically, from 17 to 8. This pattern suggests that there has been a noticeable move from linguistically basic/safe strategies to more pragmatically sophisticated strategies.

The decreasing reliance on questioning strategies in the JLE post-testing data suggests that the participants gained confidence over the course of their immersion in the target culture and became less dependent on the relatively simple strategies that they had reported they would use at the outset. One causative factor may have been that ten weeks of intensive study served to reduce the learners' cognitive load (Sweller 1988). As they gained knowledge in lexical and grammatical areas of the L2 and increased in communicative competence, they were then able to apply some cognitive resources to pragmalinguistic aspects of the L2 and to learning the relevant sociopragmatic norms.

It is interesting that token agreement remained popular as a strategy, increasing in instances of reported use rather than declining after ten weeks. Sacks (1987: 62) offers a reason for this, arguing that in the vast majority of disagreement instances one 'finds a way of providing an "agreeing" response', even when one is not agreeing. A common way to do this is by employing a partial or token agreement (Pomerantz 1984). Mori (1999), who investigated agreements and disagreements in Japanese language, notes that this type of disagreeing format is frequently employed in Japanese. She refers to the use of the connective *demo*, which is generally considered an equivalent of *but* in English (Mori 1999: 94–100). She argues that *demo* is often used as the hinge-point of a token or partial agreement, and is then followed by a disagreeing strategy:

(agreement-oriented statement) *demo* (disagreeing statement)

Considering the use of token / partial agreements is common in Japanese, it seems likely that the JLEs made use of the same strategy in English, i.e. they were transferring the strategy directly from their L1 (see section 2.8.1). Token agreements are often used by native speakers of Japanese for the same reason as they are used by English native speakers: the desire for contiguity is the most important factor in most disagreement-oriented conversations (Sacks 1987). This may explain why the pattern of offering token agreement strategies continued after ten weeks had passed.

One notable feature is that the JLEs' reported strategy selections appeared to alter appreciably in accordance with variables of power in the DCT situations. Power-equal situations appeared to encourage pragmatically sophisticated strategies, while power-unequal situations engendered a pattern of less risky strategy use. Table 4.5, below, illustrates this by condensing the post-testing strategy selection data. The eight DCT situations are compacted into two categories: power-equal and power-unequal situations. The five pragmatically sophisticated strategies which were expounded earlier are also collapsed into two categories: 1) token agreement and questioning (noted earlier as being less problematic for JLEs because of their frequent use in Japanese disagreements); and 2) stating an opinion, offering an alternative suggestion and hinting (these carry a higher risk of pragmatic failure because they are more pragmatically sophisticated).

150

	Token agreement / Questioning	Opinion / Alternative suggestion / Hint
Power-equal situations	15	13
Power-unequal situations	4	1

Table 4.5: JLEs' post-testing DCT strategy selection categorised by power-equal and power-unequal situations

The trend is quite marked: participants considered that they would respond to the power-unequal situations (*Car*, *Poster*, *Airport* and *Meeting*) using only the most common and linguistically simple strategies for reducing the force of their disagreeing utterances. By contrast, the situations which were power-*equal* (*Coffee*, *Sofa*, *Footpath* and *Cake*) extracted a wide variety of sophisticated strategies. A similar pattern is noted in the preceding section, which described high margins of shift in pragmatic sophistication in some of the power-equal DCT situations, but less notable shifts in responses to situations presenting unequal power. It seems likely that power variables may have influenced the JLE participants' strategy selection in their responses to the DCT situations. The data has shown that pragmatically sophisticated strategies were much more frequent in power-equal DCT situations than those which placed participants in a powerless position.

To sum up: the JLE participants had initially reported that they would use disagreement strategies that were pragmatically relatively straightforward, but the post-testing data has shown that they used a greater range of politeness strategies after ten weeks of intensive study at a New Zealand language school. These strategies tended also to be more pragmatically sophisticated than previously. In addition, it appears that the JLEs preferred to attempt newly-acquired and more complex strategies in power-equal situations, rather than in situations where there was an imbalance of power between themselves and their interlocutors. A viable rationale for this is that the participants were uncertain of the potential of newly-acquired, sophisticated disagreement strategies for causing pragmatic failure. This may be why they only reported using these strategies in power-equal situations, where the potential for face-damage was reduced by the parity between interlocutors.

4.5 Pragmatic sophistication in spoken production data

The patterns described in the previous section with regard to social distance and power distance can also be discerned in the role-play data. There were two patterns: one in which more sophisticated dis-agreement utterances were attempted in +D situations but not in -D situations, and a similar pattern (though not as marked) in which sophisticated utterances were attempted in -P situations but not in +P situations. This section provides a qualitative and descriptive analysis which complements the more quantitative examination carried out in section 4.4.

4.5.1 Social distance

In the situations where they had no established relationship with their interlocutors, the JLE role-play group participants generally used more pragmatically sophisticated disagreeing responses at the post-testing stage than at the pre-testing stage. This is demonstrated in examples 1.1 and 1.2 below, taken from the role-play data, in which two strangers going to the same party are disagreeing about when to get off their bus:

> (Example 1.1. Pre-testing)
> IW: Um- here's Riccarton Mall we should get off the bus now I think.
> *S1: Ah (.) I think (.) we should get five minutes more*
> IW: You think so?

(Example 1.2. Post-testing)
IW: Um (.) there's Riccarton Mall there (0.8) should we get off the bus now I think we'd better.
S1: Numm (.) I don't think it's good idea to get off now (.) um I think it's better to wait five minutes or little bit more mm
IW: Oh okay

While example 1.1 contains only a short pause followed by a small amount of redress ('Ah (.) I think') before a direct assertion of disagreement, example 1.2 is more elaborate. The participant repeatedly hedges her statements ('I don't think', 'I think') and attempts to lessen the imposition ('little bit more'). In terms of sophistication, example 1.2 is not dissimilar to a native speaker's response:

(Example 1.3. Native speaker)
IW: Oh there's the shopping centre now (.) um let's get off here and then we can walk up from there
NS: Um I think the party is a bit further on (.) if we stay on the bus till the next stop we'll be okay

Adopting strategies that are similar to the JLE post-testing statement in example 1.2, the NS in example 1.3 hedges his statement ('I think') and attempts to reduce the imposition ('a bit further on'). Thus, the role-play data reflects the finding in the DCT data that, in situations of high social distance, JLEs used more pragmatically sophisticated disagreement utterances in post-testing than they had in pre-testing.

In their responses to situations presenting *low* social distance, however, the JLEs exhibited a markedly lower degree of shift in pragmatic sophistication over their ten-week period of residence in New Zealand. This is demonstrated by the following examples taken from the spoken production data, in which two room-mates are disagreeing about whether to leave a heater on in their flat while they go out for the evening:

(Example 2.1. Pre-testing)
IW: Um (.) how about we leave the heater on in the flat so that it'll be warm when we get back
S2: Ah yes (1.5) ye- but um this house has no fireplace
IW: We can just plu- plug it into the wall though

153

(Example 2.2. Post-testing)
IW: I'd like to leave the heater on so it'll be warm when we get back (.) what
do you think?
S2: A-but- it's dangerous um
IW: No I don't think it's dangerous

Both examples 2.1 and 2.2 present a straightforward disagreement
strategy. By contrast, the NS's response in example 2.3 is to present
the potential hazard in a joking fashion:

(Example 2.3. Native speaker)
IW: How about w- how about we leave the heater on and then when we come
back from the pub it'll be nice and warm in here
NS: H-h-hh it might be warm but we might be minus a whole house
IW: You reckon?

In doing this, the NS participant lessens the strength of his illocutionary act, but also makes the point that leaving a heater on presents a
fire risk. Thus, the findings of the role-play data reflect the finding in
the DCT data that, in situations in which the interlocutors knew one
another well, the JLE participants often chose to use safe and relatively simple disagreement strategies, rather than attempting to employ
more pragmatically sophisticated strategies.

4.5.2 Power

In situations where the JLEs were to imagine they were equal in
power with their native-speaker interlocutors, the pragmatic sophistication of their role-play performances increased substantially from
pre-testing to post-testing. This is demonstrated in examples 3.1 and
3.2, in which a JLE is being short-changed in a café by a (power-
equal) shop assistant:

(Example 3.1. Pre-testing)
IW: Thanks very much (.) and four dollars fifty so that's five- fifty cents change
S3: WHAT? You said um (.) fo- four dollar fifty?
IW: Yeah (.) yeah yeah [you gave me five I gave you [fifty cents change
S3:   [Um   [I think you- ah you should
check again (.) strange

(Example 3.2. Post-testing)
IW: Thank you yep lovely (.) and that will be fifty cents change (.) thank you very much
S3: fifty cents (.) um (.) umm could you (.) have check please again?
IW: Hmm?
S3: Um did I pay a ten dollars?
IW: Ah it was five dollars um here we are (1.0) yep five dollars
S3: So maybe I can get (.) five dollars more?

The JLE's pre-testing response begins with a request for clarification, which is followed by an imperative ('You should check again'). By contrast, the post-testing response does not contain an explicit disagreeing statement, but implies disagreement by means of questioning strategies, and finally through hinting ('maybe I can get (.) five dollars more?'). The post-testing statement is arguably oriented more appropriately to the interlocutor's face than the pre-testing utterance because there is little in the JLEs' speech to imply that the assistant has made a mistake. Therefore, the role-play data reflects the finding in the written DCT data that, in power-equal situations, JLEs often chose to employ more pragmatically sophisticated disagreement utterances in post-testing than they had in pre-testing.

However, although power-equal situations may have encouraged JLE participants to attempt more sophisticated disagreeing utterances, the same was not true for situations presenting power *in*equality. In such situations, the JLE role-play group's spoken performances did not increase in pragmatic sophistication from pre- to post-testing, but continued to be relatively straightforward and simplistic. This is reflected in example 4.1 and example 4.2, in which the participants were disagreeing with their host parents over the colour of a swatch of curtain fabric destined for their bedrooms:

(Example 4.1. Pre-testing)
IW: What do you think of these- of this colour do you think that would match the (.) walls? (0.8) I think it's quite nice
S4: Oh really? Um actually I like a more light- light colour

155

(Example 4.2. Post-testing)
IW: What do you think about this? I think this is quite a nice colour [do you like it?
S4: [Oh
(0.7) I like more light colour

By contrast, the disagreeing utterances of the NS group were more sophisticated, as example 4.3 illustrates:

(Example 4.3. Native speaker)
IW: This is- this is the kind of material that I thought we would put in your room wh- what do you think I quite like it
NS: (2.3) Umm (0.9) the colour's nice but I don't know if I think it suits the room very well

In sum, the role-play data echoes the pattern revealed in the written production data. In power-unequal situations, the JLE participants were frequently reluctant to attempt pragmatically sophisticated disagreement strategies.

4.6 Discussion

This chapter has demonstrated that the variables of power and social distance may have a considerable influence on the disagreement strategies produced by the JLEs. It is worthwhile investigating some of the issues underlying these patterns.

4.6.1 Power

There are a number of possible explanations for the JLEs' apparent reluctance to use pragmatically complex strategies in power-unequal situations. It could be that i) they had not learned to accurately gauge the extent of power difference between themselves and their interlocutors; ii) they had not yet learned to respond to power-unequal interlocutors with appropriate politeness; and/or iii) power was such a salient and important variable for JLEs that anxiety about pragmatic error over-rode the desire for increase in pragmatic ability. Clearly the JLEs learned to use a range of disagreement strategies, but they were most likely to use them with power-equal interlocutors. The JLEs' reported disinclination to use any strategies except the most basic in power-unequal situations supports the notion that they were reluctant to employ pragmatically sophisticated strategies in power-unequal conversations because of the perceived risk of error.

An endemic difficulty is that when Japanese learners of English interacted with New Zealanders, they were very often in a position of reduced power. There are four reasons why this is so. Firstly, the JLEs were not native speakers. They very often lacked the linguistic re-sources to help them through conversations, and this placed them at a disadvantage when talking to people who were NSs and did have these resources (cf. Harder 1980). Secondly, they were often unfamil-iar with the cultural norms of formality, directness of utterance and appropriate degree of politeness (Bond, Zegarac and Spencer-Oatey 2000; Spencer-Oatey 2000). Thirdly, they were often lower in *social power* (French and Raven 1959) than the person they were interacting with. Many of the JLEs' interactions were with native speakers in various positions of power, such as teachers (who have *expert* power) or homestay parents (who have *legitimate* power). As a result, they were often 'talking up' to their interlocutors (see section 2.4.3 for in-formation on these types of power). Lastly, they were often dependent on the people they were interacting with. As they were all living in homestay situations, they were dependent on their host-parents for shelter, food and general well-being. They were also dependent on their teachers for instruction, for help with passing examinations and so on. So it is very probable that power was a complicating factor for the Japanese learners of English, and remained so after ten weeks had passed.

4.6.2 Social distance

There is evidence that, over ten weeks of residence in the target culture, the JLEs became more adept at managing situations in which they did not know their interlocutor. They became less indirect and more explicit in their responses to +D situations in the DCT. They also demonstrated greater pragmatic sophistication in +D situations than in -D situations. These results suggest that they had increased in confidence and were less wary of negotiating disagreements with people they did not know.

The trend toward explicit and sophisticated strategy use in situations of high social distance is initially puzzling. One would have expected that the JLEs would make the most notable shifts when communicating with people they had an established relationship with, since in such situations the face-risk is presumably minimised by the low degree of social distance between the interlocutors (Brown and Levinson 1987). In fact, the power-equal relationships discussed in the previous section follow this very pattern: the low power distance between hearer and speaker minimises the risk to face, which in turn encourages more sophisticated strategy selection. So it is surprising that the reverse seems to be true in regard to social distance. Nevertheless, the link between high social distance and direct and/or pragmatically sophisticated language use manifests repeatedly in the post-testing production data.

One possible explanation for this is that the participants were unconcerned about the potential face threat when interacting with people they did not know because they were not likely to form any strong bond with them. Conversely, a situation where the participants had formed, or were likely to form, a relationship with their interlocutor may have engendered a need for indirectness and caution in the selection of politeness strategies.

In theoretical terms, the production data from the JLEs does not appear to follow Brown and Levinson's (1987) argument that indirectness increases with social distance. Rather, it appears to follow Wolfson's (1988) model of social interaction (section 2.5.3), in which interlocutors at the two extremes of the social-distance continuum interact without regard to indirectness, but those with whom a social relationship has been formed are constrained to indirectness. For the purpose of contrast, these two models are juxtaposed in figure 4.3, below.

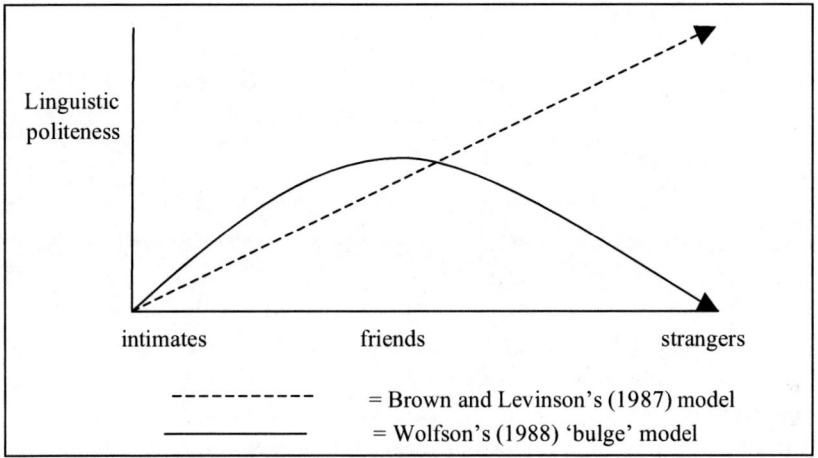

Figure 4.3: Juxtaposition of Brown and Levinson's (1987) and Wolfson's models of politeness

The JLEs' apparent lack of concern for potential face-loss in high-social-distance situations recalls Doi's (1981) concept of *enryo* (see section 2.5.3). The speech behaviour which the JLE participants reported they would use in situations of high social distance suggests that they were transferring (Faerch and Kasper 1987; see section 2.8.1 for an explanation) the Japanese concept of *enryo* to their assumptions of the target culture. The similarity is illustrated in table 4.6, below:

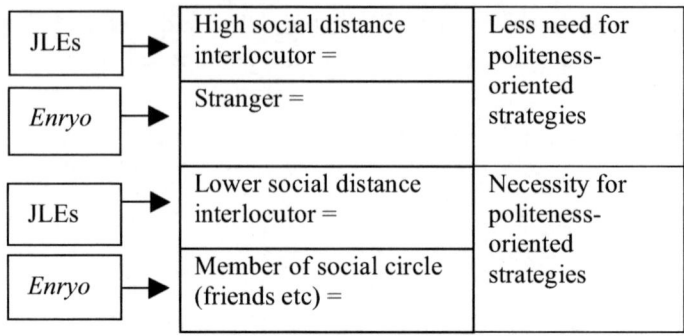

JLEs →	High social distance interlocutor =	Less need for politeness-oriented strategies
Enryo →	Stranger =	
JLEs →	Lower social distance interlocutor =	Necessity for politeness-oriented strategies
Enryo →	Member of social circle (friends etc) =	

Table 4.6: Comparing JLE politeness patterns with Doi's *enryo*

As table 4.6 shows, the trend in the JLE data in which high social distance reduces the need for politeness-oriented strategies is similar to the *enryo* principle which affirms that strangers have little need to use politeness strategies. The perception in the JLE data that lower social distance (i.e. in which interlocutors are neither strangers nor intimates) requires the use of politeness strategies is matched by the *enryo* concept that interaction with a social circle of friends, colleagues etc necessitates the use of politeness strategies.

The JLEs' tendency to adapt the principle of *enryo* from their existing store of first-culture interactional knowledge and apply it to interaction in the target culture relates to Bialystok's two-dimensional model of pragmatic acquisition. As I mentioned in section 2.8.1, this model hypothesises that adult language learners have the advantage of being able to call upon their previously-internalised pragmatic knowledge as they process new pragmatic features of the L2. It seems likely that the JLEs were transferring the *enryo* rule from their first culture in their interactions with high social distance NSs in New Zealand.

What possible causes exist for the difference between the JLEs' evaluation of social distance and that of the New Zealand native speakers? It could be partly due to differing degrees of collectivism within each culture. Gudykunst and Ting-Toomey (1988) suggest that, in general, Western styles of speech tend to stress precise, direct expression of thought, due partly to the emphasis on individualism (Hofstede 1991). However, some Asian cultures, including Japan, favour an indirect, imprecise and ambiguous style of speech-act delivery in order to preserve mutual face needs and to uphold the harmony of the group. This may be partly due to the collectivist nature of such cultures:

> The value of collectivism...constrains members of cultures such as China, Japan and Korea from speaking boldly through explicit verbal communication style. Collectivist cultures like China, Japan and Korea emphasise the importance of group harmony and group conformity [and these] are accomplished through the use of imprecise, ambiguous verbal communication behaviours (Gudykunst and Ting-Toomey 1988: 102).

So in Japanese culture ambiguous or indirect speech may partly be due to a need to preserve group harmony, which takes precedence over the individual (Triandis 1994). In terms of understanding the disagreement patterns which this chapter has been discussing, this notion has considerable importance. It may be that the JLE participants were more indirect when disagreeing with people they knew because these people were members of their 'in-group' – people with whom their social relationship was well-defined. This sociopragmatic notion may have been carried over into the JLEs' relations with native speakers of English, causing an indirect disagreement style to be employed in a conversation with someone whom they knew well. Chang (1999: 536), in a discussion of Chinese conversational styles, makes an apposite point: '[O]ne finds the puzzling conflation of two apparently contradictory qualities of speech: more well-defined role relationship systems lead to less direct verbal discourse'. Given that both Japan and China are high on Hofstede's scale of collectivism, it is probable that the same general rule applies to Japanese culture.

Fukushima (2000) discusses this notion with specific reference to Japanese culture. She argues that members of collectivist cultures tend to pay more attention to the context in which an utterance is being delivered than members of more individualist cultures would. She also notes that Japanese culture in general makes stronger distinctions between the in-group and the out-group (cf. Triandis 1994). It is not, she says, appropriate to describe Japanese people as 'indirect', nor to describe Japanese communication as 'implicit':

Instead, it would be more appropriate to characterise Japanese subjects in this study as being more responsive to the context than their British counterparts, in other words, they appear to pay more attention to context, such as power difference and social distance between S and H, on which basis they differentiate requesting strategies (Fukushima 2000: 212).

This may help to explain the apparent preference of the JLE participants to be more conscious of potential face-threat in discourse with in-group members, and less so with out-group members.

At this point, a potential anomaly needs to be addressed. According to personal communication and the responses on the participants' personal information forms (section 3.8), the JLEs' closest relationships in New Zealand were most often with friends and host family members rather than with genuine intimates such as family members or spouses. The JLEs' closest relationships in the target culture may therefore have been with members of their social sphere of interaction (within which a degree of *enryo* is required for appropriate relations), rather than members of their intimate sphere of interaction (in which *enryo* is not required). This would suggest a disparity between the intimacy of the JLEs' relationships with native speakers living in New Zealand, and the intimate relationships which they had with their relatives in Japan. After all, a mother–son relationship would probably be much more intimate than a host-mother–homestay student relationship. This disparity is, however, unlikely to affect the findings of this study. There are two reasons for this. Firstly, the focus of the present study was on the politeness strategies that the JLEs used in New Zealand with native speakers of English with whom they had relationships of varying familiarity. Their relations with their families in Japan were not relevant to the aims of this research. Secondly, the study did not focus on differences between close family relations and social relationships, but rather on variations between encounters within social relationships and encounters with outsiders. So the possible disparity is not likely to apply to this analysis.

An addendum: there may be a disparity between the JLEs' interpretations of high social distance and those of the NS reference group. Japan is a famously crowded country, and in most cases a meeting with a stranger is a one-off encounter: people are unlikely to form any social relationship except with the most local of individuals. The context is different in New Zealand because the population is much smaller and more localised. It is more likely that strangers will meet again, particularly if one of them is employed as a shop assistant or in a similar service-oriented occupation. Consequently, Japanese notions of acceptable politeness behaviour in high social distance situations may well be a source of cross-cultural pragmatic failure (cf. Thomas 1983).

4.7 Conclusion

Initially, the JLEs in the study selected disagreement strategies that were in some cases quite similar to native-speaker strategies, but in other cases markedly different. This situation changed little over ten weeks of intensive instruction in New Zealand. But the noted trend toward using more explicit and direct disagreement strategies in situations where the JLEs did not know their native-speaker interlocutor is potentially very interesting indeed, because it may signal the beginning of an increase in pragmatic competence. Further investigation is needed to determine the length of time a language learner would need to be immersed in an English-speaking culture in order for this proficiency to manifest itself. This research supports Bardovi-Harlig's (1999) call for further longitudinal studies of gains in pragmatic proficiency.

Ten weeks of study at a New Zealand language school undoubtedly enhances a non-native speaker's ability to produce pragmatically sophisticated disagreement strategies. The fact that the data indicated a shift only in situations where the participants were speaking to power-equal interlocutors may imply that their pragmalinguistic capability does not alter measurably over this period. Alternatively, it may signify that power is a significant variable for the JLEs and their desire not to commit pragmatic errors in power-unequal situations inhibits their potential for gain in ability.

This chapter has been concerned with production data elicited from DCT questionnaires and role-plays. The next chapter will shift the focus from the linguistic realisations themselves to the length of the utterances which the JLEs produced.

5 Utterance Length in Disagreements

5.1 Introduction

Utterance length is a topic of some importance in the study of speech acts because it is linked with issues of pragmalinguistic appropriateness: '[P]ragmatic failure might result from overindulgence in words, creating a lack of appropriateness which might cause the hearer to react with impatience' (Blum-Kulka and Olshtain 1986: 175). On the other hand, a very brief response may come across as curt or abrupt, causing a similarly negative reaction.

This chapter outlines some of the more prominent studies which have analysed the relationship between utterance length and negative speech acts, and compares the findings with those of the present study, i.e. JLEs producing negatively affective speech acts in an interlanguage context.

5.2 Methodology

In order to provide a substantial depiction of the utterance lengths of the JLE group, both written and spoken data were incorporated. The written data was provided by the responses of the JLE new arrival group (n=12), and the native-speaker reference group (n=10). The spoken data was elicited from two JLEs who completed the role-play tasks – see section 3.4.1), as well as from four members of the NS reference group.

5.3 Previous research focusing on utterance length

Olshtain and Weinbach (1993) used a DCT task to study how Israeli learners of English managed the speech act of complaint, compared with native speakers from Britain and the USA. They observed that non-native speech act behaviour could deviate from that of native speakers in terms of utterance length. Typically, non-native speakers reported using longer utterances than native speakers when producing negatively affective speech acts. Olshtain and Weinbach suggested that this happened because the learners believed they needed to 'say more' in order to be certain they were negotiating their intention as clearly as possible:

> Learners at the intermediate to advanced level of second language acquisition tend to be verbose and use more words than native speakers, more than they themselves would use in their own language, in order to negotiate the intentions of their speech acts in the new language. When compared to native speakers of the target language, this difference is strong (1993: 120).

Although the findings of this study appear to be applicable to Israeli learners of English, there is uncertainty about their applicability to learners from other cultures. S. Takahashi (2001), who compared the requesting strategies of JLEs with those produced by native speakers, observed that 'almost half of the [JLE] participants mentioned that the NS requests were, on the whole, longer and more elaborate than theirs' (2001: 194). Takahashi's findings are quite different to those of Olshtain and Weinbach (1993). Given this, it is possible to speculate that Israeli learners of English and Japanese learners of English may produce utterances of differing lengths, and that their utterance lengths – like other aspects of speech behaviour – are likely to be informed by social and cultural variables. To learn more about the differences in speech behaviour and to enable a more detailed analysis of the underlying variables, it is worthwhile to compare the findings of Olshtain and Weinbach's (1993) research with those of the JLEs in the present study.

5.4 Length of written disagreement utterances

This section focuses on the number of words in the JLE new arrival group's written disagreement utterances, as extracted from the DCT data. Specifically, the focus is on whether these are longer, shorter, or the same length as utterances produced by NSs in the same situational context. Additionally, because variables of power and social distance appear to have had such a pronounced effect on other aspects of the JLEs' written production (e.g. strategy selection), this section considers how these variables might affect utterance length among JLEs.

Table 5.1, below, displays the mean number of words used in each of the eight DCT situations by the native-speaker group, and compares this mean with that of the JLE new arrival group's pre-testing and post-testing data:

	NS:	SD:	JLE (pre):	SD:	JLE (post):	SD:
Car	25.6	11.7	23.3	9.2	21.7	8.8
Coffee	23.8	13.6	18.7	10.5	17.8	5.9
Computer	30.9	14.1	22.9	8.6	21.4	9.8
Sofa	20.1	12.2	14.9	5.6	15.8	8.4
Airport	17.8	3.6	15.0	7.8	16.8	6.3
Footpath	28.2	9.2	13.1	9.1	22.9	12.5
Meeting	20.5	11.0	16.9	7.1	18.6	7.2
Cake	25.5	9.1	19.6	5.3	21.3	7.2
Group mean:	*24.1*	*10.6*	*18.1*	*7.9*	*19.5*	*8.3*

Table 5.1: Mean length of DCT utterances: comparing NS with JLE (pre / post)

Table 5.1 shows clearly that neither the non-natives' pre-testing nor their post-testing utterances are as long as those produced by the native speaker participants. This is illustrated in figure 5.1, below:

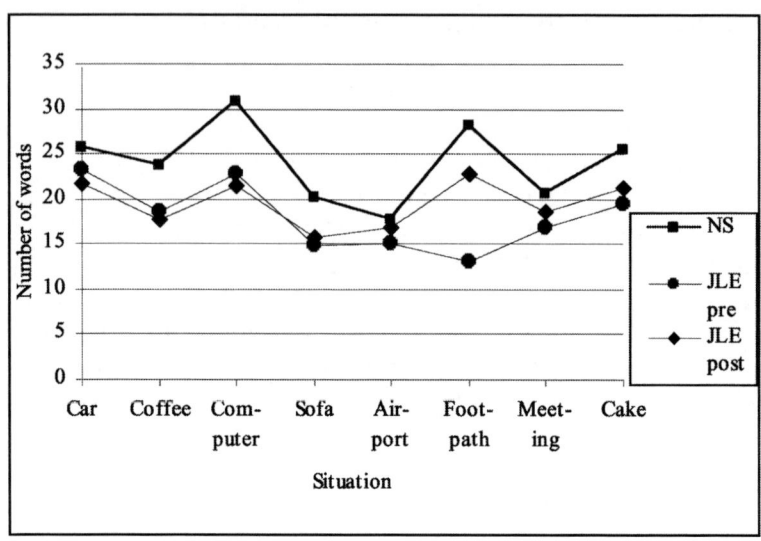

Figure 5.1: Mean number of words in DCT situations: NS compared with JLE (pre/post)

The conclusion reached by Olshtain and Weinbach (1993) – that non-native speakers would use longer utterances than native-speakers in order to express their intention as clearly as possible – appears not to be valid in the context of the present study. Rather, it seems that the JLEs preferred to keep their responses brief. Other areas of this study, which have dealt with strategy selection (section 4.3) and pragmatic sophistication (section 4.4), have also recorded a marked trend toward brevity and simplicity among JLE disagreements. It is likely that the short length of their disagreeing statements is linked to the same pattern.

5.4.1 Power and distance variables and utterance length

In order to clarify the extent to which utterance length varied in alignment with factors of power and social distance, figure 5.2 displays the JLE new arrival group's shifts in length of utterance between pre-

168

testing and post-testing. The shift in utterance length for each of the eight DCT situations is presented:

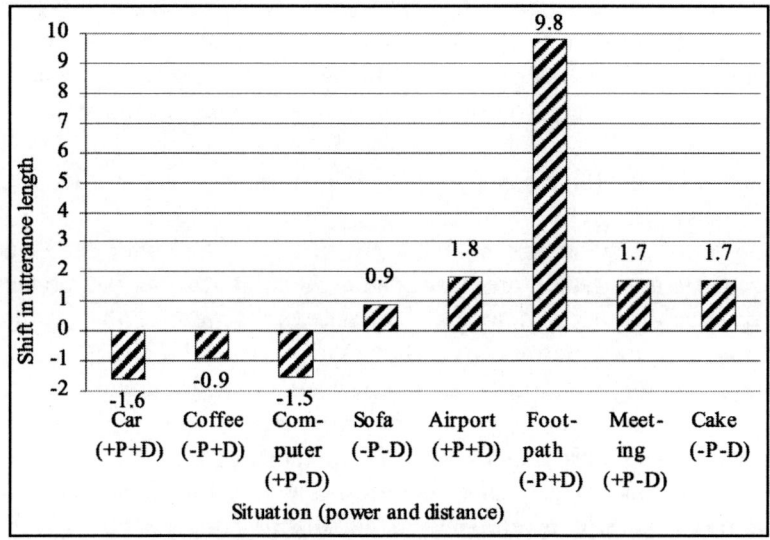

Figure 5.2: JLE shifts in length of utterance from pre-testing to post-testing

First of all, a caveat: most of the shifts in utterance length which are presented in table 5.2 were an average of only a few words. The aim in presenting this data is not to demonstrate the degree of shift, but rather to draw attention to the pattern of power and social distance variables in which the most notable shifts occurred.

'Footpath', the DCT situation which generated the highest degree of shift in utterance length from pre- to post-testing (9.8 words), is a power-equal situation, presenting a high degree of social distance between the two interlocutors. The participants were asked to disagree with a fellow-student whom they had not met previously. The marked increase in utterance length in this situation suggests that a power-equal, high-social-distance encounter is the optimum for attempting to utilise longer and potentially more pragmatically sophisticated dis-agreement strategies.

Some other situations engendered a similar pattern. The situation 'Airport', which presented a moderate degree of shift in utterance length from pre- to post-testing (1.8 words), is high in social distance: the two interlocutors in the situation did not know each other at all. The increase in utterance length in this situation supports the trend in the production data whereby the learners' responses indicated that they were more likely to use pragmatically sophisticated disagreement strategies in situations where they had not formed a relationship with their interlocutor.

Two DCT situations in table 6.2 which exhibit a minor degree of shift in utterance length are 'Cake' and 'Meeting'. 'Cake' is a power-equal situation: the participants were asked to write how they would disagree with their flatmate over the baking of a cake. The increase in utterance length (1.7 words) in a power-equal situation supports the general trend in written production data whereby JLEs reported that they would use more sophisticated disagreement strategies in power-equal situations. 'Meeting' is a power-unequal, low-social-distance situation. The shift in utterance length in this situation (1.7 words) does not appear to follow any particular pattern, and could be due to chance.

In general, there is a pattern in which some of the utterances produced by the JLE participants became closer in length to those of the NS group than others. This pattern is most salient in high social distance situations, although it is less obvious in power-equal situations.

5.4.2 Summary

In summary, it appears that the JLE new arrival group almost always used shorter utterances than NSs in formulating written disagreement speech acts. It may be that the conclusions reached by Olshtain and Weinbach (1993) are not applicable to Japanese learners of English in an interlanguage context. However, inasmuch as there was a shift in utterance length over ten weeks of intensive language learning, the shift followed a pattern common in the data concerned with production of written disagreement: most changes occurred in situations with no power differential and/or in which no relationship had been formed between the interlocutors. Let us now examine the spoken data.

5.5 Length of utterances in spoken data

The focus of this section is similar to that of section 5.4, but the emphasis is on spoken production data, i.e. data elicited from the role-play performances of the JLE role-play group. There is no guarantee that the written results will be echoed in the spoken data: In a study by Edmondson and House (1991), non-native speakers used more verbose utterances than NSs on written DCTs, but not on spoken role-plays. Edmondson and House reasoned that the learners may not have had sufficient knowledge or control of routine formulae to be able to produce and interpret utterances simultaneously, as they would have had to do during the role-play tasks, and this may have reduced their output. Consequently, it is worth analysing the role-play data in the present study separately from the DCT data, in order to compare the two sets of findings.

In the context of spoken production data, 'length of utterance' refers to the number of whole words spoken by each participant in performing each of the six role-play situations. In order to regulate what constitutes a 'whole word', verbal pauses, false starts or hesitators such as 'hmm' are not counted. Nor are partially-enunciated words. Where a participant stammers, repeating a word more than once, the word is counted only once. The words spoken by the researcher are not counted. This standardisation was introduced in order to reduce misleading results as much as possible. Only whole words are counted as contributing to utterance length.

The mean number of words used in each of the six role-play situations by each participant group is presented in table 5.2, below:

Situation	NS (n=4)	JLE group (n=2)
Sit 1 (+P+D)	58	32
Sit 2 (+P-D)	74	30
Sit 3 (-P+D)	78	50
Sit 4 (-P-D)	121	30
Sit 5 (-P+D)	52	35
Sit 6 (-P-D)	64	30
Group mean:	*75*	*31*

Table 5.2: Mean number of words in
spoken disagreement utterances (NS / JLE)

Table 5.2 indicates that the NS group's utterances were always considerably longer than those of the JLE role-play group. The mean
length of utterance for the native speakers was 75 words, as opposed
to 31 words for the JLE group. This is illustrated in figure 5.3:

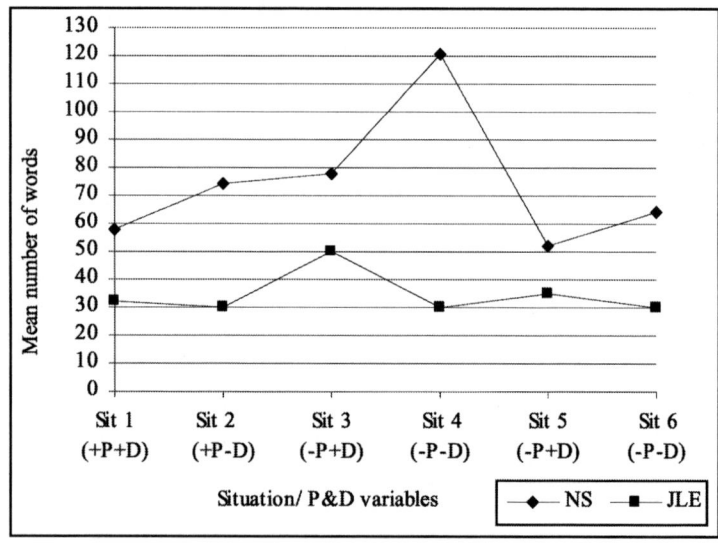

Figure 5.3: Mean length of utterances in role-plays – NS compared with JLEs

172

According to figure 5.3, there is a considerable difference between the utterance lengths of the JLE role-play group and the NS group. In general, native-speakers' spoken disagreements contained approximately twice as many words as those of JLEs.

5.6 Discussion

What might account for the difference between the findings of Olshtain and Weinbach (1993) and this study? One possibility is that the JLEs in the present study used shorter utterances purely because of a lexico-grammatical deficiency, i.e. they simply knew fewer words and grammatical patterns and were less able to formulate disagreement strategies than the native speaker group. But closer reflection suggests that this is not likely to be the case. Olshtain and Weinbach's participants, who were also second-language learners, always used utterances that were *longer* than those of NSs. So the difference between Olshtain and Weinbach's studies of Israeli second-language learners and this study of Japanese second-language learners is not explained by a lexico-grammatical deficiency.

A more plausible theory is that the results attained by the JLEs are applicable only to the case of Japanese second-language learners, and may not be transferable to other cultures. The rationale for this theory is that there is a definite and quantifiable cultural gap between Japan and Israel which might at least partially account for the discrepancy in results. This cultural gap may be illuminated using Hofstede's (1991) Power Distance Index, or PDI (section 2.7.2). According to the PDI, there is a significant difference between Japan and Israel in terms of power distance: Japan has a score of 54/104 and is ranked 33rd out of 53 countries; while Israel has a score of 13/104 and is 52nd out of 53 countries. The implication is that power is distributed much more equally in Israel than it is in Japan. Hofstede (1991: 27) says of such egalitarian cultures that there is often only limited dependence of subordinates on superiors, and that a preference for interdependence and

173

consultation is the norm. In Japan, power is distributed in a much more hierarchical manner, and there is considerable dependence of subordinates on bosses. Thus, there appear to have been cultural differences in stratification of power.

How does this dependence of subordinates on superiors translate into shorter utterances in power-unequal conversations? As Hofstede (1991) observes, hierarchical cultures such as Japan have less call for consultation and argument; employees expect to be told what to do. This may impede dialogue from lower to higher on the hierarchical strata, therefore constraining lower-status people to brevity when talking to high-power interlocutors. This theory corresponds with Beebe and Takahashi's (1989a, 1989b) finding that Japanese employees were normally brief and reticent when disagreeing with a boss. Another example is Williams' (2005) study of interaction between tutors in a university writing centre and writers (both NSs and L2 learners) who were seeking their assistance. She found that in general, tutors took longer turns than writers, and that when the writers were L2 learners the trend was even stronger, suggesting a higher degree of dominance by tutors over L2 learners. It is likely that the same trend applies to JLE utterance length in power unequal situations.

If the cultural dimension of power distance is applied to the Japanese participants in the present study and to the Israeli participants in Olshtain and Weinbach's study, it becomes clear that the JLE group are likely to be considerably more accepting of power inequality than the Israeli group. As a consequence, the JLE group are likely to use briefer utterances when speaking to a power-unequal interlocutor than the Israeli group. The spoken utterance length data suggests that this has indeed been the case. It is likely that the JLE group, when formulating a disagreement toward a higher-power interlocutor, used a strategy of pragmalinguistic transfer from their L1 (see section 2.8.1), i.e. the short utterances that were appropriate in a power-unequal situation in Japan were employed in a simulation of the same type of situation in the target culture. A comparison of mean differences in utterance length in the role-play data (table 5.3, below) compares the length of JLE utterances in power-equal situations with those of power-unequal situations.

Role-play situations	Mean # of words
Power-equal situations	36
Power-unequal situations	31

Table 5.3: Mean number of words spoken by JLEs in power-equal and power-unequal role-play situations

Although the difference is relatively minor, it demonstrates that in the role-play data, the JLEs tended to use longer utterances when disagreeing with someone who was their equal, and shorter utterances when disagreeing with a higher-power interlocutor. This supports the likelihood that the JLEs were transferring their judgments about utterance length from their L1, and recalling the pragmatic principles which they had previously internalised in their first culture (Bialystok 1993). Conversely, power inequality was much less likely to constrain the Israeli participants in Olshtain and Weinbach's (1993) study to briefer utterances. The non-hierarchical and interdependent nature of Israeli culture (as indicated by Hofstede's PDI) would likely have enabled dialogue and argument to flow freely between subordinate and superior in a manner that would be much less likely in Japan's culture. Hence, the differences in utterance length between these two studies are likely to originate – to some extent at least – in the hierarchical structure of the two cultures.

This raises the broader question of whether some cultures are likely to conform to Olshtain and Weinbach's model (i.e. NNSs using *longer* utterances than NSs), and whether other cultures are more apt to conform to the JLE model (in which NNS utterances are *shorter* than those of NSs). It seems likely that only specific types of culture are likely to match Olshtain and Weinbach's format.

To which cultures are Olshtain and Weinbach's findings most likely to apply? Although Olshtain and Weinbach do not claim that their results are globally applicable, an article by Blum-Kulka and Olshtain (1986), with similar conclusions, does imply a more general applicability. Blum-Kulka and Olshtain found that learners of Hebrew as a second language – mainly American, but also from a variety of other cultures – also used longer utterances than NSs. Blum-Kulka and Olshtain's (1986) paper is part of the Cross-Cultural Speech Act Realisation Pattern (CCSARP) project (Blum-Kulka, House and Kasper 1989) in which requesting and apologising speech act data was collected from both NSs and NNSs of seven languages: American English, Australian English, British English, Canadian French, Danish, German and Hebrew. Blum-Kulka and Olshtain pointed out that many of the countries involved in the CCSARP project revealed 'a systematic difference in length of utterance used to realise speech acts by non-native speakers as compared to native speakers' (1986: 165), i.e. NNSs used longer utterances than NSs. The implication is that Blum-Kulka and Olshtain (1986) consider that their model is likely to be applicable in a wider cultural context. The findings of Blum-Kulka and Olshtain's study corroborate the conclusions of Olshtain's later study with Weinbach. In considering this, let us reflect on the countries mentioned in the CCSARP as they rank in Hofstede's (1991) PDI. These are listed in table 5.4, below:

Country	PDI score out of 104[1]	Ranking out of 53 countries
America	40	38
Canada	39	39
Australia	36	41
Britain	35	42/44
Germany	35	42/44
Denmark	18	51
Israel	13	52

Table 5.4: Power Distance Index (PDI) values for countries studied in CCSARP project

All the countries in the CCSARP study have low PDI scores and are ranked from 38th to 52nd out of 53 countries. They are all firmly

---

1   104 was the PDI score for Malaysia, which scored highest and was ranked 1st out of 53 countries studied.

positioned at the egalitarian end of the Power Distance Index. So there appears to be a parallel between low-power-distance cultures and extended utterance length. But in a more hierarchical culture such as Japan, there is no such link. While the findings of Olshtain's research projects may be applicable to non-hierarchical, egalitarian cultures, they may apply less readily to more highly stratified cultures where there is a high tolerance for power inequality.

5.7 Conclusion

A quantitative comparison of the length of both written and spoken utterances among NSs and JLEs revealed that both the JLE new arrivals and the role-play group consistently used utterances that were much shorter in length than those of the NS reference group, in contrast with the findings of Olshtain and Weinbach's (1993) study. I proposed that this difference might be at least partly due to cultural dissimilarities between the group in Olshtain's study and the group under scrutiny in the present study.

Until now, the analysis has been concerned with the JLE participants' production of speech acts. In the next chapter, the focus shifts to the JLEs' ability to recognise and accurately interpret disagreements.

6 Recognising and Interpreting Disagreements

6.1 Introduction

In this chapter the focus shifts to the ability of the JLE participants to recognise disagreements and interpret the illocutionary strength of a disagreement speech act. Comprehension and interpretation of disagreement can be problematic because of the subtleties of this speech act, which may be hedged in a number of ways, or even implied without any specific, spoken reference to the fact that a disagreement is being performed. Riley (1989: 238) observes that 'a description of language use is only one dimension of a description of social competence, that not all communicative behaviour is verbal and that there are times when actions speak louder than words'.

Disagreements often occur over several lengthy turns at talk, involving not only a satisfactory outcome but also face-saving measures that are employed to accommodate the noncompliant nature of this speech act. Consequently, it is important that these face-saving devices be interpreted accurately. Misinterpretation may result in the opposite effect to that which was intended; the threat to one or both interlocutors' face may be exacerbated. This potential threat is magnified by some of the inherent differences between Japanese culture and New Zealand culture. As discussed in section 2.7.4, Japan is a relatively collectivist culture, while New Zealand's culture is relatively individualist (Gudykunst, Yoon and Nishida 1987; Hofstede, 1991). In societies which are oriented toward individualism, people may be distrustful of what is not said clearly (Triandis 1994: 184). Emphasis on what is said, word usage and specificity are valued. Conversely, in collectivist cultures '...[an individual] will expect his interlocutor to know what is bothering him, so that he doesn't have to be specific. The result is that he will talk around and around the point, in effect putting all the pieces in place except the crucial one. Placing it proper-ly – this keystone – is the role of his interlocutor' (Hall 1976: 113).

Due to the factors mentioned above, appropriate comprehension of disagreement between JLEs and native speakers of English requires a certain degree of linguistic and pragmatic knowledge which is often culture-specific. However, Bardovi-Harlig (1999) notes that language learners who have only just arrived in the target culture tend initially to be deficient in this knowledge. This may be true even for learners of advanced ability: '[T]he demonstration that advanced learners do not exhibit targetlike norms implies that instruction is warranted at all levels of development' (Bardovi-Harlig 1999: 681). The aim of this chapter, therefore, is to analyse how JLEs interpret disagreements that they are exposed to, and to identify some changes that take place after a period of study and immersion in New Zealand culture.

The explication of the findings of the interpretive data is divided into three sections. The first section focuses on the JLEs' ability to recognise three types of disagreement strategy: explicit disagreement; disagreement which is hedged in some manner; and implied disagree-ment, which may be expressed paralinguistically, i.e. through tone of voice or through body language. This section concludes with a statis-tical analysis, which focuses on the degree of shift in interpretive competence over ten weeks of intensive English language study. The second section examines how the JLEs who had been exposed to dis-agreement situations between two native speakers perceived the extent of politeness being utilised by those NS characters (hereafter known as 'interlocutor politeness'). The third section addresses the JLEs' per-ceptions of the relative severity of the disagreements which they had observed in the TV segments of the judgment task (hereafter known as 'situational severity'). This chapter addresses the following research question, as set out in chapter 1: What is the ability of newly-arrived JLEs in accurately interpreting the negatively affective speech act of disagreement? Specifically, this chapter

- determines the competence of the JLEs at *recognising* different types of disagreement strategy;
- investigates how the JLEs interpret the *relative interlocutor po-liteness* of various disagreement utterances;

180

– investigates how the JLEs interpret the *situational severity* of disagreement situations which they are exposed to in New Zealand; and
– compares the interpretive competence of the JLEs with that of the native speaker reference group.

6.2 Hypotheses / predictions

The following hypotheses are proposed.

1. Initially the JLE group will interpret disagreement situations as more severe and more impolite than the interpretations formulated by the native speakers of English.

This hypothesis is based on House's (2000: 151) claim that the severity of any negatively-affective speech act may be exacerbated in the process of intercultural communication because it 'involves interactants who may habitually use different, culture-specific communicative styles which are often not recognised as such'.

2. The JLE group will be able to recognise most explicitly stated expressions of disagreement, but will be less competent at recognising disagreements that are hedged or implied.

This hypothesis is based on Dascal's (1983) claim that strategies that are not stated explicitly are open to misinterpretation. In order to recognise and accurately interpret a speech act strategy, it is crucial to understand both the literal and the conveyed meaning of the statement (Searle 1975). However, this is notoriously difficult in cross-cultural interaction; in fact, the more implicit such a speech act is, the more difficult it is to accurately interpret it in cross-cultural situations. The culture-specific nature of many paralinguistic channels (e.g. breaking of eye contact) adds to this difficulty (Triandis 1994).

3. After a ten-week period of instruction in New Zealand, and immersion in the host culture, it is likely that the JLEs will interpret the magnitude of disagreement situations in a way that is to some extent more similar to the native speaker reference group than in the pre-test. The results will also become somewhat closer to those of the native speaker reference group in their interpretation of the relative interlocutor politeness of disagreement utterances. Lastly, JLEs will become more competent at recognising indirect forms of disagreement.

6.3 Methodology

The data for this section was collected through a judgment task (appendix 1). This instrument is described in more detail in section 3.5. Data was elicited from the JLE new arrival group (section 3.4.1). These 12 participants also provided the data discussed in chapters 4 and 5.

6.4 Previous research focusing on interpretation

There is a growing body of literature which has focused on how L2 learners interpret and negotiate negatively-affective speech acts. For example, Frescura (1991), in her discussion of how L2 learners develop sociopragmatic competence, argues that comprehension and interpretation are not focused on in L2 classrooms to the extent they should be. She cites four reasons for this:

1. there is no neat methodology with skills and plans outlined clearly in a textbook;

2. the speaking of the target language, rather than the understanding, is considered the primary goal of L2 instruction;

3. developing listening competence not only reduces precious time available for speaking, but goes against the common-sense notion of learning 'from simple to difficult' (1991: 119); and

4. in first-language instruction, listening comprehension is held to be a given, 'something that will somehow develop "naturally"' (1991: 119).

This lack of classroom teaching of comprehension and interpretation has been echoed by a paucity of studies of cross-cultural pragmatic interpretation. The majority of pragmatics-oriented studies seem to have focused on production of speech acts, rather than interpretation. The ability to accurately interpret speech acts, however, is clearly crucial to attaining sociopragmatic competence in a second-language setting:

> ...even advanced language learners often show a marked imbalance between their grammatical and their pragmatic knowledge or, more specifically, between the lexico-grammatical microlevel and the 'macrolevel of communicative intent and sociocultural context' (Bardovi-Harlig and Dornyei 1998: 234).

Those studies which have concentrated on comprehension of L2 indirect speech acts suggest that there are numerous differences in processing indirect speech acts between native and non-native speakers. Research by Kasper (1984) and Schraw et al (1988) indicates that second language learners use a word-by-word literal process to understand L2 speech acts. Kasper (1984) found that German learners of English, utilising this process, often failed to identify the illocutionary intent of their native-speaker interlocutors. A good example is an utterance by a native speaker of English, addressed to a German English learner, 'You're drinking a beer there'. A logical inference for a native speaker of English would be that the NS wanted to join the German speaker for a drink, or perhaps that s/he wanted the German speaker to buy him/her a pint (cf. Barron 2002). However, the response by the German learner of English was a simple 'yes', thus indicating a literal interpretation of the utterance, and a failure to comprehend the native speaker's hint. Takahashi and Roitblat (1994), who focused specifically on interpretation of language by Japanese learners of English, pointed out that little is known about the acquisition of *conventional* (i.e. nonliteral) language in either L1 or L2 learners. It is not known whether Japanese learners of English process the literal meaning of an utterance before the conventional meaning, process the conventional meaning before the figurative meaning, or interpret both meanings simultaneously.

In summary, the studies mentioned above have underlined the importance of research into interpretation of negative speech acts, particularly in terms of cross-cultural speech behaviour.

6.5 Format

6.5.1 Interpreting severity in the judgment task scenarios

The social variable of severity (i.e. ranking of imposition – see section 2.4.3) is not controlled in the judgment task scenarios because it is 'culturally and situationally defined' (Brown and Levinson 1987: 77); a situation that is relatively innocuous in terms of face-threat in New Zealand's culture may engender a more severe face-threat in Japan's culture, and vice versa. Therefore, instead of making my own pronouncements of situational severity, I elicited the perceptions of the participants. This enabled a comparison of native and non-native speakers' judgments of situational severity.

6.5.2 Problems and modifications in implied-disagreement situations

Two of the judgment task implied-disagreement segments, situations 16 and 17, proved to be problematic in that they contained other disagreement strategies which had not been excluded or accounted for in the design of the questionnaire. In order to avoid confusion, it was decided that the data from situations 16 and 17 would not be used in the analysis. The reasons for excluding these two situations, and the consequences of having done so, are briefly discussed in this section[1].

Situation 16 was a short extract from a New Zealand TV medical drama, containing a conversation between a senior nurse and a senior doctor. The conversation took place shortly after they had reprimanded another doctor:

> Senior Doctor: I'll speak to the other doctors, they won't pull a stunt like this again.
> Senior Nurse: If they did, you'd be the last to know.
> Senior Doctor: Sorry?

In the second problematic extract, situation 17, a woman and a doctor were arguing about whether or not another doctor had stolen money from the hospital:

> Woman: You doctors are all the same. What's he done, promised you a percentage next time?
> Doctor: You know, for your information, Victor didn't pocket that money.
> Woman: Yeah, right.

Situation 16 contained what was perceived to be an implied disagreement: The doctor was ostensibly making a request for clarification, but it is more likely that he was preparing to take issue with the nurse's statement. Such repair initiators are often employed as delay devices, prefacing an impending disagreeing statement: 'In the course of producing a disagreement, a recipient may request clarification with "what?", "hm?", questioning repeats, and the like' (Pomerantz 1984:

---

1   These problems apply exclusively to the judgment task but not to any of the other data-collecting instruments. For this reason, they are discussed here rather than in the methodology chapter.

185

71). Situation 17 had been included to determine whether the participants could recognise the woman's sarcastic comment on the proposition (i.e. 'Yeah, right') as connoting disagreement. However, both situations contained additional cues which may have indicated to participants that the characters in the segments were disagreeing. The characters' tones of voice and facial expressions, for instance, were clues that the situation was negatively affective. Significantly, a considerable number of participants were able to identify that the two situations contained a disagreeing strategy of some kind. This suggested that they had attained a degree of pragmatic skill, in that they were able to identify the situations as being negatively affective. However, there was no way to determine whether the participants had noticed the 'default' disagreeing strategies, or had noticed some other aspect which signalled that the situation was negatively affective. To avoid possible misinterpretation of these results, these two situations were excluded from the analysis.

There are both negative and positive consequences of having excluded these two situations. The main negative effect is that although there are four explicit- and hedged-disagreement situations in the judgment task, there are only two implied-disagreement situations (situations 7 and 13). Hence, the amount of data from the implied disagreement situations is reduced.

Fortunately, both of the two remaining implicit situations focus on unspoken disagreement (see section 2.6.1). Those who utilise implied disagreement strategies of any kind run the risk of their interlocutor a) not realising that they are disagreeing; b) not understanding the reasons behind the disagreement; and/or c) misinterpreting the intended strength of the disagreement (cf. Dascal 1983). Needless to say, paralinguistic methods of expressing disagreement exacerbate this risk because they are even more susceptible to misinterpretation. So even though it has not been possible to obtain useful data about verbalised implicit disagreement, there are some interesting findings to be discussed regarding paralinguistic disagreement strategies.

In retrospect, creating a judgment task which focuses on implied disagreement seems to have been just as complex and difficult as using implied disagreement strategies in a conversation! Implied disagreement is, by its very nature, ambiguous; it is always open to misinterpretation, misconstruction and misunderstanding (House 2000, 2003). In creating a method of measuring how disagreements are implied, I found that I ran into problems which were similar to those afflicting language learners who attempt to manage implied disagreements.

6.6 Recognition of disagreement speech acts

Table 6.1, below, displays the three types of disagreement strategy (i.e. explicit, hedged and implied disagreement) which were presented in the judgment task situations. The table also shows the percentage of participants in each of the three groups (the native speakers, the JLE pre-testing group, and the JLE post-testing group) who were able to identify the disagreement. The bottom row (in bold) indicates the degree to which the non-native speaker participants' ability to identify each kind of disagreement increased over the ten-week period. Note, however, that the JLE sample size is only 12 people, so the conclusions that may be drawn from these results are necessarily limited, and must be treated with caution. All percentages are aggregated.

Group	Explicit %	Hedged %	Implied %
NS group (n=10)	95 (38/40)	85 (34/40)	90 (18/20)
JLE pre (n=12)	81 (39/48)	60 (29/48)	25 (6/24)
JLE post (n=12)	85 (41/48)	71 (34/48)	42 (10/24)
JLE pre-post shift (%)	*4*	*11*	*17*

Table 6.1: Percentages of each participant group who could recognise disagreement strategies of increasing indirectness

Figure 6.1, below, illustrates the degree by which the JLE participants increased in ability to identify each type of disagreement:

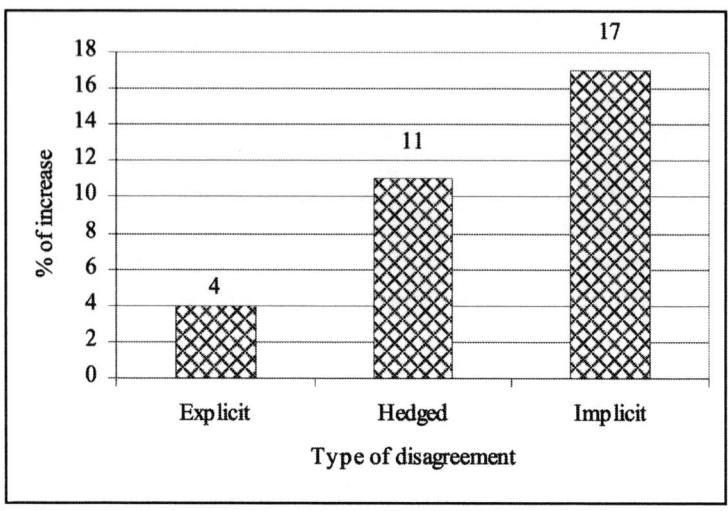

Figure 6.1: JLE pre-to-post shift in ability to recognise
disagreement utterances

As figure 6.1 shows, the JLE new arrival group made gains in recognising disagreement strategies at all three levels of transparency over their ten-week instruction period. The least notable gains were made in recognising explicit disagreements; average gains were made in recognising hedged disagreements; and the most prominent gains were made in recognising implied disagreements. These are discussed in turn.

6.6.1 Explicit disagreement

From the outset, a high proportion of the 12 JLE new arrival group participants could identify explicitly-stated disagreement utterances. At the beginning of the period of research, 81% of JLEs were able to identify explicit disagreement. After ten weeks, this had risen to 85%, indicating a shift of 4%. The small degree of shift is likely to be due to a 'ceiling effect', i.e. since the participants' ability to recognise this kind of disagreement was high from the beginning, there was little opportunity for shift.

6.6.2 Hedged disagreement

Initially, 60% of the JLE new arrival group were able to identify hedged disagreement – a relatively low percentage. The result after the ten-week period of study was 71%, indicating a shift of 11% in their capacity to identify hedged disagreement strategies. This result on its own does not imply that the JLEs had learned how to appropriately interpret the severity of a negatively affective situation, or the level of interlocutor politeness used – only that they could recognise that the utterance was intended as a disagreement. The most useful data about interpretation of hedged disagreements is likely to be found in JLE interpretations of interlocutor politeness and situational severity in hedged situations, which are discussed in sections 6.7 and 6.8.

6.6.3 Implicit disagreement

The 12 JLE participants made relatively high gains in the category of implicit disagreement. Table 6.1 illustrates that at the beginning of the ten weeks of study in New Zealand, only 3 of the 12 (25%) participants were able to identify strategies of implied disagreement. After ten weeks, this had risen to 5 (42%). The increase of 17% in identifying implicit disagreement is the highest out of the three categories of disagreement. The ability of the JLE new arrival group to recognise implied disagreement appeared to alter considerably – although with such a small sample size it is difficult to gauge the import of this shift.

What factors could be responsible for this shift? It is well-known that communicative behaviour is by no means solely verbal: it is very often paralinguistic and understanding the verbal aspect of a speech act is only one element of general social competence (Gass and Houck 1999; Goodwin and Goodwin 1987; Riley 1989). It is therefore worth

189

examining some excerpts recorded from TV programmes in some more detail.

As mentioned earlier, the judgment task contained two TV segments in which disagreement was implied: situations 7 and 13. In both, paralinguistic channels were used to express the speaker's opposition. In situation 7, a politician expressed his disagreement with his interlocutor by shaking his head throughout the other's turn at speaking. In situation 13, a man appeared to disagree with a woman by breaking eye contact with her, looking down at the ground and responding to her statement in a weary, resigned tone of voice (see appendix 1 for transcripts of these situations). The judgment task paper asked participants to select three specific paralinguistic cues – facial expression, sound or loudness of voice, and hand or body gestures – which they thought may have contributed to the delivery of disagreement in each TV segment. In the questionnaire, participants were asked to select paralinguistic cues which:

1. indicated the situational severity of the disagreement; and
2. marked the interlocutor politeness / impoliteness of the main speaker.

I am using these results to illustrate the participants' awareness of paralinguistic cues in *identifying* disagreement.

Table 6.2 (below) presents the percentage of native speakers and JLEs (both pre-testing and post-testing) who identified these cues. Note that it is not the percentages themselves that are important. Rather, the important point is to compare the number of JLEs who recognised each category of implicit disagreement with the number of NSs who did so.

Table 6.2 demonstrates how similar to the NS responses the JLE new arrival group's responses had become after ten weeks. As the two samples are different sizes, the percentages have been aggregated.

190

Paralinguistic cue:	JLE Pre-testing (n=12)	JLE Post-testing (n=12)	Native speakers (n=10)
Facial expression	3 (25%)	6 (50%)	8 (80%)
Tone / loudness of voice	1 (8%)	2 (17%)	5 (50%)
Hand / body gestures	1 (8%)	3 (25%)	5 (50%)
Total cues noticed	*5*	*11*	*18*

Table 6.2: JLE and NS – recognition of paralinguistic cues in implicit
disagreement situations

Facial expression was perceived as indicative of disagreement by 80% of NSs. Among the JLEs only 3 (25%) identified facial expressions as denoting disagreement, but this increased to 6 (50%) by the end of the ten-week instruction period. There was a slight shift in the ability of the JLE participants to recognise disagreement which was implied through tone of voice (from 8% to 17%, i.e. one more participant). Of course, only one of the two implied-disagreement segments (situation 13) actually contained a vocalised disagreement, which is no doubt part of the reason why so few participants noticed it! While only one (8%) JLE was originally aware of hand or body movements as signalling a disagreement, this awareness increased to 3 (25%) after ten weeks had passed, indicating a shift in ability to identify and interpret hand gestures or body language.

The shift mentioned above may denote the beginning of an upsurge in ability to recognise disagreement expressed through para-linguistic channels. It is quite probable that the JLE new arrival group developed this ability, at least to a certain degree, during their ten-week period of instruction and immersion in the host culture. The culture-specific and largely non-verbal nature of paralinguistic chan-nels makes them difficult to understand in a cross-cultural milieu (cf. Gass and Houck 1999; Littlewood 2001), suggesting they would be difficult to teach as part of a classroom-based curriculum (see section 7.5.2). The likelihood is that the participants acquired this knowledge through their immersion in the host culture.

It is unfortunate that only two situations in this judgment task presented strategies of implied disagreement (as noted earlier, the remaining two were excluded from the analysis due to ambiguity). This is clearly a possible area for further research.

6.6.4 Recognition of disagreement: How substantial was the pre-post shift?

To determine whether there was a statistically significant change from pre-testing to post-testing in terms of the JLE new arrival group's recognition of disagreement strategies, three statistical analyses were carried out on the interpretation (judgment task) data: a sign test, a Wilcoxon (paired) signed rank test, and a paired t-test. The sign test was applied in order to see whether there was either a positive (+) difference or a negative (-) difference between pre-testing and post-testing. The Wilcoxon (paired) signed rank test and the paired t-test were applied to determine the size of the changes from pre-testing to post-testing, assuming any such changes existed. These two tests were selected because they took into account the relative sizes of such changes: the t-test measured the change explicitly, and the Wilcoxon test examined the ranks of the measurements. In general, these three tests are not entirely appropriate for this kind of data, but when they are used in conjunction with one another the conclusion is likely to be quite robust.

Test	Probabilities (p-values)
Sign test:	0.2744
Wilcoxon (paired) signed rank test:	0.0737
Paired t-test:	0.0801

Table 6.3: Recognising disagreement: results of statistical testing
to measure differences between JLE pre-testing and post-testing

In many areas of research, a p-value of 0.05 (i.e. a 5% probability of error) is considered to be a 'borderline acceptable' level of significance. The test results do not present this level of significance. The result of the sign test, 0.2744, is not significant at all. However, the

Wilcoxon test and the paired t-test both show a difference at the 10% level of significance (though not at the more usual 5% level). Put simply, there is a 10% probability that the relation between the variables found in the sample is due to chance. Though this probability is higher than ideal, it is nevertheless quite low.

While it appears that a ten-week period of study in the host culture is not enough to facilitate a statistically significant shift in ability to recognise disagreements, there is definitely a marked positive shift over that period. I would surmise that a longer period of time spent in the host culture would result in a statistically significant improvement in ability. How long that period should be remains to be investigated; however, given the advances made by the participants over even such a short time as ten weeks, it is likely that a significant change would take place within a relatively short time.

6.6.5 Summary

The JLE new arrival group's ability to recognise explicit disagreement altered only a little, possibly because their ability was high to begin with. They made some gains in recognising hedged disagreements. They made considerable gains in ability to recognise implied disagreement, which suggested that their ability to recognise paralinguistic signals as part of a disagreement strategy had increased over the ten week instruction period. The general shift made by the JLEs from pre-testing to post-testing was not in itself statistically significant, but the results did suggest that a significant shift in recognising ability could take place within a relatively short period of time.

6.7 Perceiving interlocutor politeness in disagreement situations

6.7.1 Introduction

Understanding the intended politeness of an utterance can be problematic, even when there is no cultural gap between hearer and speaker. Leech (1983: 30) says the following about interpreting politeness in an utterance:

> We cannot ultimately be certain of what a speaker means by an utterance. The observable conditions, the utterance and the context, are determinants of what S means by the utterance U; it is the task of H to diagnose the most likely interpretation. Since...utterances are liable to illocutionary indeterminacy, it is not always possible for H...to come to a definite conclusion about what S means. Interpreting an utterance is ultimately a matter of guesswork.

Leech is referring to the potential difficulty of using politeness utterances within one single cultural context. In a cross-cultural context, interpreting the politeness value of an utterance is rendered even more problematic because each culture has its own unique conceptualisation of appropriate politeness and the social variables which may inform this. Language learners who have only been in a target culture for a short time are often deficient in knowledge about how the new culture manages pragmatic appropriateness in general (Bardovi-Harlig 1999), and appropriate politeness in particular (Arndt and Janney 1992). For the purposes of this study, then, it is useful to gain some idea of the JLE participants' perceptions of interlocutor politeness to which they were exposed and how these perceptions altered over the ten-week period of instruction.

This section provides a brief outline of the format used in the judgment task to collect information on assessments of interlocutor politeness. It then discusses the results obtained through analysis of that data. Lastly, it discusses the likely value of these results for understanding JLE cognition regarding the speech act of disagreement.

6.7.2 Format for obtaining politeness data

Section 6.2 hypothesised that the JLE new arrival group's perceptions of the degree of politeness employed by characters in the judgment task video was likely to be less tolerant than the perceptions of the native speaker group. This was due to the likelihood that the severity of a speech act may be exacerbated by different, culture-specific communicative styles. (House 2000: 151). It was also hypothesised that the JLEs' perception would alter after ten weeks of immersion in the target culture. In order to obtain constructive data relating to perceptions of interlocutor politeness, all participants were asked to indicate how polite or otherwise they considered the main speaker in each TV segment to have been.

Example:

Is Nick being appropriately polite for this situation? Circle a number below.

1	2	3	4	5
Too polite		Appropriately polite		Not polite at all

The participants gauged politeness values on a five-point Likert scale, as in the above example. The participants also indicated paralinguistic cues in each segment which they perceived as signifying the interlocutor politeness of the situation. In considering the politeness values of each situation, the participants took into account the relative power of the two interlocutors (P), and whether the speaker and the listener knew one another (D). The participants also noted how severe (R) they perceived the situation to be. Consideration of these variables enabled the participants to make a subjective determination of the politeness or impoliteness of the language used by the speakers in each TV segment.

If the politeness values of the JLE new arrival group had become lower after ten weeks, the group as a whole was seen as being more 'tolerant'. If, on the other hand, the politeness value became higher, the group was viewed as being more 'stringent'. These are the terms I

195

shall use in this chapter in discussing whether perceptions of politeness became higher or lower on the 5-point scale.

6.7.3 Results

Table 6.4, below, presents the mean interlocutor politeness values from the four combinations of P and D variables for each participant group:

	NS (n=10)	SD	JLE pre (n=12)	SD	JLE post (n=12)	SD
-P-D	2.9	0.84	3.3	0.78	3.4	0.64
+P-D	4.0	0.69	3.9	1.04	3.9	0.85
-P+D	4.2	0.67	4.1	0.90	3.9	0.97
+P+D	3.6	0.85	3.7	1.00	3.5	1.01
Group mean:	*3.7*	*0.55*	*3.7*	*0.36*	*3.7*	*0.26*

Table 6.4: Perceptions of interlocutor politeness in judgment task situations, categorised by P and D variables

The combined means of all three groups (the bottom row of table 6.4) were virtually identical. There was little pattern of change in perceptions of interlocutor politeness between pre-testing and post-testing. The hypothesis mentioned earlier – that JLEs would initially hold more severe perceptions of politeness than NSs but that this would alter over the ten-week period of study – is not supported.

However, closer reflection reveals a distinctive pattern of JLE perceptions of interlocutor politeness. In specific situations, the JLE new arrival group's initial perception of politeness was high (4 or 5) on the scale, indicating that they considered the primary interlocutor in the TV segments to have been quite impolite. However, their post-testing perception had become lower on the scale, suggesting that i) their perceptions were less stringent then ten weeks previously; and ii) they were no longer conforming to a preconceived notion of what constituted appropriate politeness.

196

The situations presenting this pattern corresponded to certain combinations of power and social distance within the segments. The pattern was present in situations of high social distance (+D), but not in low social distance situations. The pattern was also present in situations that depicted two power-equal (-P) interlocutors, though the effect was less marked. The following tables present the difference between JLEs' pre-testing perceptions of politeness and their post-testing perceptions. Note that in all except one case, the post-testing assessments are lower than the pre-testing assessments, suggesting that the JLEs deemed the interlocutors to have been less impolite than they had previously. Table 6.5.1 depicts high social distance situations:

	JLE pre	JLE post	Pre-post difference
-P+D	4.13	3.92	0.21 lower
+P+D	3.66	3.54	0.12 lower

Table 6.5.1: Mean perceived interlocutor politeness – high social distance situations

Table 6.5.2 depicts power-equal situations:

	JLE pre	JLE post	Pre-post difference
-P-D	3.28	3.39	0.11 higher
-P+D	4.13	3.92	0.21 lower

Table 6.5.2: Mean perceived interlocutor politeness – power-equal situations

In situations that were high in social distance, JLE new arrival group's perceptions of politeness became lower (i.e. less stringent). The same trend, albeit less pronounced, was evidenced in JLE interpretations of power-equal situations. Conversely, in situations that portrayed low social distance or power-unequal relationships, the JLEs' perceptions remained as stringent as previously. This pattern seems to suggest that the JLE participants were initially cautious in their assessments of interlocutor politeness values. After ten weeks of study, the JLEs' assessments of politeness and impoliteness appeared to become more tolerant. It is possible that their capacity for accurately interpreting the intended politeness of an utterance had increased over their ten-week period of study. As a result of this increase, the JLEs were less inclined to be cautious in their interpretation of politeness – but only in situations which posed the least risk in terms of potential face-loss.

Crucially, this pattern is very similar to that manifested in both the written and spoken production data. Both types of production data demonstrated that JLE participants were able to use pragmatically sophisticated utterances, but preferred to attempt them only in situations of high social distance or power-equality, where the potential for face-damage was minimal. In short, the pattern which was previously identified in the production data appears to also be present in the interpretation data.

It is possible to speculate that after a longer period of time spent in the target culture, this downward shift will adjust itself to an assessment of politeness akin to that of the native-speaker group. Once a certain amount of time has passed and a certain amount of acculturation has taken place, the JLEs are likely to be able to form a more precise impression of the target culture's politeness norms. Consequently, they may feel less need to form conservative judgments; their assessments of negatively affective situations may not be as stringent as they had been previously. Tables 6.5.1 and 6.5.2 demonstrate the initial stages of this downward shift. Further investigation is necessary to determine the length of time JLEs would need to be immersed in the target culture in order for their perceptions of interlocutor politeness to approximate those of the native-speaker group.

6.7.4 Summary

The most important finding of this section has been the pattern of JLE participants' interpretations of interlocutor politeness when viewing disagreements between NS interlocutors. I will now discuss the second variable elicited by the judgment task: the JLEs' perceptions of situational severity in the TV extracts to which they were exposed.

6.8 Assessing the severity of disagreement situations

6.8.1 Introduction

As mentioned in section 6.1, 'situational severity' refers to the seriousness, or magnitude, of a disagreement scenario, i.e. how extreme the consequences of the disagreement are likely to be. The notion of 'situational severity' is based on Brown and Levinson's (1987) variable of ranking of imposition (defined in section 2.4.3). Brown and Levinson note that severity is both situationally and culturally defined: 'these intra-culturally defined costings of impositions on an individual's preserve are in general constant only in their rank order from one situation to another' (1987: 77).

In a cross-cultural context, assessing the severity of a disagreement situation is problematic because notions of which factors add to or detract from the severity of a situation are calibrated differently by each individual culture. Second-language learners who have only recently been immersed in the target culture tend to have limited culture-specific knowledge about factors which might mitigate or exacerbate severity in social situations, such as rights or obligations to perform an FTA (see section 2.4.3). For the purposes of this study, then, it is useful to obtain information about the JLE new arrival group's assessments of severity in the judgment task situations and how these assessments alter over the ten-week period of instruction.

6.8.2 Format for obtaining data about situational severity

The judgment task questionnaire required the participants to make a judgment about the severity of disagreement scenarios which they had viewed. They were asked to indicate their assessment on a five-point scale:

Example:
2. How <u>serious</u> do you think this disagreement is? Circle a number below.

Not serious at all   1   2   3   4   5   Very serious

                       serious

The situational severity scale employed a somewhat different format from that used to obtain assessments of interlocutor politeness (see the example in section 6.7.2). The politeness scale was a five-point Likert scale which comprised a mid-point of 'normal' politeness, and two extremes (i.e. too polite, or not polite at all) on either side of this mid-point. By contrast, the situational severity scale is a continuum. Low severity is indicated at one end of the continuum, and high severity is indicated at the other. Piloting of this task suggested that participants were not confused by this.

In estimating the severity of the disagreement in each TV segment, participants took into account several factors. Firstly, they read a short introduction on each page of their questionnaires, which offered a brief description of the background in each scenario under consideration. Secondly, they listened to the dialogue in each segment for any indication of the weight of the disagreement (such as through raised voices or coarse language). Thirdly, they observed the paralinguistic cues in the TV segment which may have denoted its severity: facial expression, tone or loudness of voice, and head or body movements. Through attention to these factors, participants were able to formulate a subjective assessment of the situational severity of each segment.

As in the previous section, I employ the terms 'stringent' and 'tolerant' to denote whether the JLEs' perceptions of situational severity became higher or lower on the severity scale.

6.8.3 Results

Examination of the present interpretation data indicates that the JLE new arrival group's post-testing assessments of severity were similar to NS assessments, although only in certain combinations of social variables. Table 6.6, below, compares the JLE group's post-testing assessments of severity with those of the native speaker group. This table presents each group's mean assessments of severity at two decimal places for purposes of clarity.

Power / distance variables	NS assessments	JLE (post-testing) assessments	Difference between JLE and NS assessments
-P / -D	2.88	3.52	0.64
+P / -D	3.35	3.59	0.24
-P / +D	3.72	3.80	0.08
+P / +D	3.40	3.32	0.08

NS n = 10; JLE n = 12

Table 6.6: Difference between JLE (post-testing) and NS perceptions of situational severity, categorised by power and social distance

The JLE participants' post-testing assessments of situational severity were similar to NS assessments in some cases, but less similar in others. In the two bottom categories, power-equal / high social distance (-P / +D) and power-unequal / high social distance (+P / +D), the JLEs' perceptions were within 0.08 points of the NS perceptions. The JLE assessments most closely matched the NS assessments in responses to TV segments in which the interlocutors did not know one another.

There is a similar pattern of shift between the JLEs' pre-testing and post-testing assessments of severity. Table 6.7, below, presents the mean situational severity value of all the TV segments as judged by the NSs and by the JLEs (pre-testing and post-testing) on a five-point scale. The bottom row of table 6.7, labelled 'Group mean', indicates the total and combined mean situational severity values for

201

all the disagreement situations. The column on the far right, labelled 'Average pre-post shift', refers to the average difference between the JLEs' pre-testing and post-testing estimates. A value that was reduced after ten weeks would indicate that, in general, the JLE group's perception of situational severity had become more tolerant over that period of time. Conversely, a higher value would indicate that the JLE group's perception of situational severity had become more stringent.

	NS (n=10)	JLE pre (n=12)	JLE post (n=12)	Mean JLE pre-post shift
-P-D	2.9	2.8	3.5	0.8 higher
+P-D	3.4	3.7	3.6	0.1 lower
-P+D	3.7	4.1	3.8	0.3 lower
+P+D	3.4	3.7	3.3	0.4 lower
Group mean	*3.4*	*3.6*	*3.6*	

Table 6.7: Mean severity of all disagreement scenarios, categorised by power and social distance variables

Section 6.2 hypothesised that there would be a shift among the JLE group toward lower perceptions of situational severity after ten weeks had passed, and that the JLEs would become more similar to the NSs in their assessments of severity. However, in general the anticipated shift was not supported in the data. The mean severity value presented by the NS group was 3.4, as opposed to that of the JLEs, which was 3.6 both at the pre-testing and post-testing stages. Evidently, the JLE new arrival group had a more stringent perception of situational severity than the NS group did, and ten weeks of intensive study in New Zealand hardly altered this perception. This suggests that an understanding of a second culture's sociopragmatic norms and values takes time to develop.

However, a more thorough analysis reveals a distinctive pattern of JLE assessments of situational severity between the pre-testing and post-testing stages. In certain situations, the JLEs' initial perceptions of severity were high (i.e. stringent) on the severity scale, but their post-testing perceptions had become lower (i.e. more tolerant) on the scale. The situations presenting this pattern corresponded to certain combinations of power and social distance variables within the segments. The pattern was evident in situations of high social distance, but not in those presenting low social distance. The pattern was also evident in situations depicting two power-equal interlocutors, though the effect was not as noticeable.

Table 6.8.1 presents the difference between the JLE new arrival group's pre-testing assessments of situational severity and their post-testing assessments in situations of high social distance:

	JLE pre	JLE post	Pre-post difference
-P+D	4.1	3.8	0.3 lower
+P+D	3.7	3.3	0.4 lower

Table 6.8.1: Mean perceived severity – high social distance situations

Table 6.8.1 reflects a marked drop in judgments of perceived severity between pre-testing and post-testing in situations in which the TV interlocutors had not established a relationship.

Table 6.8.2 below, demonstrates the difference between the JLE group's pre-testing and post-testing assessments of situational severity in power-equal situations:

	JLE pre	JLE post	Pre-post difference
-P-D	2.8	3.5	0.7 higher
-P+D	4.1	3.8	0.3 lower

Table 6.8.2: Mean perceived severity – power-equal situations

There is a drop in perceived severity in power-equal situations, but the shift is only evident in one of the power-equal categories (-P+D). In the other, -P-D, there is a definite *rise* in perceived severity. This outcome suggests that power-equal situations were less threatening to a JLE's face than power-unequal situations, but participants continued to exercise a certain degree of caution. In general, then, the post-testing data indicates a trend towards lower and more tolerant assessments of severity in two kinds of disagreement situation: those in which the two TV interlocutors had not formed a relationship; and (to a lesser extent) those in which the interlocutors were equal in power.

The results in terms of evaluating interlocutor politeness (as presented in section 6.7.3) formed a very similar pattern to that noted in this section. The JLE group's assessments of politeness values had changed most in their responses to high social-distance situations and power-equal situations. As in the section on politeness values, the patterns described in this section may suggest that the JLE participants were initially cautious in their assessments of situational severity, but later altered their assessments. It is likely that, by the post-testing stage, the JLEs' ability to accurately interpret situational severity had increased. Consequently, they were less inclined to be conservative in their interpretations of severity. However, this inclination was evident only in high-social-distance situations and power-equal situations, i.e. those least likely to result in face-loss for the JLEs. This implies that, as with politeness assessments, the JLE group only tended to revise their assessments in situations where incorrect perceptions were unlikely to cause face-loss. Where the potential for face-loss was high, i.e. in low social-distance situations or power-unequal situations, their assessments were as severe as previously. The participants may have deliberately formulated cautious assessments of situational severity, overestimating severity rather than risk underestimating it. It is possible that such a shift in the JLEs' perceptions of situational severity may eventually come to correspond with the perceptions of the NS group, although an extended period of participant observation and assessment would be required to determine whether this was actually the case.

6.9 Discussion

6.9.1 The information processing procedure

From a cognitive viewpoint, the shift in judgments of perceived impoliteness and severity which are discussed in the previous sections could be regarded as part of the information processing procedure (McLaughlin 1988; McLaughlin and Heredia 1996) (section 2.8.1 describes this in more detail). In the course of this process, repeated practice in various language skills engenders gains in performance, and sub-skills become automated, allowing the learner to concentrate on internalising more complex linguistic skills. It is likely that the JLE new arrival group underwent an initial stage of consciously processing both lexical-grammatical and pragmatic knowledge (*controlled* processing). The JLE participants were thereby able to lay a foundation for automatic processing through internalising items of language and moving on to more difficult and complex linguistic items.

As I said in section 2.8.1, I have extended McLaughlin's model to account for both grammatical and pragmatic acquisition. The extension is logical because of the interconnection between linguistic and pragmalinguistic processes. However, these two processes may not be equal in priority for processing by second language learners. Levelt (1989) proposed that conversation was hierarchical in structure. Significantly, Levelt ranked the understanding of pragmatic conventions as the lowest priority in terms of hierarchical structure (see table 6.9, below):

First-order goal:	to express a particular intention
Second-order goal:	to decide on a topic
Third-order goal:	to formulate a series of phrases
Lower-order goals:	to retrieve the lexicon needed
	to activate articulatory patterns
	to utilise appropriate syntactic rules
	to meet pragmatic conventions

Table 6.9: Levelt's (1989) hierarchical task structure of speaking

Hence, it seems reasonable to presume that acquisition of grammatical processes may, initially at least, take precedence over that of pragmatic processes.

In order to provide a more detailed explanation of how these two processes are reflected in the present data, I will discuss them in two sections: Firstly, the processes of acquisition of lexical / grammatical rules; secondly, the processes of acquisition of pragmatic knowledge.

Processes of acquiring lexical / grammatical rules
During the initial weeks of their period of study in New Zealand, the JLE new arrival group needed to develop rather complex cognitive mechanisms for managing conversations in the L2. These mechanisms are described in detail by McLaughlin and Heredia (1996). According to McLaughlin and Heredia, the first goal for language learners is to express a particular intention. To do this, they need to select a topic and select a syntactic arrangement for delivering the topic. In turn, the realisation of this syntactic arrangement requires the development of sub-activities, such as formulating grammatical phrases to express various facets of the topic to be delivered. However, to utter these phrases there is a need for 'lexical retrieval, the activation of articulatory patterns, utilisation of appropriate syntactic rules, and so forth' (McLaughlin and Heredia 1996: 215). The participants in the present study would have had some linguistic skills already, having studied English as a Foreign Language for at least six years as part of their secondary education in Japan. But clearly, time was required in order for these newly-acquired grammatical / lexical items and their myriad applications to be automatised. In the interim, there appeared to be a period of uncertainty while these skills were being learned, practiced and routinised. Only once these lexical-grammatical rules had been internalised were the learners able to concentrate on pragmatic aspects of their talk. This partly explains the JLEs' inclination to consciously formulate cautious assessments of politeness or situational severity, as noted in sections 6.7.3 and 6.8.3. While they were still actively assimilating new lexical or grammatical items, they employed a sociopragmatic / pragmalinguistic 'safety device' in order to avert face-loss due to misinterpretations of politeness utterances or situational severity. (This 'safety device' will be discussed further in sections 7.2 and 7.3.)

However, over the ten weeks of intensive study in New Zealand, the JLE new arrival group appeared to automatise a number of grammatical and lexical processes. Once they had integrated these processes, they were then able to concentrate on other, more advanced processes, including pragmatic processes.

Processes of acquiring pragmatic knowledge
Although the JLEs' primary concern during their ten-week testing period was most likely the linguistic aspects of their language learning, it is probable that they also learned to recognise and routinise a number of pragmatic aspects of conversations during this time, as a result of their immersion in the target culture. The language learners would have been exposed to pragmatic norms through interacting with native speakers and through observing native speakers interacting with one another.

Automaticity may be viewed as the acquisition of domain-specific knowledge. McLaughlin and Heredia (1996: 219) posit that this type of knowledge 'accumulates through separate instances, each of which leaves episodic traces on memory'. The JLE participants were provided exposure to a number of these instances as a consequence of their immersion in the target culture. However, it is possible that, during the initial few weeks of their immersion in the target culture, the conscious acquisition of pragmatic competence took second place because there were so many other purely linguistic aspects of language that required controlled processing. Indeed, Bardovi-Harlig and Dornyei (1998) suggest that NNSs who had just arrived in the target culture, having previously only studied in their own culture, may not have seen value in attaining pragmatic competence, instead viewing the internalising of lexico-grammatical information as being the primary objective in second language acquisition. Bardovi-Harlig and Dornyei's (1998: 223) study of pragmatic versus grammatical awareness in second language learning revealed that EFL learners and their teachers consistently identified and ranked grammatical errors as more serious than pragmatic errors. So during the beginning stages of the JLEs' stay in New Zealand, pragmatic acquisition may have been a lesser priority. However, we have seen a shift in assessments of interlocutor politeness and situational locutor politeness and situational severity as the JLEs adjusted their conceptions of appropriate politeness over this period of exposure to authentic communication in English.

6.9.2 Recognising implied disagreement: an extracurricular acquisition

It seems possible that a certain amount of the JLEs' shift in ability has been the result of immersion in the target culture. As section 6.6.3 explains, the JLEs exhibited a reasonably marked shift (17%) in their ability to recognise strategies of implied disagreement. A likely causative factor in this shift was an increase in the participants' ability to recognise and interpret paralinguistic channels. Understanding such channels requires a degree of often culture-specific pragmatic competence. However, according to the literature, it is quite unlikely that pragmatic knowledge had been explicitly taught as part of a classroom curriculum. Gass and Houck (1999: 200), for instance, mention a widespread assumption that the emphasis in a classroom will be on phonology, lexicon and syntax, and that pragmatics are often 'perceived to be universal'. Kasper (2001: 22) concurs with this, arguing that a teacher-fronted learning milieu 'is an unproductive interactional format for the learning of pragmatics and discourse'. So the JLEs are likely to have acquired more interpretive and productive competence through frequent and repeated contact with native speakers of English than through classroom instruction.

According to Ochs' (1986) language socialisation model (outlined in section 2.8.2), this process of acquisition may have had as much to do with interaction with native speakers as to classroom instruction. Language socialisation, which is concerned with the process of acquiring the linguistic and pragmatic principles of a new culture, emphasises the relationships which language learners have with 'experts' (who may include peers, friends, teachers and host family members, among others) with whom they frequently interact. Classroom-based instruction may also have contributed to this process, but conversation and other interactive communication are seen as the primary source for exposure to linguistic, pragmatic and sociocultural resources (Swain and Lapkin 1998; Jordens 1996). Littlewood observes that

> [F]orms include not only words and structures but also different kinds of pitch or intonation. Socialised speakers can then use these forms to *index* (in the sense of encode or invoke) particular situational meanings (2001: 193).

Clearly, a high degree of socialisation is essential in order to be able to index these situationally-specific meanings. This type of socialisation with native speakers of New Zealand English appears to have engendered considerable shifts in the JLEs' ability to recognise implied disagreement strategies.

6.9.3 Shifts in perceptions of politeness and severity

My initial hypothesis that the newly-arrived JLE participants' perceptions of politeness and severity in the TV segments would become similar to those of NSs was not supported by the data. However, there was a pattern of reduction in JLE perceptions which, I suggested, may eventually come to emulate the perceptions of NSs. According to sections 6.7.3 and 6.8.3, the most marked pre-to-post changes in perceived interlocutor politeness and situational severity occurred in the situations in which there was a) high social distance and b) power-equality between the TV interlocutors. It is worth considering in some detail why these shifts were only noticeable in situations presenting certain configurations of these social variables.

Firstly, the power-equal situations did not require the JLEs to make a judgment about power-distance between the interlocutors. Encounters between equals are likely to be more straightforward to judge than encounters with a large power-distance value because there is less need for conscious interpretation of politeness devices such as brevity or indirectness. It is likely that this facilitated an interpretation of politeness and situational severity that was more tolerant than previously. Secondly, the power-equality in the TV situations may have served to reduce the JLEs' estimation of the potential weight of any FTA that was committed (Brown and Levinson 1987). Thus, if the

JLEs made any errors of judgment about politeness values or values of situational severity, these errors would be less conspicuous than the same errors of judgment made in a power-unequal situation. Thirdly, it is possible that the JLEs perceived direct disagreement as being acceptable in the power-equal situations, perhaps due to a pragmatic transfer from their L1. This possibility is supported by Beebe and Takahashi's (1989a, 1989b) research, which concluded that Japanese people may be accustomed to reticence in power-unequal situations, but more at ease with direct strategies in disagreement with equals or subordinates. So in witnessing direct disagreements between power-equal NSs, the JLE new arrival group may not have perceived direct and forthright language as being excessively impolite. A fourth possibility also presents itself: the JLE participants may have received prior instruction from Japanese teachers of English about the 'directness stereotype' sometimes attributed to Westerners. This may have affected how the JLEs perceived the politeness values of utterances in the judgment task segments. Beebe and Takahashi specifically mention this phenomenon as a potential influence on the responses of their own JLE participant group:

> In some instances...the student was formally taught the stereotype (e.g. 'Americans are very direct, so be direct when talking to them'). In this case, we have...'transfer of training' (Selinker 1972) and 'teacher-induced error' (Stenson 1974). Many Japanese learners have reported to us that they were, in fact, taught by their Japanese teachers of English to 'be direct when using English' (1989b: 214–215).

It is feasible that, due to this factor, at least some members of the JLE new arrival group perceived directness as normal in interaction between two Westerners. This may have influenced their judgments of direct speech in the TV segments.

In high social distance encounters, the JLEs were witnessing disagreements between TV characters who did not know one another and were not likely to form a relationship. Possibly, the participants were conscious that in a parallel situation between two Japanese interlocutors, the necessity for *enryo* would be low (Doi 1981). As mentioned in section 2.5.3, *enryo* is normally a necessity in the social sphere of interaction in Japanese culture, but not in cases where there is no

210

established relationship. Hence, it is likely that, over the ten-week period of instruction, the JLE participants altered their relatively stringent perceptions of people who were not members of their in-group, i.e. people with whom they had no close and continuing relationship (Triandis 1986). As mentioned in section 4.6.2, Japanese culture tends to place more importance on in-group relationships than out-group relationships (Hofstede 1991). This can affect how social relationships are conducted:

> [M]embers of collectivistic cultures draw sharper distinctions between members of in-groups (e.g. those with whom they go to school or work) and out-groups and perceive in-group relationships to be more intimate than members of individualistic cultures. In-group relationships include co-worker and colleague…or classmate…while out-group relationships include, but are not limited to, interactions with strangers (Gudykunst, Yoon and Nishida 1987: 296).

Given this, it is likely that the JLE participants interpreted the encounters between people who did not know one another as having less value than those between people who had a close relationship. This may have reduced their evaluation of the weight of any potential FTA, allowing more latitude for interpretation of values of interlocutor politeness and situational severity.

Why were these two patterns not evident in the pre-testing data? It is possible that in the pre-testing data the JLEs were making conservative judgments of all the TV situations they were exposed to, while in the post-testing data they were making conservative judgments only in situations which they perceived as particularly face-threatening. I posited in sections 6.7.3 and 6.8.3 that during the initial period the participants adopted a strategy of overestimating severity or impoliteness values rather than underestimate them, a strategy which Brown and Levinson refer to as 'tak[ing] out the maximum insurance policy' (1987: 74). This is not necessarily the best option: Discussing production, Brown and Levinson suggest that 'the off-record strategy leads to ambiguities and unclarities, while redressive action takes time, foresight and effort' (1987: 74). So overestimating severity, impoliteness, or the indirectness of a required reply may have the paradoxical effect of *increasing* the weight of an FTA.

Nonetheless, it appears that over the ten-week period of study the JLE new arrival group may have gained a more detailed understanding of sociopragmatic and pragmalinguistic factors influencing speech behaviour in native-speaker disagreements. But they continued to 'take out the maximum insurance policy' in interpreting situations which they perceived as potentially highly face-threatening, i.e. those presenting power inequality, and/or those which presented a high degree of social distance.

6.10 Conclusion

In general, the JLE new arrival group's ability to identify disagreement had increased to a certain degree between pre-testing and post testing, although this shift was not statistically significant (as section 6.6.4 discusses). The most marked shift was in the participants' ability to recognise implied disagreements, which are expressed 'off-record' (Brown and Levinson 1987), often through paralinguistic methods rather than through a verbalised speech act. Section 6.9.2 has posited that the ability to identify and interpret these paralinguistic channels was largely the result of immersion and interaction in the target culture, rather than classroom instruction.

There was a noticeable modification in the participants' classifications of interlocutor politeness in situations which presented factors of high social distance or power-equality. However, these assessments did not begin to correspond with the assessments made by the NS group. The hypothesis that JLEs' perceptions of politeness would become similar to NS perceptions was not upheld. The participants' ability to accurately interpret the situational severity of TV segments *did* become similar to that of the native-speaker group after a ten-week period, but once again the shift was only evident in the JLEs' responses to situations of high social distance and those which were power-equal. The hypothesis was only partially supported.

I suggested that the patterns of shift in high social-distance situations and power-equal situations might imply a strategy of avoiding unnecessary face-loss by overestimating assessments of politeness and severity rather than underestimating them. This would account for the fact that shifts only occurred in situations which contained the lowest threat of potential face-damage. It is possible that this phenomenon of downward shift in low-face-threat situations could be a precursor to eventual emulation of NS perceptions of interlocutor politeness and situational severity in disagreements. Further research is required in order to determine how long this change in assessment would take, or indeed if it would happen at all.

7 Discussion

7.1 Introduction

This project was constructed in order to formulate a qualitative and quantitative account of a) the ability of JLEs to employ disagreement strategies appropriately, and b) their ability to accurately interpret the sociopragmatic contexts underlying disagreement strategies. Another focus of the research was on shifts in the ability of the JLEs to interpret and express disagreement over a period of time spent residing and studying ESL in the host culture. As the data has been analysed and discussed in chapters 4 to 6, it is now possible to construct a general summary of what the findings reveal about the JLE group's pragmatic ability. Specifically, this chapter considers what patterns of change have been identified and what these patterns might signify.

Firstly, I will briefly summarise and discuss the steps taken and the methods used in carrying out the analysis.

7.1.1 Recapitulating the theoretical framework

The theoretical framework of this study comprised four facets: i) theories of politeness; ii) the use of disagreement speech acts; iii) the potential effect of cultural dissimilarities between Japan and New Zealand on the JLE group's disagreement strategy selections; and iv) pertinent theories of second language acquisition which help to illuminate the patterns of pragmatic change noted in this study.

In terms of theories of politeness, this study has largely adhered to Brown and Levinson's (1987) framework of three social variables: power, social distance and weight of imposition. However, I argued that for understanding social distance and indirectness in the context of Japanese learners of English, an alternative structure, Doi's (1981)

215

concept of *enryo* (restraint) appeared more appropriate. This notion suggested that in cases where social distance was either very high or very low there was little need for indirectness in a speech act. In relationships which fell between these two extremes (such as with friends, colleagues and acquaintances), indirectness was appropriate. It is noteworthy that the JLE new arrival group continued to use *enryo* as a social-distance reference point when they were immersed in another culture. The JLEs appeared to transfer (Faerch and Kasper 1987) their L1 social distance norms to the L2 milieu. This, in turn, may have influenced the type of disagreement strategies selected.

Strategies for delivering the negatively affective speech act of disagreement were listed on a continuum of indirectness, ranging from explicit strategies to implied (off-record) strategies. The results indicated that by the post-testing stage JLE participants were likely to use more explicit disagreements. This pattern was particularly evident in +D and -P situations (see sections 7.2 and 7.3 for a detailed discussion of this phenomenon). One interpretation of this finding is that the JLE participants had more confidence in their communicative ability at the post-testing stage, and this manifested in more explicit disagreeing statements. I conjectured that after a suitable interval of study and immersion in the target culture, this trend towards explicitness would begin to approximate NS norms (see section 4.3.3).

Disagreement strategy selection depended in large measure on cultural notions of appropriate speech behaviour. Indeed, many of the differences between JLE and NS speech behaviour could be attributed to cultural dissimilarities. One of those considered was collectivism, i.e. the degree to which a culture is oriented to the needs of the group or the individual. According to Hofstede (1991), Japan's culture was only moderately collectivist, but it was in contrast with the very individualistic culture of New Zealand. This may have affected how each group perceived the social relationship between themselves and their interlocutors, and consequently how they selected strategies in disagreement-oriented talk. The other relevant cultural dimension was that of power distance, i.e. the disparity between the powerful and the powerless people in a society. New Zealand is a very egalitarian culture, while Japan is quite hierarchical (Hofstede 1991; Triandis 1994). This factor is likely to have influenced how JLEs perceived disagree-

ment situations with power-unequal interlocutors, the potential consequences of making a pragmatic error, and thus the kind of disagreeing
strategy that they considered appropriate. The inability to accurately
determine these things in a cross-cultural or interlanguage milieu is, as
Thomas (1983) says, a catalyst for cross-cultural pragmatic failure.

Although these theories provided information about some of the
cultural stimuli which influenced the JLE new arrival group's speech
act strategies, it was crucial to be able to glean information about how
their speech behaviour changed over ten weeks, and about some of the
processes underlying these changes. To this end, I adapted two theories of second language acquisition which appeared to correlate with
patterns of pragmatic change revealed in this study: McLaughlin's
(1988) cognitively informed information-processing model, and Ochs'
(1986) socially and culturally informed language socialisation model.
The information-processing model posited that a language learner may
develop a set of well-learned, effective cognitive procedures for dealing with information so that more attention-demanding processes are
freed up for new and more complex tasks. The model was useful for
illuminating some of the cognitive processes underlying the JLEs'
language learning and pragmatic development. The language socialisation model argued that novices in society acquire knowledge about
cultural rules regulating conversation and pragmalinguistic appropriateness by participating in repeated social interaction with experts.
The model was used in this study to identify some of the cultural and
sociolinguistic processes underlying the JLE group's pragmatic development.

Two other models were employed. The first was Bialystok's
(1993) two-dimensional model of pragmatic development. This model
was used to demonstrate how JLEs were able to refer to previously internalised pragmatic knowledge, which they then transferred (though
not always appropriately) to situations in their second language. The
second model to be applied to this study was the interlingual transfer
hypothesis (Faerch and Kasper 1987), which is defined as 'the process
by which L2 learners' activate L1 knowledge in developing or using
their interlanguage' (O'Malley and Chamot 1990: 148). This hypothesis was applied to pragmatic aspects of the JLE participants' L2
(Kasper 1997), wherein they may have utilised pragmatic knowledge

217

from their L1 in order to assist in the comprehension of sociopragmatic principles or pragmalinguistic forms in the L2. Depending on whether or not the knowledge from the first language was appropriate in the second language, pragmatic transfer may have either supported (positive transfer) or detracted from (negative transfer) learning. (Section 2.8.1 describes these models in greater detail.)

7.1.2 Reviewing the methods used

The data collection tools used in this study were designed to tease out aspects of the JLE group's ability to recognise, interpret and produce the speech act of disagreement in an interlanguage context. They extracted information about shifts in pragmatic ability which occurred over the newly-arrived JLEs' ten-week period of study, and also investigated facets of socialisation into the new cultural environment which may have had some bearing on these shifts.

The discourse completion task and the role-plays were designed to collect data on the participants' production of disagreement speech acts, and to determine the comparability of their sociopragmatic politeness norms with those of an NS reference group. These instruments were effective in gathering data and appeared to be easily understood by the non-native speakers, perhaps due to extensive piloting. A particular advantage was that the findings produced by the written data were able to be compared with those elicited by way of the spoken data, providing a more multi-faceted perspective on disagreement production. In general, one type of data was able to corroborate the other, e.g. in chapter 4, the study of spoken utterance length was descriptively compared with the study of written utterance length. On the other hand, some of the situations depicted in the DCT and the role-play instruments were less likely than others to occur in reality. This was a consequence of having inserted power and social distance variables into the scenarios in order to measure variation in participants' responses. In the relatively common situations, the participants' responses were likely to be a more accurate representation of their actual speech behaviour in such a situation. In the less probable situations, the participants' responses may have been less representative of their likely speech behaviour. Fortunately, none of the situations was so extraordinary as to be implausible, and it is doubtful whether this difference was of very much importance.

Another data-gathering tool, the judgment task was developed to measure the JLEs' ability to identify and accurately interpret speech act strategies. It exposed the participants to New Zealand grammatical, lexical and pragmatic disagreement formats through having them observe short clips of New Zealand TV programmes. Participants were then asked to estimate the politeness of the utterances spoken, as well as the severity of the situations. The judgment task proved to be innovative in that it was able to elicit data about paralinguistic cues such as eye contact or head movement. Paralinguistic cues such as these are a common way to convey disagreement, but presenting them in a traditional written task is difficult because participants cannot actually see the interlocutors. The judgment task overcame this problem by depicting people acting out conversations as part of TV programmes, thus adding a visual element to the task. On the other hand, it was difficult to present examples of language and politeness norms that were representative of naturally-occurring speech patterns. Although efforts were made to ensure that the TV segments used in the task were as 'authentic' as possible, most of the segments were scripted and acted out. As such, they cannot be considered truly authentic. As Comstock (1980) observed, TV sitcoms and dramas invariably present a somewhat warped version of the world: one that is more Caucasian, more male and often more violent than the culture it is meant to depict. Some of the segments used in the judgment task did come from unscripted TV programmes (e.g. interviews or chat shows); however, the majority should only be viewed as a generalised caricature of authentic New Zealand speech behaviour.

All of the primary data-gathering tasks – the DCT, the role-plays and the judgment task – were limited in length, in order to ensure that they did not take an excessive amount of time to complete. Had the tasks been longer, a wider range of responses could have been elicited, encompassing a greater range of variables; a more robust representation of JLE group's gains in pragmatic competence could have been formulated. On the other hand, longer tasks could have exacerbated the participants' rate of fatigue, preventing them from giving adequate

thought to their responses and thus reducing the quality of the collected data. Therefore it was necessary to limit the duration of these three
tasks in order to maximise the value of the data which they elicited.

Having reviewed the theoretical framework used in this study,
and assessed the efficacy of the data-collecting methods, I will now
discuss the findings and speculate on what they may indicate. This is
the focus of the following section.

7.2 *Enryo*-based assessments of pragmatic variation

7.2.1 Introduction

The JLE group made evident shifts in their ability to recognise and
produce disagreement speech acts. But the data repeatedly points to a
preference for applying newly-learned pragmatic principles to interactions with strangers rather than with those in their social sphere.
Conversely, there was a reluctance to attempt 'risky' (i.e. potentially
face-damaging) speech act strategies with people they knew. The DCT
data and the role-play data both indicate that when the JLEs produced
disagreement speech acts, they often employed relatively explicit and
sophisticated strategies at the post-testing stage, but only in high social distance situations. The judgment task data reveals that the JLE
group were cautious in their interpretations of polite or impolite utterances and situational severity, which they tended to overestimate.
There was a shift in this pattern after ten weeks, but it generally
manifested when the participants were reporting their perceptions of
TV interlocutors who had no relationship with each other.

The JLEs appeared to be transferring the *enryo* principle from
their store of first-culture pragmatic knowledge to the negative situations in the target culture. As I said in section 2.5.3, *enryo* (Doi 1981)
means verbal and/or behavioural restraint or indirectness. It is not
required among intimates, but it is necessary in work-based or socially-based relationships. Conversely, an encounter between strangers

220

necessitates a much lower degree of *enryo* since strangers are not members of an in-group. Since the JLE participants' assessments of sociopragmatic and pragmalinguistic variation frequently correlated with the *enryo* principle, instances of this kind of transfer will hereafter be called '*enryo*-based assessments of pragmatic variation'. I will argue that these *enryo*-based assessments act as a pragmatic 'safety device' for the JLEs, in that they minimise the potential for face-loss in negatively-affective situations.

In the preceding chapters, each facet of this pattern of variation has been presented in its own context: 1) the pattern of *enryo*-based assessments in production data; 2) the associated pattern of utterance lengths; and 3) the same *enryo*-based pattern as it manifested in the interpretation data. This section will draw together the types of *enryo*-based assessment discussed previously, in order to provide a coherent overall representation of how this pattern manifests itself in the JLE data. I will then speculate on some of the underlying reasons for this pattern.

7.2.2 Enryo-based assessments in production data

I will look first at some examples of *enryo*-based assessments in the written DCT data and the spoken role-play data. The following two examples (1.1 and 1.2) were extracted from the written data. They are reported responses to an imaginary interlocutor with whom the JLE had no relationship. The interlocutor was driving with the JLE to the airport to pick up a foreign student, and was about to make a wrong turn:

(Example 1.1. Pre-testing)
I think we should turn left here. It's shorter [if] we turn left.

(Example 1.2. Post-testing)
Excuse me, [head teacher's name], I think we should turn left here. If we turn right here, we will be late meeting the student.

The post-testing example was considerably more pragmatically sophisticated than the pre-testing example had been, suggesting that the

221

JLE participant had more confidence in her ability to use an appropriate form of politeness when speaking to someone she did not know. These examples support the probability (as noted in sections 4.4.3 and 4.6.2) that, by the post-testing period, the JLE participants had become more confident at employing pragmatically sophisticated disagreement strategies in high social distance situations.

7.2.3 Enryo-based assessments in interpretation data

In interpretation data, *enryo*-based assessments manifested through shifts in the JLE new arrival group's perceptions of the judgment task situations. Two types of shift were identified. Firstly, the JLEs initially perceived the situational severity of the TV segments as relatively high (i.e. on a 5-point scale) during pre-testing, but perceived these segments in a more tolerant light (i.e. lower on the scale) at the post-testing stage. For example, the JLE group's general mean score of situational severity in high social distance situations dropped from 3.7 to 3.3 (table 6.8.1). Secondly, the JLEs tended to judge disagreement utterances as impolite, but considered these utterances less impolite and more neutral during post-testing ten weeks later. For example, the JLEs' overall mean score of impoliteness in high social distance situations dropped from 3.66 to 3.54 (table 6.5.1).

The findings above demonstrate that during the pre-testing phase of the study, the JLE participants frequently overestimated (as compared to the NS reference group) the severity of a situation and / or the impoliteness of the TV interlocutors. During the post-testing phase the JLEs' assessments of appropriate politeness and situational severity often shifted in the direction of the NS reference group's judgments. But in both types of assessment, the shift was consistently most discernible in situations depicting a disagreement between interlocutors who were high in social distance.

7.2.4 Explaining shifting assessments of politeness and situational severity

This section will discuss some of the possible explanations for this pattern. In line with Doi's (1981) and Wolfson's (1988) findings, situations in which no relationship had been established appeared to carry less importance in terms of face-threat than situations in which an established relationship needed to be maintained. From a sociocultural perspective, the JLE new arrival group were more flexible in their responses to unfamiliar interlocutors because these were not part of their in-group (see Gudykunst and Ting-Toomey 1998; Gudykunst, Yoon and Nishida 1987; Hofstede 1991; Triandis 1986, 1994). Brown and Levinson's (1987) claim that indirectness would increase proportionately with social distance was not supported by the JLE data.

It is possible to speculate that the JLEs were willing to experiment with newly-acquired politeness strategies because they perceived that the weight of any potential FTA was reduced in high social distance situations. They were also more likely to report less stringent perceptions of interlocutor politeness and situational severity in their interpretation data. This trend was manifested repeatedly throughout the research, in both production and interpretation data. In post-testing production data, the JLE participants' disagreement strategies with high social distance interlocutors became less indirect and more on record. They attempted more sophisticated strategies than in the pre-testing sessions. They also delivered lengthier utterances in high social distance situations than in other situations, suggesting that they were more at ease in those situations and were therefore less constrained to brevity in their disagreeing responses (see section 5.4.1). In the post-testing interpretation data, the JLEs interpreted interlocutor politeness and situational severity less strictly, as indicated by lower scores on the 5-point scale. In the data relating to low social distance situations, no such trend was discernible.

One possible reason for the shifts was that the newly-arrived participants had undergone a certain degree of language socialisation (see section 2.8.2) during their period of residence and study in New Zealand. In other words, ten weeks of immersion in the host culture had enabled them to take some sociopragmatic cues from the host culture, rather than having to transfer them from their own culture to situations in the host culture. Other studies had reached a similar conclusion:

> [S]ince some studies suggest that length of stay influences second language pragmatic behaviour in a non-linear fashion (Olshtain and Blum-Kulka 1985; Blum-Kulka and Olshtain 1986), it can be assumed that this factor has an impact on pragmatic transfer also (Maeshiba, Yoshinaga, Kasper and Ross 1996: 157).

On the other hand, retention of some elements of first language communicative style does not necessarily indicate a deficiency in intake of pragmatic principles. Maeshiba, Yoshinaga, Kasper and Ross (1996: 157) suggest that advanced learners may *deliberately* use first language pragmatic transfer to maintain their cultural identity as separate from the community at large. Other studies (e.g. Clyne 1979; Blum-Kulka and Sheffer 1993) have suggested that even linguistically fluent long-term residents of a second-language community may preserve a certain amount of their first language communicative style, and even pass it on to the second generation of immigrants. This appears to express the need of the language users to keep their cultural identity distinct from that of the second language community in which they are immersed. This makes sense from a standpoint of preserving one's culture in the face of another which is larger and more pervasive. It enables people to guard against what Triandis (1994: 241) calls 'subtractive multiculturalism', in which individuals are forced to abandon some of their original cultural principles in forging their new cultural identity. However, the relevance of this to the present study is limited because the JLE participants were generally in New Zealand for a relatively short time, and there was less threat to their cultural identity than if they had been permanent immigrants. We can only speculate that ten weeks of immersion in the host culture may have enabled the JLEs to take some sociopragmatic cues from the host culture, rather than having to transfer L1 pragmatic norms to situations in the L2 culture.

Another possible explanation (section 6.9.1) is that the intensive study of English at a language school reduced the participants' cognitive load (Sweller 1988), enabling them to apply more attention to the pragmatic intent of the TV characters' talk. In other words, because the newly-arrived JLE participants had not yet become used to hearing English, they would have initially had to concentrate on the content of what was being said in the judgment task situations, rather than the force of the illocutionary acts. Ten weeks later they would likely have a) become more accustomed to listening to English, and b) assimilated more sophisticated grammatical strategies, as well as increasing their lexicon. These two factors were identified as being at least partially responsible for the apparent drop in perceptions of situational severity and interlocutor impoliteness.

7.3 Power-risk assessments of pragmatic variation

7.3.1 Introduction

The JLE participants produced newly-learned, pragmatically sophisti-cated and potentially face-threatening utterances when they disagreed with power-equal interlocutors, but in situations where they had to disagree with higher-power interlocutors they would frequently revert to using pre-internalised, formulaic strategies which carried a lower face-threat. They were also cautious in their interpretations of polite and impolite utterances, and situational severity. There was a shift in this pattern after ten weeks (though it was not as salient as the shift recorded in high social distance situations), but this shift generally manifested only when the participants were reporting their perceptions of power-equal interlocutors. When forming judgments about higher-power interlocutors, the JLE group continued to interpret impoliteness and situational severity cautiously.

I will refer to instances of this pattern as 'power-risk assessments of pragmatic variation', since the JLE group's assessments of prag-matic variation in these instances appear to have been based on their perception of the power distance between themselves and their inter-locutors, as well as the potential face-threat. Power-risk assessments and *enryo*-based assessments (discussed in the previous section) are different in that the former is concerned with the vertical scale of power distance between speakers, and the latter with the horizontal scale of social distance. The JLEs' assessments of pragmatic variation are invariably based on a combination of these factors, since the DCT tasks, the role-plays and the judgment task all present situations which combine power distance and social distance. They have been artificially separated here for analytical purposes.

7.3.2 Power-risk assessments in production data

The two following examples (2.1 and 2.2), taken from the written production data, provide an illustration of power-risk assessment in the JLE group's data. In the examples, the JLE was reporting on a disagreement with a power-equal interlocutor over the attractiveness of a sofa in a second-hand shop:

(Example 2.1. Pre-testing)
Um…It's not my type but it's suitable to you.

(Example 2.2. Post-testing)
Um…I actually don't think that pink and purple are good colours. It's just my opinion. I know you are different from me. If you want to buy it, you'll be able to buy it.

Note that the post-testing response was considerably more pragmatically sophisticated than the pre-testing response. The speaker made clear that she was only offering an opinion, and encouraged her friend to buy the sofa if s/he liked it. Her speech in example 2.1 might have appeared brisk and short to a native-speaker interlocutor, while her language in example 2.2 was considerably more fluent. It was perhaps more likely to be regarded as pragmatically appropriate by a native speaker interlocutor, in that it '[used] routinised pragmatic phenomena…namely gambits, discourse strategies and speech acts [as well as] ability to show appropriate uptaking…replying and responding behaviour' (House 1996: 229).

Two similar examples are taken from the spoken production data. Examples 2.3 and 2.4 depict a disagreement with a power-equal interlocutor who has short-changed her:

(Example 2.3. Pre-testing)
JLE: I ga- no (.) a ten dollars
NS: Ten dollars?
JLE: Yes
NS: Are you sure?
JLE: Yes I'm sure

(Example 2.4. Post-testing)
JLE: Ah I'm sorry I'm afraid you're- you are making a mistake (...) I gave you ten dollars

The participant's post-testing response demonstrated a greater degree of pragmatic sophistication: she began with an apology, and hedged her disagreement with negative politeness ('I'm afraid'). These four examples support the likelihood (discussed in section 4.6.1) that, by the post-testing phase, the JLE participants had become more confident at utilising pragmatically sophisticated disagreement strategies in power-equal situations.

A similar phenomenon was noted in an earlier study concerning Japanese learners of English. Matsumura (2001) investigated whether Japanese EFL learners used advice-giving strategies differently after eight months of residence in an English-speaking culture. He discovered that the participants' strategies became more target-like in situations involving equal- or lower-status interlocutors, but this was not evident when the interlocutors were higher in status. In such situations, 'the L2 socialisation pattern expected in the ESL context was not observed' (2001: 665). Matsumura suggested that the JLEs in his study were transferring their L1 pragmatic norms to the host culture, i.e. they were treating higher-status interlocutors in the target culture just as they would in their own culture. This result correlates with the findings of the present study: in situations where the face-risk was low the students were quick to alter their strategy use, but in situations where it was high they continued to employ more basic strategies.

7.3.3 Power-risk assessments in interpretation data

The JLEs' assessments of power and face-threat shifted between the pre-testing and post-testing stages, though once again the shift was not as prominent as the shift in assessments of social distance. The shift was most noticeable in power-equal situations. In higher-power situations the JLE participants' assessments remained cautious.

The participants' general mean score of impoliteness in power-equal situations declined from 4.13 at the pre-testing stage to 3.92 at the post-testing stage (table 6.5.2), indicating that they may have interpreted these utterances in a more neutral light at the later stage. There was no such shift in scores from power-unequal situations. The participants' general mean score of situational severity in power-equal situations dropped between pre- and post-testing from 4.1 to 3.8 (table 6.8.2), suggesting that they perceived power-equal situations in a more tolerant light at the post-testing stage. Again, this shift did not manifest in scores from power-unequal situations.

7.3.4 Explaining shifts in assessments of power

As section 4.6.1 noted, it is likely that the JLE new arrival group perceived power-equal situations as having a reduced potential for face-loss. The reduced weight of any potential FTA may therefore have enabled the JLEs to attempt newly-acquired politeness strategies without obligation to be reticent or indirect – strategies that would have been necessary if their interlocutors had been higher in power than they (Beebe and Takahashi 1989a; Rees-Miller 2000; Spencer-Oatey 1996). This has been a consistent finding in both the production data and the interpretation data. In the production data, participants who disagreed with power-equal interlocutors frequently attempted to utilise newly-acquired politeness strategies and to apply lengthier and more complex sentence structures than did JLEs who were interacting with power-unequal interlocutors. When they were asked to interpret power-equal disagreement situations, they frequently gave liberal interpretations of interlocutor politeness and situational severity. The likelihood that the JLEs perceived power-equal situations as poten-

228

tially less face-threatening also explains why the participants continued to perceive politeness and severity stringently in power-*un*equal disagreement situations. The consequences of pragmatic failure were likely to be more pronounced if the face-disadvantaged interlocutor was a teacher or an employer, than if the interlocutor was a student or a colleague (Beebe and Takahashi 1989a, 1989b; Brown and Levinson 1987; Rees-Miller 2000; Spencer-Oatey 1996).

There has been much study of how language may be used as a vehicle for conveying and demonstrating power over another interlocutor (e.g. Blommaert 2005; Fairclough 1989, 1992; Ng and Bradac 1993; Thornborrow 2002). From this perspective it may be argued that JLEs' use of longer, more complex, and pragmatically sophisticated responses in power-equal situations was not simply due to the need to avoid face-loss, but the desire to express power over someone else – 'to impress and influence' (Ng and Bradac 1993: 5) or even to dominate. It is possible that the participants in the JLE new arrival group were employing a powerful style rather than a powerless style in their responses to the DCT and the role-plays because the low potential for face-loss in a power-equal situation gave them the opportunity to do this. This seems unlikely, however. As I noted in section 4.6.1, JLEs frequently seem to be lower in power than their NS interlocutors due to a disparity in language skills and a lack of familiarity with the cultural norms of politeness, formality and directness of utterance (Bond, Zegarac and Spencer-Oatey 2000; Spencer-Oatey 2000). Consequently, although it is feasible that JLEs exploited low-face-threat situations to demonstrate a higher degree of power in the manipulative and persuasive manner with which Ng and Bradac are concerned, it is more likely that they were simply taking advantage of the low face threat to attempt more sophisticated utterances and test their estimations of the pragmatic norms of the host culture.

7.3.5 Summary

I will briefly summarise the key findings of the data in relation to social distance and power distance. It is likely that the JLE participants were more confident about using complex or newly-acquired disagreement strategies in high social distance situations because they had no relationship with their interlocutors and were unlikely to meet them again. The JLEs also appeared to become more secure about the appropriate use of disagreement strategies in power-equal situations because the potential of any FTA for causing face-loss was reduced in power-equal situations. It is therefore likely that such situations provided opportunities for the participants to experiment with the use of pragmatically sophisticated utterances. They could also make liberal estimations of interlocutor politeness and situational severity, instead of being constrained to overestimate these values as an 'insurance policy' in order to ensure that the potential for face-loss was minimised (Brown and Levinson 1987: 74).

7.4 The relationship between *enryo*-based / power-risk assessment and utterance length

In chapter 5 I hypothesised that JLE utterances would be longer than NS utterances. This hypothesis was based on the results of Olshtain and Weinbach's (1993) study of Israeli second-language learners (see section 5.3), in which non-native subjects used longer utterances than native speakers 'in order to negotiate the intentions of their speech acts in the new language' (Olshtain and Weinbach 1993: 120). These findings were compared with the findings of the current research.

In both written and spoken disagreement utterances, JLEs invariably used considerably *fewer* words than the NS reference group. This pattern did not alter from pre-testing to post-testing; there were no instances of JLE utterances being longer than those of the NS group. The hypothesis seemed to be dramatically invalid in the case of Japanese learners of English. However, one notable finding was presented in written utterance-length data: in JLEs' responses to DCT situations that were a) power-equal and/or b) high in social distance, there was a slight shift from pre- to post-testing in number of words used in utterances. It is possible to speculate that the JLEs were applying power risk assessments or *enryo*-based assessments in the length of their utterances. The participants seemed to formulate longer utterances when the potential face-threat was low, i.e. when the JLEs were equal in power to their interlocutors or those in which they did not know their interlocutor and were unlikely to meet them again. Conversely, in situations which had the potential to aggravate a possible face-threat, the JLEs' utterances were brief.

It is likely that the differences in utterance length between the present study and that of Olshtain and Weinbach (1993) were due to cultural dissimilarities, particularly in perceptions of power-distance. Hofstede's (1991) Power Distance Index (section 2.7.2) indicates that the Japanese participants in this study hailed from a very interdependent and high power-distance culture (Hofstede 1991; Triandis 1994). By contrast, the Israeli subjects came from a culture that was much more egalitarian in terms of power-distance. This cultural difference may have influenced how participants in each study interpreted power between interlocutors in conversational interaction, and consequently how they discerned appropriate utterance lengths. It is possible that Olshtain and Weinbach's (1993) findings may have been applicable to cultures that are similar to Israel (i.e. non-hierarchical, egalitarian cultures), while the findings of this study might be more applicable to high power-distance, interdependent countries that are culturally similar to Japan.

7.5 Factors influencing the process of pragmatic acquisition

7.5.1 Introduction

The current findings suggest that after ten weeks of intensive studying and living in the target culture there was a marked reduction in the cognitive load (Sweller 1988) of the JLEs which may have allowed them to focus on pragmatic issues to a greater extent than previously.

This section will examine some of the factors underlying this shift, referring to relevant literature where appropriate.

This section is divided into three subsections. The first subsection discusses the likely effects of classroom instruction on pragmatic development. The second considers the process of language socialisation, specifically the degree to which daily interaction with NSs and homestay accommodation (which all the JLEs experienced) may have influenced pragmatic development. The third subsection reflects on ways in which the JLEs' linguistic proficiency in the L2 may have influenced their attainment of pragmatic competence.

7.5.2 Did classroom instruction influence pragmatic awareness?

Certain aspects of classroom instruction / interaction are likely to have been valuable for increasing the JLEs' knowledge of items that were strictly linguistic in nature. The classroom has been shown to equip L2 learners with fundamental language skills, without which communication would not be possible. It also 'provides participants with positive attitudes needed to motivate participation in exchanges and the self-confidence to attempt communication with...NSs' (MacFarlane 1999: 2). Lastly, it provides a sheltered 'real' context for practicing their language skills with NS teachers and with other ESL learners (MacFarlane 1999; Tanaka 1997). These elements of classroom instruction may have assisted in raising the communicative competence of the JLEs in this study.

However, there are questions as to how useful this artificial situation is in preparing L2 learners for naturally-occurring disagreement situations. A study of Australian students who were learning Japanese as exchange students at Japanese high schools revealed that out-of-class interaction was much more valuable than in-class instruction (Marriott and Enomoto 1995). Other studies have suggested that the classroom is inadequate for the purpose of increasing pragmatic competence in second language learners. Bardovi-Harlig and Dornyei (1998) compared learners in their own country (who would have been learning most of their language skills in a classroom) with learners in an English-speaking country (who would have been exposed to pragmatic items both inside the classroom and in daily interaction with native speakers). They concluded that L2 learners gained much of their pragmatic discernment through face-to-face interaction with NSs, rather than through classroom teaching:

> [T]he pragmatic awareness of [second-language learners who are studying in the host culture] may have come from the friction of their daily interactions: the pressure not only of making themselves understood but also of establishing and maintaining smooth relationships with NSs in the host environment (1998: 253).

Bardovi-Harlig and Dornyei noted that in all probability, language learners who were forced to establish relationships with target language speakers were more likely to pay close attention to pragmatic input and to struggle to understand than those who were learning in their own country and were not thus compelled (cf. Schmidt 1993). House (1996), who studied classroom teaching of pragmatics in a learner's native culture, concluded that it was difficult, time-consuming and appeared to produce only a negligible shift in the learners' pragmatic ability. I should note, however, that this may not be true to the same extent in an ESL milieu, where the friction of daily interaction may encourage language learners to learn more and faster. Boxer (2002a), in her discussion of cross-cultural pragmatic discourse issues, asserted that it was not possible to simply educate newly-arrived immigrants into a new set of pragmatic norms. Rather, 'social, educational and workplace networks that support[ed] successful communication' (2002a: 162) needed to be established. Additionally, the teacher-centred Initiation-Response-Feedback (IRF) model of interaction which predominates in many EFL/ESL classrooms was considered to be a poor format for the learning of pragmatic items (Hall 1995; Kasper 2001; Ohta 1995).

Even the explicit, deductive teaching of pragmatic items of language has met with only limited success. Liddicoat and Crozet (2001) explicitly taught French interactional norms to learners of French as a second language. These learners gained a measure of proficiency in both content and form, but a delayed post-test after a year revealed that the learners' knowledge of form had largely been lost. Rose and Ng Kwai-fun (2001) investigated whether EFL learners could benefit from explicit instruction in complimenting strategies. They found that learners were able to produce compliments when tested with a DCT instrument, but a questionnaire designed to assess the learners' meta-pragmatic competence demonstrated that their understanding of form remained deficient. Yoshimi (2001) explored the use of explicit class-room instruction to facilitate comprehension and production of discourse markers among learners of Japanese as a foreign language. The instruments of instruction included explanatory handouts, NS models, communicative practice tasks and corrective feedback. Yet learner use of the target discourse markers in extended turns at talk remained extremely limited. These findings support the likelihood that classroom instruction is not an adequate medium for learning and retaining pragmatic features of language.

The studies mentioned in this section are diverse in terms of the phenomena being studied, the methods used to collect data, the sample sizes etc, so the comparison with the current research is necessarily generalised. Nonetheless, they clearly suggest that classroom instruction may have been less useful for increasing pragmatic capability than one might expect.

7.5.3 The role of socialisation in increasing pragmatic knowledge

For purposes of clarity, this section is divided into two subsections. The first discusses the evidence in literature that shifts in pragmatic proficiency are most frequently the result of daily interaction with 'expert' native speakers (see section 2.8.2). The second discusses types of accommodation which may have provided impetus for these shifts.

Interaction with NSs

As section 6.6 discussed, there was a considerable shift in the ability of the JLE participants to recognise disagreements that were hedged or implied rather than explicitly stated. I had speculated that the gain in pragmatic proficiency was largely the result of interaction with native speakers of English outside the classroom, as they underwent a pro-

234

cess of language socialisation (Ochs 1986). A similar conclusion was reached by Shea (1994), who argued that conversation between native speakers and non-native speakers is crucial for advancement of the non-native speakers' language proficiency because it enables them to use native-speaker utterances to structure their own discourse. Also relevant is MacFarlane's (1999) research of interethnic exchanges between Canadian learners of French and native speakers of Canadian French. MacFarlane found that whereas classroom instruction appears to be mainly limited to grammar and vocabulary, the milieu of social interaction expands the range of grammatical items and vocabulary learned by introducing L2 application contexts which are unavailable in the classroom:

> Because these various interlocutors are mainly native-speaking peers, participants are motivated to converge to native-speaker norms rather than the non native-like version of L1 classmates (1999: 3).

These authors maintain that experience of language-mediated interaction with NSs is crucial in order for learners to acquire L2 norms rather than transferring the pragmatic norms of their L1.

Even advanced learners often exhibit a marked imbalance between grammatical knowledge (to which L2 learners can be exposed in a classroom) and pragmatic knowledge (to which classroom learners are less likely to be exposed):

> [S]tatus-appropriate input is often limited or absent from the status-unequal encounters that characterise talk in advising sessions and classrooms, which would imply that learners do not acquire a sufficient level of L2 pragmatic competence because the target language they encounter in the L2 classroom simply lacks a sufficient range and emphasis of relevant exemplars (Bardovi-Harlig and Dornyei 1998: 234).

Bardovi-Harlig and Dornyei note that even language-teaching course books are lacking in this respect (Bardovi-Harlig, Hartford, Mahan-Taylor, Morgan and Reynolds 1996; Boxer and Pickering 1995).

A potentially useful area for further research would be to measure the ability of JLEs studying on English-language courses in Japan in recognising hedged or implied disagreement. The judgment task used in the present study (appendix 1), or a similar instrument, could be administered for this purpose. These findings could then be compared with those of the participants in the present study, i.e. JLEs who were studying ESL in New Zealand. These two groups could then be post-tested after a certain period of time to determine which group had advanced the most in ability to recognise hedged and implied disagreement strategies. A research project of this type would be similar to that of Bardovi-Harlig and Dornyei (1998) in that it would measure differences in interpretative competence between EFL students and ESL students.

Homestay accommodation and pragmatic development

For the JLE group, living in homestay situations may have been one of the key factors contributing to pragmatic acquisition, since their repeated interaction with host family members is likely to have aided in the language socialisation process. Part of this process involves the acquisition of sociopragmatic principles, since 'adults who arrive in a particular context in a new community may not be fully aware of what conventions, including what acts and what stances, are considered appropriate for the different social roles enacted in that context' (Yates 2005: 68). This process also entails the learning of pragmalinguistic aspects of the L2, in which learners assign situational meanings to particular forms such as interrogative forms, diminutive affixes, raised pitch and so on (Ochs 1996: 411). In Ochs' (1986) terminology, second language learners are 'novices' in a new community who rely on interaction with 'expert' others to aid them in the socialisation process (see section 2.8.2). Host family members are ideal 'experts' in their role as linguistic and social models for the 'novice' L2 learners. The learners have the advantage of frequent language-based interaction with individual host family members or as part of the family group, e.g. around the dinner table. As the social distance is normally low, L2 learners have opportunities to ask about conventions of interaction in the target culture. Acquisition of interactional principles or pragmalinguistic items can also occur indirectly – through listening to conversations between host-family members, exposure to English through TV programmes and so on. The JLEs in this study are likely to have assimilated a considerable amount of pragmatic information through their homestay interaction.

It is possible, though, that even in interaction with host-family members the processing of purely linguistic items may have taken precedence over the processing of pragmatic items. Levelt (1989) postulated that conversation was hierarchical in structure (see table 6.9) and that pragmatic conventions were likely to be one of the lower priorities in acquisition. Levelt implies that linguistic structures need to be automatised before pragmatic structures can be considered. However, other research (e.g. Bardovi-Harlig and Dornyei 1998) suggests that in a milieu in which language learners are immersed in the host culture, the pragmatic conventions take on a great deal more importance than they would in a milieu where English was being taught as a foreign language. Given this, it is possible that the relevance of Levelt's hierarchical model is dependent upon the sociocultural background in which the learner is acquiring the new language. If this were the case, it would be less applicable to the subjects of the present study, who were learning in the target culture.

Section 4.6.1 pointed out one possible drawback to homestay accommodation: that the JLEs may have been in a position of reduced power, relative to their host-parents. Homestay host-fathers and host-mothers were often considerably older than the JLEs, and they could have been perceived as possessing *legitimate power* (French and Raven 1959) which enabled them to exert influence upon the younger and less life-experienced JLEs. Furthermore, the JLE participants depended on their host-parents for food, shelter and general wellbeing. Consequently, the JLEs may sometimes have been obliged to perceive homestay hosts as higher-power interlocutors rather than power-equal interactive partners. This may have led to a need to 'talk up', i.e. to use a linguistic register appropriate for a higher-power interlocutor. The perceived potential for face-damage if the JLEs used an inappropriate linguistic form or made a sociopragmatic mistake may have restricted the linguistic forms which were available to them in interaction with their host-parents. As section 7.3 describes, there would have been a marked preference for strategies that were previously-internalised and safe, rather than newer, untried strategies. In sum, the JLEs may have believed that the linguistic forms which they could use

237

with their host-parents were restricted to a certain degree by the power distance factor.

Apart from this disadvantage, however, it is probable that continuous association with native speakers through homestay situations has been an important factor in the JLE participants' pragmatic development.

7.5.4 How JLE linguistic proficiency may have influenced pragmatic development

In section 6.9.1 I suggested that an increase in the JLEs' linguistic proficiency may have enabled them to focus on the pragmatic appropriateness of the disagreement utterances which they encountered. This may have occurred through progressive cycles of conscious processing followed by automatic processing. Initially the JLEs would consciously process lexical and grammatical items. Once these items were automatised, cognitive resources would have been freed up for processing more complex pragmalinguistic features of the L2. Previous research findings (McLaughlin 1990; McLaughlin and Heredia 1996; Skehan 1998) have shown that this is a familiar pattern in language learning. Kasper and Rose (2002: 26–7) support this notion:

> Internal modification through grammaticalised material requires a highly-developed control of processing. Before learners have reached the necessary levels of control, they select fewer politeness markers, and the politeness markers they do choose demand less attention to produce.

It is possible that the JLE participants initially used formulaic, on-record forms of disagreement which required only the linguistic skills they already possessed. As they increased in grammatical and lexical competence, they may have learned to employ hedging strategies or external modifiers. Later, once they had a clearer grasp of the socio-pragmatic norms of the L2, they might attempt more pragmatically sophisticated strategies such as conventional indirectness. The shifts in their lexical and grammatical competence may have helped to engender shifts in their pragmatic capability.

7.6 Conclusion

This chapter has drawn together the findings in the three preceding chapters. This final section will summarise these findings.

The first part of this chapter examined trends in the JLEs' production of disagreement strategies between pre- and post-testing. In general, the JLEs were most likely to attempt pragmatically sophisticated disagreement strategies in high social distance situations, since they had no relationship with their interlocutor. In low social distance situations, short and formulaic strategies were more common. I posited that the JLE participants perceived a lower degree of face threat in high social distance situations, as a result of transferring the *enryo* principle from their L1. In addition, the participants' assessments of pragmatic variation may also have been based on perceived situational power distance and degree of face-threat. As a result, they were likely to attempt pragmatically sophisticated strategies in power-equal situations but less likely in power-unequal situations.

The second part of this chapter investigated some of the factors which could have influenced the JLEs' pragmatic acquisition, drawing on relevant second language acquisition theory and research. Classroom instruction was not thought to have been a major factor in the JLEs' pragmatic acquisition, though it may have had some beneficial effects. I argued that repeated and sustained interaction with native speakers, particularly within a homestay context, is likely to have been considerably more effective in this respect. Finally, I speculated that increases in the JLEs' grammatical and lexical competence may have enabled them to process new pragmalinguistic items more quickly.

Before closing this chapter, it is necessary to address the possibility that the results described and discussed in this chapter are partially due to a testing effect. During the pre-testing session the JLE new arrival group were watching the judgment task video and completing the discourse completion task for the first time; they were thus required to utilise certain cognitive resources in order to ensure they understood what was required of them. The post-testing session differed from the pre-testing session in two respects, aside from shifts that may be attributed to processes of second language acquisition. Firstly, the participants were completing the tasks for the second time, and may therefore not have had to concentrate to the same extent in order to understand it. This may have allowed the participants to utilise previously unavailable cognitive resources in considering the tasks. Secondly, the participants were considering for the second time the variables of power, social distance and severity of the situations in the tasks. They were also reconsidering their perceptions of the politeness represented in the tasks. Their perceptions in the pre-testing may have affected their cognition in forming perceptions in the post-testing.

Although these issues may have had some influence on the JLEs' responses, there are a number of mitigating factors. There was a substantial time-lapse between the two testing periods; participants were not aware that they would be receiving the same testing materials twice; they received no feedback on their performances after the pre-testing sessions; and they were not given access to the data-gathering materials in the interim. In future research, however, it may be possible to overcome this problem by employing two separate groups of JLEs. Each group would complete the tasks only once. One group would complete them immediately, while the other group would complete them after they had been studying in New Zealand for the requisite ten weeks. It would then be possible to compare the data from the two groups. A method such as this would reduce the possibility of a testing effect.

8 Conclusion

8.1 Introduction

This chapter summarises the findings of the current study, and also evaluates some of the strengths and limitations of the present study and the methods by which it was carried out. Finally, this chapter considers some of the possible implications of this study's findings.

8.2 Summarising the findings

At the beginning of this book (section 1.3), four research questions were posed. This section summarises the answers revealed by the data obtained during this project.

8.2.1 Managing politeness in talk with NSs

The first research question was concerned with how JLEs managed politeness when involved in situations of disagreement with NSs. The collected data suggested that the JLE new arrival group's management of politeness strategies tended to follow the pattern expounded in Wolfson's (1988) 'bulge' theory. That is, if the JLEs did not know their interlocutor, or knew him/her very well, they were frequently brief and direct in their use of disagreement strategies. But when interacting with interlocutors with whom they had a social relationship – colleagues, friends, acquaintances – they were often much more circumspect in their disagreement utterances. I posited that this pattern of behaviour was grounded in Doi's (1981) concept of *enryo*, or 'restraint', which the JLEs may have been transferring from their first culture. The JLEs were also less likely to attempt sophisticated utterances or employ newly-learned language when interacting with low social distance interlocutors, due to the potential face-threat. This phenomenon was termed *enryo*-based assessment of pragmatic variation (see section 7.2).

The data also suggested that the JLEs' disagreement response patterns depended on the degree of power inequality between interlocutors, though not to the same extent as social distance. JLEs appeared to be somewhat more likely to use direct disagreement utterances with power equals, rather than with power-unequals. Similarly, the JLE new arrival group were, to some extent, more willing to attempt newly-learned and relatively complex disagreement strategies with power-equal interlocutors than with those who were unequal in power. The pattern of *enryo*-based assessment appeared to be present here as well.

8.2.2 Expressing disagreement

The second research question was concerned with identifying the ability of newly-arrived JLEs in accurately expressing disagreement speech acts. It was observed that in general, the JLE group initially selected less explicit disagreement strategies than the native speaker group selected in the same situations (see table 4.1). There were some exceptions: in some high social distance situations the JLE group used more explicit strategies than the NSs did, possibly because they perceived the face-threat in these situations to be comparatively low. However, this was the exception rather than the rule in the JLEs' disagreement strategy selection. JLEs were normally less explicit in their responses than NSs.

Additionally, the disagreement strategies initially utilised by the JLEs were considerably less pragmatically sophisticated than those of the NS group. Table 4.2 indicates that the NS group scored a mean of 4.5 out of 5 for sophistication, while the JLEs scored a mean of only 2.8. In particular, the JLE new arrival group demonstrated a preference for using token agreements (such as *yes but*) prior to offering a

242

disagreeing statement, possibly transferring from their L1 (as posited in section 4.4.4). As well as being uncomplicated, the JLE utterances were also invariably shorter than those of the NS group. NS utterances were a mean of 24.1 words, while utterances by the JLEs were a mean of 18.1 words (see table 5.1).

The JLE group's initial tendency to avoid explicit disagreement strategies and to employ brief and pragmatically unsophisticated utterances suggests two things: Firstly, that the JLEs' knowledge of New Zealand pragmatic norms was very limited when they arrived; and secondly, that they were cautious about making both syntactic and pragmatic errors in disagreement-oriented conversations with native speakers in the host culture.

8.2.3 Interpreting disagreement

The third research question was concerned with identifying the ability of newly-arrived JLEs in accurately interpreting disagreement speech acts to which they were exposed. Initially, the JLEs were able to recognise most explicit disagreements presented in the judgment task, but as the disagreement strategies increased in opacity the JLE group's ability to recognise them decreased. Sequences that presented an implied disagreement strategy often passed unnoticed.

There were also differences between JLE participants and the NS reference group in interpretation of situational variables. Although the JLEs' perceptions of interlocutor politeness were generally quite similar to those of the NS group (see table 6.4), the JLE group's initial judgments of situational severity were frequently higher than those of the NS group (see table 6.6).

The JLE new arrival group appeared to possess only the ability to recognise and interpret the most obvious pragmatic strategies when they first arrived in New Zealand. Those that were implied or delivered through paralinguistic channels seem to have been much more difficult to recognise or interpret. This suggests that, compared to native speakers, their sociopragmatic understanding of implicature and their pragmalinguistic ability to manipulate language using implied strategies were deficient at this early stage (Bouton 1992, 1994). Pos-

243

sibly as a consequence of this, JLEs were often conservative in their judgments of situational severity.

8.2.4 Increases in productive and interpretive ability

The fourth research question dealt with the extent to which expressing and interpreting ability increased after a period of residence and study in New Zealand. In general, the JLEs became more adept at recognising disagreements that were hedged or implied. In addition, their initially high perceptions of situational severity became lower over the ten-week testing period, and more similar to the perceptions of the native-speaker group. However, this shift in perception of severity was only salient in low-face-threat situations in which the interlocutor was not known to the JLE, or was equal in power. In other situations, i.e. those which presented a low amount of social distance (requiring *enryo*) and those with two power-unequal interlocutors, judgments of severity remained high.

The JLE new arrival group demonstrated an increased ability to employ pragmatically sophisticated disagreements: their mean Sophistication score increased from 2.8 out of 5 to 3.3 (see table 4.2). There was a decline in the use of questioning strategies, and a gain in the use of more complex strategies such as framing disagreements as opinion, offering alternative suggestions, or hinting. These changes indicate that the ability of the JLEs to manage more complex disagreement strategies had increased, and that they now had a foundation of sociopragmatic knowledge to assist them in accurately estimating how these strategies should be employed. However, their utilisation of recently-acquired and / or pragmatically complex strategies continued to depend on the perceived face-threat. If there was a high probability that erroneous use of a disagreement strategy would cause face-loss to either interlocutor, a more simple strategy would often be employed instead.

8.3 Evaluating this study

Invariably, there are both strengths and limitations in a study such as this. This section will consider some of these, beginning with the strengths. As the strengths and limitations of the methodology of this project have already been addressed in section 7.1.2, this section will not focus on methodological issues.

8.3.1 Strengths

One of the strengths of this study is in the specifications of the participant sample. This sample was designed to ensure the greatest possible uniformity in terms of i) the primary variables, i.e. age, language ability and level of education; and ii) similarity of age and education level between the JLE participants and the NS reference group. This contrasts with some studies done previously (e.g. Hashimoto *et al* 1992; Leet-Pellegrini 1980), in which the background and characteristics of the participants were not precisely specified. As a result, the data from these studies appeared nebulous and overly-generalised, despite the clarity of their findings. In order to avoid this problem in the present study, I stipulated that both NS and JLE participants should be aged between 18 and 25 years, and should all have attained a similar level of post-secondary education. As a consequence, all the native speakers were university undergraduates, and all the JLEs were undertaking full-time study (though not necessarily at a university). The goal of this measure was to ensure that readers and researchers would be able to understand to which ethnic, educational, linguistic ability and age categories this study was intended to apply.

A second benefit is that the participants in this study were able to construct their own assessments of situational severity in the various data-gathering tasks. The rationale for this measure was that there was likely to be cross-cultural variation in what each group considered a 'severe' situation. A set of circumstances judged quite innocuous by a New Zealand participant would perhaps be interpreted as more serious by a Japanese subject, and vice versa. Indeed, the findings of this

245

study supported this possibility: the JLEs' perceptions of situational severity were consistently higher than those of the NS reference group (see section 6.8.3). The self-assessment of situational severity in this project contrasts with some previous studies (e.g. Blum-Kulka, Ganet and Gherson 1985; Holmes 1990; Trosborg 1987; Wood and Kroger 1991), where severity was based on the researcher's own assessment, and the participants were not given the opportunity to assess it themselves. A second advantage was that allowing subjects to make their own assessments of situational severity enabled cross-cultural comparisons of the assessments. This in turn may have provided a more accurate depiction of how this variable was likely to influence politeness strategy selection in each culture.

However, like any research project, there are limitations to the scope of the present study. It is important to mention these, in order to present an accurate indication of the applicability of the study and its conclusions.

8.3.2 Limitations

The first limitation is that the size of the JLE sample was limited to 14 participants: 12 completing the DCT and judgment task, and 2 completing the role-plays. Although this number may be adequate for a descriptive study such as this, a larger sample group would have reinforced the study's construct validity. As mentioned previously, the guidelines for subjects were quite stringent: JLE participants had to be between 18 and 25 years; they had to be full-time language learners; and they had to be of at least intermediate ability in English. Additionally, participants were required to be studying in Christchurch for at least ten weeks after the initial testing so that follow-up testing could be done. This restricted the number of suitable candidates, and as a result, the size of the sample is relatively small. To an extent, however, the small sample size may have been compensated for through the use of diverse and multi-dimensional methods of testing.

Secondly, of course, it is not possible to generalise the findings of this project to Japanese second-language learners as a whole. Although the JLE subjects were all Japanese nationals, in reality they

246

represented only a small section of Japan's diverse and highly popu-
lous society. This was also true of the reference group of New Zealand
university students. If the data were elicited from people of a different
age group, occupation, socioeconomic status or level of education, the
results could well be different. Although this study has used 'New
Zealander' and 'Japanese' as labels, the findings are not intended to
represent the whole of the societies concerned. As Fukushima (2000:
216) has pointed out, patterns of speech behaviour may differ from
region to region, even within the same culture. Accordingly, it must be
stressed that this study is intended as a broad-based investigation of
two specific groups, rather than a comparison of two entire cultures.

8.4 Implications of this study

This section outlines some of the implications of the findings of this
study.

8.4.1 Implications for the teaching of English as a second language

The first implication is that English language education in the JLEs'
home country does not provide sufficient opportunity for considering
the pragmatic boundaries of an English-speaking country. The results
of this research suggest that learning polite, formulaic expressions –
which is the norm in most Japanese EFL textbooks – may not be
conducive to understanding how politeness is conceived and perceived
in an English-speaking milieu. This supports House's (1996) finding
that teaching second-language pragmatic information was problematic
in an EFL context. The present data indicates that despite at least six
years of English language tuition at junior and senior high school, the
JLEs' initial ability to accurately produce or interpret pragmatically
appropriate disagreements was often quite deficient. One possible explanation for this is that the JLEs initially viewed the attainment of

pragmatic competence as less important than expanding lexical or grammatical competence (Bardovi-Harlig and Dornyei 1998).

The second implication is that an understanding of how language is influenced by cultural context is essential for language learning, and immersion in the target culture is the most efficient method for raising consciousness about cultural contexts. This study has indicated that some comprehension of pragmalinguistic forms of politeness was necessary in order for the JLEs to increase in pragmatic competence. This needed to be underpinned by an understanding of the cultural norms and values of the L2 culture, since as Malinowski (1923: 305) stated, 'language is essentially rooted in the reality of culture'. Evidently, a period of immersion in the target culture is likely to be beneficial for the attainment of pragmatic capability. According to the findings of the current study, a period of only ten weeks of such experience may positively influence a second-language learner's speech act behaviour and his/her ability to accurately interpret the speech acts of others. Homestay accommodation was revealed to be particularly beneficial because it provided the participants with constant reinforcement of both linguistic and pragmatic tenets for managing negatively affective situations.

The third implication is that JLEs studying at New Zealand language schools would benefit from more explicit classroom instruction about some of the politeness norms in the host culture. Understanding language in its appropriate context could usefully be integrated as one of the explicit aims of ESOL curricula in English-speaking countries. This idea is endorsed by Lee-Wong (2000: 317), who maintains that '"who is speaking to who in what kind of setting regarding what" [needs] to be an explicit part of text design'. Thomas (1983: 110) also corroborates this notion: explicitly coaching learners to expect cross-cultural differences in the linguistic manifestations of politeness 'takes the teaching of language beyond the realms of mere training and makes it truly educational'. So the explicit teaching of culture-specific rules of politeness could usefully be made an integral aspect of ESOL curricula in New Zealand. Clyne (1983: 147) suggests two categories for this: i) general rules which express broad aspects of culture and its institutions; and ii) specific rules, or individual formulae for speech acts. Examples of these are: 1) rules pertaining to general cultural concepts which may influence communication, such as trust, honour etc; 2) different routines for entire speech act fields – such as persuasion – which are central to human action, such as requests, flattery etc. As language and culture are inextricably intertwined, it is important that the teaching of these two things also be connected to one another.

The fourth implication is that ESOL teachers should be made aware of JLEs' tendency to make assessments about appropriate politeness based on *enryo* and on power-risk. This study has shown that JLEs became more disposed to use pragmatically sophisticated utterances, were more conscious of appropriate degrees of directness, and were more liberal and natural in their interpretations of utterances delivered by high-social-distance interlocutors and power-equal interlocutors. These patterns were referred to as *enryo*-based assessments (in the case of high social distance interlocutors) and power-risk assessments (in the case of power-equal interlocutors) of sociopragmatic variation (see sections 7.2 and 7.3).

These findings illuminate two points of potential interest for ESOL teachers. Firstly, as teachers are always in a power-*un*equal (i.e. teacher-student) relationship with their JLE students, they may not be aware of JLEs' shifts in pragmatic competence because these shifts are less likely to be displayed to them. According to the findings of this study, JLEs would be more likely to be brief and circumspect and to avoid attempting risky disagreement strategies when talking to their teacher. This may give teachers the impression that the JLEs' ability to formulate disagreements is not increasing. In fact, though, this may not be the case. It may simply be that JLEs are reluctant to attempt a disagreement with a person they view as a higher-power interlocutor in a situation with potentially face-damaging consequences.

Secondly, if teachers were aware of JLEs' predisposition to avoid disagreement-oriented talk with members of their social sphere or higher-power interlocutors, they could perhaps tailor certain aspects of the classroom-based learning curriculum to take account of this factor. For example, teachers might introduce role-play tasks in which JLEs could practice various negatively-affective scenarios with both power-equal and power-unequal interlocutors, as well as both high and low social distance interlocutors.

This explicit instruction and repeated practice could encourage the JLEs to concentrate on interacting appropriately, not just in situations which pose the lowest risk to face, but also in situations that are potentially face-threatening. Role-plays are useful for instruction in pragmatic aspects of language because they have few real-life consequences. Roles are simply acted out. Also, roles can be changed, allowing students to experience a variety of roles and attempt a number of linguistic styles. In addition, retrospective feedback is possible: once a scenario has been acted out, the teacher can comment on the appropriateness of the linguistic politeness used and point out possible areas of error (Walkinshaw 2006).

8.4.2 Cultural stereotyping

Thomas (1983: 106) contends that it is foolish to suggest that one ethnic group can be viewed as inherently more 'polite' than another simply because they use more elaborate linguistic formulae: 'We are not dealing with moral or spiritual qualities, only with the linguistic encoding of certain attitudes and values'. Nonetheless, cultural stereotypes abound about the Japanese, as they do with all ethnic groups and nationalities. Beebe and Takahashi (1989b: 200) noted some of the more prominent stereotypes: '"Americans are more direct than Japanese." "Americans are more explicit than Japanese." "Japanese do not make critical remarks to someone else's face. They avoid disagreement. And, they are always apologising."' However, the present study of Japanese learners of English found that levels of indirectness and degrees of avoidance of disagreement depended very much on the interplay of power and social distance variables between the interlocutors. The JLE participants were often indirect with people they knew socially, but more direct with people they did not know at all. Hence, the stereotypes of Japanese people as being indirect, reticent and apologetic have not been confirmed in this study. The reality is a great deal more complex. Indeed, the findings of this study reinforce Beebe and Takahashi's (1989b: 200) insistence that such stereotypes are based on exaggeration and misperception.

One of the most common stereotypes, both in the literature and in general thinking, appears to be that Japanese people are often forbearing, indirect, acquiescent and timid. Deutsch (1983: 182), for instance, advises the following to Americans doing business with Japanese:

> It is not appropriate, according to Japanese custom, to criticise someone openly, thus causing him to lose face; embarrassment should be avoided whenever possible by refraining from negative or combative statements that will make the Japanese look wrong or foolish.

However, my personal experience of living in Japan and my previous research (Walkinshaw 2000) suggested that Japanese are not always 'indirect', either in their own language or in English. The present study has confirmed this; while the JLE participants were indirect in some situations, in others they were often just as direct as native speakers, or even more so. This study has drawn attention to the many different strategies for negotiating the speech act of disagreement, and shown that these do not necessarily conform to popular characterisations.

8.5 Concluding remarks

Cross-cultural disparity in politeness is arguably one of the most important issues in the field of pragmatics, because interlocutors from different cultures often hold to very different norms and rules of interaction. This study has highlighted the case for Japanese learners of English, but there are many other cultural / social groups studying in New Zealand's language schools and tertiary institutions, and employed in various capacities in New Zealand's workplaces. Rapidly expanding multiculturalism, and attendant population growth, has been one of the hallmarks of New Zealand society at the beginning of the 21st century. We cannot afford to ignore, or fail to comprehend, how pragmatic norms differ according to culture. In a society where cross-cultural interaction is becoming so prevalent, different rules of speaking have the potential to 'cause stereotypes, prejudice, and discrimination against entire groups of people' (Boxer 2002a: 150). So it is important to understand the differences in speech behaviour between these cultures in order to begin to establish the social, educational and workplace networks that support successful cross-cultural communication.

The sphere of second-language education is a focal point for teaching politeness strategies that are sociopragmatically and pragmalinguistically appropriate in a given culture without the threat of stereotyping or prejudice. It is in this domain that second language learners have opportunities to experiment with negatively affective strategies without the threat of face-loss: 'this sphere [i.e. of education] is the locus of many gatekeeping encounters' (Boxer 2002a: 154).

In conclusion, I hope that this study will provide people with some knowledge of how Japanese learners of English manage disagreement situations in conversation with native speakers of New Zealand English, and that this study will be of some use in reducing misunderstanding between people from different cultural/ethnic backgrounds and styles of communication.

Bibliography

Adler, N. J. (1997): *International Dimensions of Organisational Behaviour.* Cincinnati: South-Western College Publishing.

Arndt, H. and R. W. Janney (1985): 'Politeness revisited: Cross-modal supportive categories.' *International Review of Applied Linguistics* 23 (4), pp. 281–300.

—— (1992): 'Universality and relativity in cross-cultural politeness research: a historical perspective.' *Multilingua* 11.

Bardovi-Harlig, K. (1999): 'Exploring the interlanguage of interlanguage pragmatics: A research agenda for acquisitional pragmatics.' *Language Learning,* 49 (4), pp. 677–713.

—— and Z. Dornyei (1998): 'Do language learners recognise pragmatic variations? Pragmatic versus grammatical awareness in instructed L2 learning.' *TESOL Quarterly,* 32 (2), pp. 233–262.

—— and B. Hartford (1993): 'Learning the rules of academic talk: A longitudinal study of pragmatic change.' *Studies in Second Language Acquisition,* 15, pp. 279–304.

—— and B. Hartford (eds) (2005): *Interlanguage Pragmatics: Exploring Institutional Talk.* New Jersey: Erlbaum.

——, B. Hartford, R. Mahan-Taylor, M. Morgan and D. Reynolds (1996): 'Developing pragmatic awareness: Closing the conversation.' In T. Hedge and N. Whitney (eds), *Power, Pedagogy and Practice,* pp. 324–337. Oxford: Oxford University Press.

Barnouw, V. (1982): *An Introduction to Anthropology.* Homewood, Illinois: Dorsey Press.

Barron, A. (2002): *Acquisition in Interlanguage Pragmatics: Learning How to Do Things with Words in a Study Abroad Context.* Amsterdam: Benjamins.

Baxter, L. A. (1984): 'An investigation of compliance gaining as politeness.' *Human Communication Research* 10 (3), pp. 427–456.

Beebe, L. M. (1985): 'Speech act performance: A function of the data collection procedure.' Paper presented at the sixth annual TE-SOL and sociolinguistics colloquium at the international TESOL convention, New York.

—— and M.C. Cummings (1996): 'Natural speech act data versus written questionnaire data: How data collection method affects speech act performance.' In S. Gass and J. Neu (eds), pp. 65–83.

—— and T. Takahashi (1989a): 'Do you have a bag? Social status and patterned variation in second language acquisition.' In S. Gass, C. Madden, D. Preston and L. Selinker (eds), *Variation of Second Language Acquisition: Discourse and Pragmatics*, pp. 104–120. Clevedon: Multilingual Matters.

—— and T. Takahashi (1989b): 'Sociolinguistic variation in face-threatening speech acts.' In M. R. Eisenstein (ed), *The Dynamic Interlanguage*, pp. 199–216. New York: Plenum.

——, T. Takahashi and R. Uliss-Weltz (1990): 'Pragmatic transfer in ESL refusals.' In R. Scarcella, S. D. Krashen and E. Anderson (eds), *On the Development of Communicative Competence in a Second Language*, pp. 55–73. Cambridge, MA: Newbury House.

Bergman, M. L. and G. Kasper (1993): 'Perception and performance in native and non-native apology.' In G. Kasper and S. Blum-Kulka (eds), pp. 82–107.

Bialystok, E. (1993): 'Symbolic representation and attentional control in pragmatic competence.' In G. Kasper and S. Blum-Kulka (eds), pp. 43–59.

Blommaert, J. (2005): *Discourse*. Cambridge: Cambridge University Press.

Blum-Kulka, S. (1982): 'Learning how to say what you mean in a second language.' *Applied Linguistics* 3, pp. 29–59.

—— (1987): 'Indirectness and politeness in requests: same or different?' *Journal of Pragmatics* 11, pp. 131–146.

—— (1997a): 'Discourse pragmatics'. In T. A. Van Dijk (ed), *Discourse as Social Interaction: Discourse Studies: A Multidisciplinary Introduction Volume 2*. pp. 38–63. London: Sage Publications.

—— (1997b): *Dinner Talk*. Mahwah, NJ: Erlbaum.

—— (2005): 'Metapragmatic definitions: "I don't think it's polite to be hypocritical"'. In R. W. Watts, S. Ide and K. Ehlich (eds), pp. 257–280.

——, B. Ganet and R. Gherson (1985): 'The language of requesting in Israeli society.' In J. Forgas (ed), pp. 113–141.

—— and J. House (1989): 'Cross-cultural and situational variation in requesting behaviour.' In S. Blum-Kulka, J. House and G. Kasper (eds), pp. 123–154.

——, J. House and G. Kasper (eds) (1989): *Cross-Cultural Pragmatics: Requests and Apologies.* Norwood, NJ: Ablex Publishing Corporation.

—— and E. Olshtain (1984): 'Requests and apologies: a cross-cultural study of speech-act realisation patterns (CCSARP).' *Applied Linguistics* 5 (3), pp. 196–213.

—— and E. Olshtain (1986): 'Too many words: length of utterance and pragmatic failure.' *Studies in Second Language Acquisition* 8, pp. 165–180.

—— and H. Sheffer (1993): 'The metapragmatic discourse of American-Israeli families at dinner.' In G. Kasper and S. Blum-Kulka (eds), pp. 196–223.

Bond, M. H., V. Zegarac, and H. Spencer-Oatey (2000): 'Culture as an explanatory variable: problems and possibilities.' In H. Spencer-Oatey (ed), pp. 47–71.

Bouton, L. F. (1992): 'Culture, pragmatics and implicature.' *AFinLa Yearbook 1992*, pp. 35–61.

—— (1994): 'Conversational implicature in the second language: learned slowly when not deliberately taught.' *Journal of Pragmatics* 22, pp. 157–167.

Boxer, D. (1993): 'Social distance and speech behaviour.' *Journal of Pragmatics* 19, pp. 103–125.

—— (2002a): 'Discourse issues in cross-cultural pragmatics.' *Annual Review of Applied Linguistics* 22, pp. 150–167.

—— (2002b): *Applying Sociolinguistics: Domains and Face-to-Face Interaction.* Amsterdam: John Benjamins.

—— and L. Pickering (1995): 'Problems in the presentation of speech acts in ELT materials: The case of complaints.' *ELT Journal* 49, pp. 44–58.

255

Brown, H. D. (2000): *Principles of Language Learning and Teaching* (4th edition). New York: Longman.

Brown, J. D. (2001): 'Pragmatics tests: Different purposes, different tests.' In K. R. Rose and G. Kasper (eds), pp. 301–325.

Brown, P. and S. Levinson (1978): 'Universals in language usage: Politeness phenomena.' In E. N. Goody (ed), *Questions and Politeness: Strategies in Social Interaction,* pp. 56–289. Cambridge: Cambridge University Press.

—— (1987): *Politeness: Some Universals in Language Usage.* Cambridge: Cambridge University Press.

Brown, R. and A. Gilman (1972): 'Pronouns of power and solidarity.' In P. Giglioli (ed), *Language and Social Context*, pp. 252–282. Harmondsworth: Penguin.

Cansler, D. C. and B. S. Stiles (1981): 'Relative status and interpersonal presumptuousness.' *Journal of Experimental Social Psychology* 17, pp. 459–471.

Chang, H. C. (1999): 'The "well-defined" is "ambiguous": indeterminacy in Chinese conversation.' *Journal of Pragmatics* 31, pp. 535–556.

Chen, R. (1993): 'Responding to compliments: a contrastive study of politeness strategies between American English and Chinese speakers.' *Journal of Pragmatics* 20, pp. 49–75.

Clyne, M. (1979): 'Communicative competence in contact.' *ITL* 43, pp. 17–37.

—— (1983): 'Communicative competences in contact.' In L. Smith (ed), *Readings in English as an International Language*, pp. 147–163. Oxford: Pergamon Press.

Cohen, A. (1996): 'Investigating the production of speech act sets.' In S. Gass and J. Neu (eds), pp. 21–43.

—— and E. Olshtain (1981): 'Developing a measure of sociocultural competence: the case of apology.' *Language Learning* 31, pp. 113–134.

—— and E. Olshtain (1993): 'The production of speech acts by EFL learners.' *TESOL Quarterly* 27 (1), pp. 33–55.

—— and E. Olshtain (1994): 'Researching the production of L2 speech acts.' In E. E. Tarone, S. M. Gass and A. D. Cohen (eds), *Research Methodology in Second Language Acquisition*, pp. 143–156. Hillsdale, NJ: Lawrence Erlbaum.

Comstock, G. (1980): *Television in America.* Beverly Hills: Sage Publications.

Craig, R., K. Tracy and F. Spisak (1986): 'The discourse of requests: assessment of a politeness approach.' *Human Communication Research* 12 (4), pp. 437–468.

Crealock, E., T. M Derwing and M. Gibson (1999): 'To homestay or stay home: the Japanese Canadian experience.' *TESL Canada Journal,* pp. 53–61.

D'Amico-Reisner, L. (1983): 'An analysis of the surface structure of disapproval exchanges.' In N. Wolfson and E. Judd (eds), *Sociolinguistics and Language Acquisition.* Rowley, MA: Newbury House.

—— (1985): *An Ethnolinguistic Study of Disapproval Exchanges.* Dissertation, University of Pennsylvania.

Dascal, M. (1983): *Pragmatics and the Philosophy of Mind 1: Thought in Language.* Amsterdam: John Benjamins.

Deutsch, M. F. (1983): *Doing Business with the Japanese.* New York: New American Library.

DiPietro, R. (1987): *Strategic Interaction: Learning Languages Through Scenarios.* Oxford: Oxford University Press.

Doi, T. (1981): *The Anatomy of Dependence.* Tokyo / New York: Kodansha International.

DuFon, M. A. (1999): 'The acquisition of linguistic politeness in Indonesian as a second language in a naturalistic context.' Unpublished PhD dissertation, University of Hawaii at Manoa.

Duranti, A. (1988): 'Ethnography of speaking: towards a linguistics of the praxis.' In F. J Newmeyer (ed), *Linguistics: The Cambridge Survey Volume IV: Language – The Sociocultural Context*, pp. 210–228. Cambridge: Cambridge University Press.

Edmondson, W. and J. House (1991): 'Do learners talk too much? The waffle phenomenon in interlanguage pragmatics.' In R. Phillipson, E. Kellerman, L. Selinker, M. Sharwood Smith and M. Swain (eds), *Foreign / Second Language Pedagogy Research*, pp. 273–286. Clevedon, UK: Multilingual Matters.

Eelen, G. (2001): *A Critique of Politeness Theories*. Manchester: St Jerome.

Eisenstein, M. and J. W. Bodman (1986): '"I very appreciate": expressions of gratitude by native and non-native speakers of American English.' *Applied Linguistics* 7 (2), pp. 167–185.

—— (1993): 'Expressing gratitude in American English.' In G. Kasper and S. Blum-Kulka (eds), pp. 64–81.

Faerch, C. and G. Kasper (1987): 'From product to process: introspective methods in second language research.' In C. Faerch and G. Kasper (eds), *Introspection in Second Language Research*, pp. 523. Philadelphia: Multilingual Matters.

—— (1989): 'Internal and external modification in interlanguage request realisation.' In S. Blum-Kulka, J. House and G. Kasper (eds), pp. 221–247.

Fairclough, N. (1989): *Language and Power*. London: Longman.

—— (1992): *Discourse and Social Change*. Cambridge: Polity Press.

Fraser, B. (1985): 'On the universality of speech act strategies.' In S. George (ed), *From the Linguistic to the Social Context*, pp. 43–49. Bologna: CLUEB.

—— (1990): 'Perspectives on politeness.' *Journal of Pragmatics* 14 (2), pp. 219–236.

French, J. R. P. and B. Raven (1959): 'The bases of social power.' In D. Cartwright (ed), *Studies in Social Power*, pp. 150–167. Ann Arbor: University of Michigan.

Frescura, M. (1991): 'Listening comprehension and the development of sociopragmatic competence: a proposal for Italian as a second language.' *The Canadian Modern Language Review / La Revue Canadienne des Langues Vivantes*, 48 (1), pp. 119–134.

Fukushima, S. (2000): *Requests and Culture*. Bern: Peter Lang.

Gardner, R. (2000): 'Resources for delicate manoeuvres: learning to disagree.' *Australian Review of Applied Linguistics* Series S, 16, pp. 31–47.

Gass, S. M. and N. Houck (1999): *Interlanguage Refusals: A Cross-Cultural Study of Japanese English*. New York: Mouton de Gruyter.

Goffman, E. (1967): *Interaction Ritual: Essays on Face-to-Face Behaviour*. New York: Garden City.

Goodwin, C. and M. H. Goodwin (1987): 'Concurrent operations on talk: notes on the interactive organisation of assessments.' *Papers in Pragmatics* 1 (1): pp. 1–54.

Grice, H.P. (1975): 'Logic and conversation.' In P. Cole and J. L. Morgan (eds), *Syntax and Semantics 3: Speech Acts*, pp. 41–58. New York: Academic Press.

Gudykunst, W. B. and S. Ting-Toomey (1988): *Culture and Interpersonal Communication*. Newbury Park, CA: Sage.

——, Y. Yoon and T. Nishida (1987): 'The influence of individualism-collectivism on perceptions of communication in ingroup and outgroup relationships.' *Communication Monographs* 54, pp. 295–306.

Gumperz, J. J. (1982): *Discourse Strategies*. Cambridge: Cambridge University Press.

Hall, E. T. (1976): *Beyond Culture*. Garden City, NY: Doubleday Anchor Books.

Hall, J. K. (1995): 'Aw, man, where you goin'?: Classroom interaction and the development of L2 interactional competence.' *Issues in Applied Linguistics* 6, pp. 37–62.

Hamza, A. (2002): A review of Eelen, G (2001). In *Working Papers on the Web: Linguistic Politeness and Context*. Retrieved 31/1/03 from http://www.shu.ac.uk/wpw/politeness/reviews.htm#1

Harder, P. (1980): 'Discourse as self-expression on the reduced personality of the second-language learner.' *Applied Linguistics* 1, pp. 262–270.

Hashimoto, Y. and Intercultural Communication Study Group (1992): 'Enkyokuteki communication houryaku no ibunkakan hikaku (Euphemistic communication strategy: cross-cultural studies on indirect speech acts).' *Tokyo University Shakai Jouhou Kenkyujo Chousa Kenkyu Kiyou* 1, pp. 107–159.

Hassall, T. J. (1997): *Requests by Australian Learners of Indonesian.* Unpublished doctoral dissertation, Australian National University, Canberra.

Hill, B., S. Ide, S. Ikuta, A. Kawasaki and T. Ogino (1986): 'Universals of linguistic politeness: quantitative evidence from Japanese and American English.' *Journal of Pragmatics* 10, pp. 347–371.

Hill, T. (1997): 'The development of pragmatic competence in an EFL context.' (Doctoral dissertation, Temple University Japan.) *Dissertation Abstracts International* 58, p. 3905.

Hofstede, G. (1991): *Cultures and Organisations: Software of the Mind.* London: McGraw-Hill.

—— (2001): *Culture's Consequences: Comparing Values, Behaviours, Institutions, and Organisations Across Nations* (2nd edition). London: Sage Publications.

—— and M. H. Bond (1984): 'Hofstede's culture dimensions: an independent validation using Rokeach's Value Survey.' *Journal of Cross-Cultural Psychology* 15 (4), pp. 417–433.

Holliday, A. (2005): *The Struggle to Teach English as an International Language.* Oxford: Oxford University Press.

Holmes, J. (1986): 'Compliments and compliment responses in New Zealand English.' *Anthropological Linguistics* 28 (4), pp. 485–508.

—— (1990): 'Apologies in New Zealand English.' *Language in Society* 19, pp. 155–199.

—— (1995): *Women, Men and Politeness.* Singapore: Longman.

—— (2001): *An Introduction to Sociolinguistics* (2nd edition). London / New York: Longman.

—— (2002): 'Politeness, power and provocation: how humour functions in the workplace.' *Discourse Studies* 2, pp. 159–185.

Holtgraves, T. (1986): 'Language structure in social interaction: perceptions of direct and indirect speech acts and interactants who use them.' *Journal of Personality and Social Psychology* 51, pp. 305–313.

—— and J. Yang (1990): 'Politeness as universal: cross-cultural perceptions of request strategies and inferences based on their use.' *Journal of Personality and Social Psychology* 59 (4), pp. 719–729.

Hornby, A.S. (1995): *Oxford Advanced Learner's Dictionary* (5th edition), Oxford: Oxford University Press.

Houck, N. and S. Gass (1996): 'Non-native refusals: a methodological perspective.' In S. Gass and J. Neu (eds), *Speech Acts Across Cultures: Challenges to Communication in a Second Language*, pp. 45–63. New York: Mouton de Gruyter.

House, J. (1979): 'Interaktionsnormen in deutchen und englischen alltagsdialogen.' *Linguistische Berichte* 59, pp. 76–90.

—— (1993): 'Toward a model for the analysis of inappropriate responses in native / non-native interactions.' In G. Kasper and S. Blum-Kulka (eds), pp. 161–183.

—— (1996): 'Developing pragmatic fluency in English as a foreign language.' *Studies in Second Language Acquisition* 18 (2), pp. 225–252.

—— (2000): 'Understanding misunderstanding: a pragmatic-discourse approach to analysing mismanaged rapport in talk across cultures.' In H. Spencer-Oatey (ed), pp. 145–164.

—— (2003): 'Misunderstanding in intercultural university encounters.' In J. House, G. Kasper and S. Ross (eds), *Misunderstanding in Social Life: Discourse Approaches to Problematic Talk*. Harlow, UK: Longman / Pearson Education.

—— and G. Kasper (1981): 'Politeness markers in English and German.' In Florian Coulmas (ed.), *Conversational Routine: Explorations in Standardised Communication Situations and Prepatterned Speech,* pp. 157–185. New York: Mouton de Gruyter.

Hudson, T. (2001): 'Indicators for pragmatic instruction: Some quantitative tools.' In K. R. Rose and G. Kasper (eds), pp. 283–300.

——, E. Detmer and J.D. Brown (1995): 'Developing prototypic measures of cross-cultural pragmatics.' *Technical Report* 7, Honolulu: Second Language Teaching and Curriculum Centre, University of Hawaii at Manoa.

Hymes, D. H. (1986): 'Discourse: scope without depth.' *International Journal of the Sociology of Language* 57, pp. 49–89.

Ide, S. (1989): 'Formal forms and discernment: two neglected aspects of universals of linguistic politeness.' *Multilingua* 8, pp. 223–248.

Janney, R. W. and H. Arndt (2005): 'Intracultural tact versus intercultural tact.' In R. J. Watts, S. Ide and K. Ehlich (eds), pp. 21–41.

Jordens, P. (1996): 'Input and instruction in second language acquisition.' In P. Jordens and J. Lalleman (eds), *Investigating Second Language Acquisition*. Berlin: Mouton de Gruyter.

Kasper, G. (1984): 'Pragmatic comprehension in learner–native speaker discourse.' *Language Learning* 34, pp.1–20.

—— (1990): 'Linguistic politeness: current research issues.' *Journal of Pragmatics* 14, pp. 193–218.

—— (1994): 'Politeness.' In R. Asher and J. Simpson (eds), *The Encyclopedia of Language and Linguistics*, pp. 3206–3211. Oxford: Pergamon Press.

—— (1997): 'The role of pragmatics in language teacher education.' In K. Bardovi-Harlig and B. Hartford (eds), *Beyond Methods: Components of Second Language Teacher Education*, pp. 113–136. New York: McGraw-Hill.

—— (1999): 'Data collection in pragmatics research.' *University of Hawaii Working Papers in ESL* 18 (1), pp. 71–107.

—— (2001): 'Four perspectives on pragmatic development.' *Applied Linguistics* 22, pp. 502–530.

—— and S. Blum-Kulka (eds) (1993): *Interlanguage Pragmatics*. Oxford: Oxford University Press.

—— and M. Dahl (1991): 'Research methods in interlanguage pragmatics.' *Studies in Second Language Acquisition* 13 (2), pp. 215–247.

—— and K. R. Rose (1999): 'Pragmatics and SLA.' *Annual Review of Applied Linguistics* 19, pp. 81–104.

—— and K. R. Rose (2001): 'Pragmatics in language teaching.' In K. R. Rose and G. Kasper (eds), pp. 1–9.

—— and K. R. Rose (2002): *Pragmatic Development in a Second Language*. Michigan: Blackwell Publishing.

—— and R. Schmidt (1996): 'Development issues in interlanguage pragmatics.' *Studies in Second Language Acquisition* 18, pp. 149–169.

Knapp-Potthoff, A. (2005): 'Secondhand politeness.' In R. Watts, S. Ide and K. Erlich (eds), pp. 203–218.

Koike, D. A. (1989): 'Pragmatic competence and adult L2 acquisition: speech acts in interlanguage.' *Modern Language Journal* 73, pp. 79–89.

Kotthoff, H. (1993): 'Disagreement and concession in disputes: on the context sensitivity of preference structures.' *Language in Society* 22, pp. 193–216.

Lakoff, R. (1973): 'The logic of politeness, or minding your Ps and Qs.' In *The Ninth Regional Meeting of the Chicago Linguistic Society*. Chicago: Chicago Linguistic Society.

—— (1975): *Language and Woman's Place*. New York: Harper and Row.

Lebra, T. S. (1976): *Japanese Patterns of Behaviour*. Honolulu: University of Hawaii Press.

Leech, G. (1983): *Principles of Pragmatics*. London: Longman Group.

Leet-Pellegrini, H. M. (1980): 'Conversational dominance as a function of gender and expertise.' In H. Giles, P. Robinson and P. Smith (eds), *Language: Social Psychological Perspectives*, pp. 97–104. Oxford: Pergamon Press.

Lee-Wong, S. (2000): *Cross-Cultural Communication: Politeness and Face in Chinese Culture*. Frankfurt am Main: Peter Lang.

Leichty, G. and J. L. Applegate (1991): 'Social-cognitive and situational influences on the use of face-saving persuasive strategies.' *Human Communication Research* 17 (3), pp. 451–484.

Levelt, W. J. M. (1989): *Speaking: From Intention to Articulation*. Cambridge: The MIT Press.

Liddicoat, A. J. and C. Crozet (2001): 'Acquiring French interactional norms through instruction.' In K. R. Rose and G. Kasper (eds), pp. 125–144.

Levinson, S. (1983): *Pragmatics*. Cambridge: Cambridge University Press.

Lim, T. and J. Bowers (1991): 'Facework, solidarity, approbation and tact.' *Human Communication Research* 17 (3), pp. 415–450.

Littlewood, W. (2001): 'Cultural awareness and the negotiation of meaning in intercultural communication.' *Language Awareness* 10 (2–3), pp. 189–199.

LoCastro, V. (1990): 'Intercultural pragmatics: a Japanese-American case study.' Unpublished PhD thesis, University of Lancaster.

Locher, M. A. (2004): 'Power and Politeness in Action: Disagreements in Oral Communication.' Berlin: Mouton de Gruyter.

MacFarlane, A. (1999): 'Brief interethnic exchanges and classroom language learning.' Paper presented at *Acts of the Colloquium / Actes du Colloque*, November 27th 1999, Second Language Education Centre, University of New Brunswick. Retrieved 2/2/03 from http://www.unb.ca/slec/Events/Actes/MacFarlane.html

Maeshiba, N., N. Yoshinaga, G. Kasper and S. Ross (1996): 'Transfer and proficiency in interlanguage apologising.' In S. Gass and J. Neu (eds), pp. 155–187.

Malinowski, B. (1923): 'The problem of meaning in primitive languages.' In Ogden and Richards (eds), *The Meaning of Meaning*, pp. 451–510. London: Routledge and Kegan Paul.

Manes, J. and N. Wolfson (1981): 'The compliment formula.' In F. Coulmas (ed), *Conversational Routine*. The Hague: Mouton de Gruyter.

Mao, L. R. (1994): 'Beyond politeness theory: "Face" revisited and renewed.' *Journal of Pragmatics* 21, pp. 451–486.

Markus, H. R. and S. Kitayama (1991): 'Culture and the self: implications for cognition, emotion and motivation.' *Psychological Review* 98, pp. 224–253.

Marriott, H. and S. Enomoto (1995): 'Secondary exchanges with Japan: exploring students' experiences and gains.' *Australian Review of Applied Linguistics (Series S)* 12, pp. 64–82.

Matsumoto, Y. (1988): 'Re-examination of the universality of face: politeness phenomena in Japan.' *Journal of Pragmatics* 12, pp. 403–426.

—— (1989): 'Politeness and conversational universals – observations from Japanese.' *Multilingua* 8, pp. 207–221.

Matsumura, S. (2001): 'Learning the rules for offering advice: a quantitative approach to second language socialisation.' *Language Learning* 51 (4), pp. 635–679.

McLaughlin, B. (1990): 'Restructuring.' *Applied Linguistics* 11, pp. 113–128.

——, T. Rossman and B. McLeod (1983): 'Second language learning: an information-processing perspective.' *Language Learning* 33, pp. 135–158.

—— and R. Heredia (1996): 'Information-processing approaches to research on second language acquisition and use.' In W. C. Ritchie and T. C. Bhatia (eds).

Mori, J. (1994): 'Functions of the connective *datte* in Japanese conversation.' In N. Akatsuka (ed), *Japanese Korean Linguistics* 4, pp. 77–94. Stanford: CSLI Publications.

—— (1995): 'Interactional functions of *kedo* clauses in Japanese conversation.' Paper presented at the Annual Conference of the American Association for Applied Linguistics, Long Beach, California.

—— (1996): 'Historical change of Japanese connective *datte*: its form and functions.' In N. Akatsuka, S. Iwasaki and S. Strauss (eds), *Japanese Korean Linguistics* 5, pp. 208–218. Stanford: CSLI Publications.

—— (1999): *Negotiating Agreement and Disagreement in Japanese: Connective Expressions and Turn Construction.* Amsterdam: John Benjamin.

Myers, G. (1998): 'Displaying opinions: topics and disagreement in focus groups.' *Language in Society* 27, pp. 85–111.

Nakajima, Y. (1997): 'Politeness strategies in the workplace: which experiences help Japanese businessmen acquire American English native-like strategies?' *Working Papers in Educational Linguistics* 13 (1), pp. 49–69.

Nakane, C. (1972): *Tekio no Joken [Conditions of Adjustments].* Tokyo: Kodansha.

Nation, I. S. P. (1996): *Vocabulary Lists.* Victoria University of Wellington, English Language Institute.

Ng, S. H. and J. J. Bradac (1993): *Power in Language: Verbal Communication and Social Influence.* Newbury Park: Sage Publications.

Ochs, E. (1986): 'Introduction.' In B. B. Schieffelin and E. Ochs (eds), *Language Socialization Across Cultures,* pp. 1–13. New York: Cambridge University Press.

—— (1996): 'Linguistic resources for socialising humanity.' In J. J. Gumperz and S. L. Levinson (eds), *Rethinking Linguistic Relativity*, pp. 407–437. Cambridge: Cambridge University Press.

Ohta, A. S. (1995): 'Applying sociocultural theory to an analysis of learner discourse: learner–learner collaborative interaction in the zone of proximal development.' *Issues in Applied Linguistics* 6, pp. 93–121.

—— (2001): 'A longitudinal study of the development of expression of alignment in Japanese as a foreign language.' In K. Rose and G. Kasper (eds), *Pragmatics in Language Teaching*, pp. 103–120. New York: Cambridge University Press.

Olshtain, E. (1989): 'Apologies across languages.' In S. Blum-Kulka, J. House and G. Kasper (eds), pp. 155–173.

—— and S. Blum-Kulka (1985): 'Degree of approximation: nonnative reaction to native speech act behaviour.' In S. Gass and C. G. Madden (eds), *Input and Second Language Acquisition*, pp. 303–325. Rowley, MA: Newbury House.

—— and L. Weinbach (1993): 'Interlanguage features of the speech act of complaining.' In G. Kasper and S. Blum-Kulka (eds), pp. 108–122.

O'Malley, J.M. and A. U. Chamot (1999): *Learning Strategies in Second Language Acquisition*. Cambridge: CUP.

Planken, B. (1997): A review of Gass, S and J. Neu (eds) (1996). *The Clarion*, 3 (2), pp. 10–15.

Pomerantz, A. (1984): 'Agreeing and disagreeing with assessments: some features of preferred / dispreferred turn shapes.' In J. M. Atkinson and J. Heritage (eds), pp. 57–101.

Ranney, S. (1992): 'Learning a new script: An exploration of sociolinguistic competence.' *Applied Linguistics* 13, pp. 25–50.

Rees-Miller, J. (2000): 'Power, severity and context in disagreement.' *Journal of Pragmatics* 32, pp. 1087–1111.

Rehbein, J. (1987): 'Multiple formulae: Aspects of migrant Turkish workers' German in intercultural communication.' In K. Knapp et al (eds), *Analysing Intercultural Communication*, pp. 215–248. Berlin: Mouton de Gruyter.

Riley, P. (1989): 'Well don't blame me! On the interpretation of pragmatic errors.' In W. Olesky (ed.) *Contrastive Pragmatics,* pp. 231–249. Amsterdam: John Benjamins.

Rintell, E. M. and C. J. Mitchell (1989): 'Studying requests and apologies: An enquiry into method.' In S. Blum-Kulka, J. House and G. Kasper (eds), pp. 248–272.

Robinson, G. L. (1988): *Cross-Cultural Understanding.* New York: Prentice Hall.

Robinson, M. A. (1992): 'Introspective methodology in interlanguage pragmatics research.' In G. Kasper (ed.), *Pragmatics of Japanese as Native and Target Language.* Honolulu: University of Hawaii Press.

Rose, K. R. and G. Kasper (eds) (2001): *Pragmatics in Language Teaching.* Cambridge: Cambridge University Press.

—— and C. Ng Kwai-fun (2001): 'Inductive and deductive teaching of compliments and compliment responses.' In K. R. Rose and G. Kasper (eds), pp. 145–170.

Sacks, H. (1987): 'On the preferences for agreement and contiguity in sequences in conversation.' In G. Button and J. R. E. Lee (eds), *Talk and Social Organisation,* pp. 54–69. Cleveland: Multilingual Matters.

Salsbury, T. and K. Bardovi-Harlig (2000): 'Oppositional talk and the acquisition of modality in L2 English.' In B. Swierzbin et al (eds), *Social and Cognitive Factors in Second Language Acquisition,* pp. 57–76. Somerville, MA: Cascadilla Press.

Salzmann, A. (1989): 'Oh, darn! I'd love to come, but I already have plans: Television invitations as conversation models.' *Issues and Developments in English and Applied Linguistics* 4, pp. 157–186.

Sarangi, S. K. and S. Slembrouck (1992): 'Non-cooperation in communication: A reassessment of Gricean pragmatics.' *Journal of Pragmatics* 17, pp. 117–154.

Schiffrin, D. (1984): 'Jewish argument as sociability.' *Language in Society* 13, pp. 311–335.

—— (1985): 'Everyday argument: The organisation of diversity in talk.' In T. van Dijk (ed), *Handbook of Discourse Analysis vol 3: Discussion and Dialogue,* pp. 35–46. London: Academic Press.

Schmidt, R. W. (1983): 'Interaction, acculturation and the acquisition of communicative competence.' In N. Wolfson and E. Judd (eds), *Sociolinguistics and Second Language Acquisition,* pp. 137–174. Rowley, MA: Newbury House.

—— (1993): 'Consciousness, learning and interlanguage pragmatics.' In G. Kasper and S. Blum-Kulka (eds), pp. 21–42.

Schraw, G., W. Trathen, R. E. Reynolds and R. T. Lapan (1988): 'Preferences for idioms: Restrictions due to lexicalisation and familiarity.' *Journal of Psycholinguistic Research.*

Schwebel, D. C. (1997): 'Strategies of verbal duelling: how college students win a verbal battle.' *Journal of Language and Social Psychology* 16, pp. 326–343.

Scollon, R. and S. W. Scollon (1995): *Intercultural Communication.* Oxford: Blackwell.

Scott, S. (1998): *Patterns of Language Use in Adult Face-to-Face Disagreements.* Unpublished PhD thesis, Northern Arizona University.

—— (2002): 'Linguistic feature variation within disagreements.' *Text,* 22 (2): pp 301–328.

Searle, J. R. (1969): *Speech Acts: An essay in the Philosophy of Language.* Cambridge: Cambridge University Press.

—— (1972): 'What is a speech act?' In P. P. Giglioli (ed), *Language and Social Context,* pp. 136–154. Harmondsworth: Penguin Publishing.

—— (1975): 'Indirect speech acts.' In P. Cole and J. Morgan (eds), *Syntax and Semantics 3: Speech Acts,* pp. 59–82. New York: Academic Press.

Selinker, L. (1972): 'Interlanguage.' *International Review of Applied Linguistics* 10, pp. 209–230.

Shea, D. P. (1994): 'Perspective and production: Structuring conversational participation across cultural borders.' *Pragmatics* 4 (3), pp. 357–389.

Sifianou, M. (1992): *Politeness Phenomena in England and Greece: A Cross-Cultural Perspective.* Oxford: Clarendon Press.

Skehan, P. (1998): *A Cognitive Approach to Language Learning.* Oxford: Oxford University Press.

Slugoski, B. and W. Turnbull (1988): 'Cruel to be kind and kind to be cruel: Sarcasm, banter and social relations.' *Journal of Language and Social Psychology* 7 (2), pp. 101–121.

Sornig, K. (1977): 'Disagreement and contradiction as communicative acts.' *Journal of Pragmatics* 1, pp. 347–374.

Spencer-Oatey, H. D. M. (1996): 'Reconsidering power and distance.' *Journal of Pragmatics* 26, pp. 1–24.

—— (ed) (2000): *Culturally Speaking: Managing Rapport Through Talk Across Cultures.* London: Continuum.

Sperber, D. (1996): *Explaining Culture: A Naturalistic Approach.* Oxford: Blackwell.

Stalpers, J. (1995): 'The expression of disagreement.' In K. Ehlich and J. Wagner (eds), *The Discourse of Business Negotiation.* Berlin: Mouton de Gruyter.

Stenson, N. (1974): 'Induced errors.' In J. Schumann and N. Stenson (eds), *New Frontiers of Second Language Learning,* pp. 54–70. Rowley, MA: Newbury House.

Swain, M. and S. Lapkin (1998): 'Interaction and second language learning: two adolescent French immersion students working together.' *Modern Language Journal* 82, pp. 320–337.

Sweller, J. (1988): 'Cognitive load during problem solving: Effects on learning.' *Cognitive Science* 12, pp. 257–285

Takagi, T. (1997): 'What "questions" do in argument talk in Japanese.' Paper presented at Ethnomethodology and Conversation Analysis: East and West, Tokyo, Japan.

Takahashi, S. (1996): 'Pragmatic transferability.' *Studies in Second Language Acquisition* 18, pp. 189–223.

—— (2001): 'The role of input enhancement in developing pragmatic competence.' In K. R. Rose and G. Kasper (eds), pp. 171–199.

—— and H. L. Roitblat (1994): 'Comprehension process of second language indirect requests.' *Applied Psycholinguistics* 15, pp. 475–506.

Takahashi, T. and L. Beebe (1987): 'Development of pragmatic competence by Japanese learners of English.' *Journal of the Japan Association of Language Teachers* 8 (2), pp. 131–155.

Tanaka, K. (1997): 'Language learning experiences of Japanese students in Auckland.' *The TESOLANZ Journal* 5, pp. 37–49.

Tanaka, S. and S. Kawade (1982): 'Politeness strategies and second language acquisition.' *Studies in Second Language Acquisition* 5 (1), pp. 18–33.

Tannen, D. (1994): *Talking From 9 to 5: How Women's and Men's Conversational Styles Affect Who Gets Heard, Who Gets Credit, and What Gets Done at Work.* London: Virago.

—— and C. Kakava (1992): 'Power and solidarity in modern Greek conversation: agreeing to disagree.' *Journal of Modern Greek Studies* 10 (1), pp. 11–34.

Tarone, E. (2005): 'English for specific purposes and interlanguage pragmatics.' In K. Bardovi-Harlig and B. Hartford (eds), pp. 157–169.

Tateyama, Y. (2001): 'Explicit and implicit teaching of pragmatic routines: Japanese *sumimasen.*' In K. R. Rose and G. Kasper (eds), pp. 200–222.

Thomas, J. (1983): 'Cross-cultural pragmatic failure.' *Applied Linguistics* 4, pp. 91–111.

—— (1994): 'Cooperative principle.' In R. Asher and J. Simpson (eds), *The Encyclopaedia of Language and Linguistics*, pp. 3206–3211. Oxford: Pergamon Press.

—— (1995): *Meaning in Interaction.* London: Longman Group.

Thornborrow, J. (2002): *Power Talk: Language and Interaction in Institutional Discourse.* London: Longman.

Triandis, H. C. (1986): 'Collectivism vs individualism: a reconceptualisation of a basic concept in cross-cultural psychology.' In C. Bagley and G. Verma (eds), *Personality, Cognition and Values: Cross-Cultural Perspectives of Childhood and Adolescence.* London: MacMillan.

—— (1994): *Culture and Social Behaviour.* New York: McGraw-Hill.

Trompenaars, F. (1993): *Riding the Waves of Culture: Understanding Cultural Diversity in Business.* London: Nicholas Brealey Publishing.

Trosborg, A. (1987): 'Apology strategies in natives/non-natives.' *Journal of Pragmatics* 11, pp. 147–167.

Turner, K. (1996): 'The principal principles of pragmatic inference: politeness.' *Language Teaching* 29, pp. 1–13.

Vollmer, H. and E. Olshtain (1989): 'The language of apologies in German.' In S. Blum-Kulka, J. House and G. Kasper (eds), pp. 197–217.

Walkinshaw, I. S. (2000): 'Immersion in an English-speaking culture: learning to swim in the deep end.' *IATEFL Issues* December 1999–January 2000, pp. 16–19.

—— (2006): 'Learning and rehearsing negative speech acts in language classrooms.' *Modern English Teacher,* 15:4, pp. 34–38.

Washburn, G. (2000): 'Pragmatic language use in television sitcoms.' Manuscript in preparation, New York: Syracuse University.

—— (2001): 'Using situation comedies for pragmatic language teaching and learning.' *TESOL Journal* 10 (4), pp. 21–26.

Watts, R. J. (1989): 'Relevance and relational work: linguistic politeness as politic behaviour.' *Multilingua* 8 (2-3), pp. 131–166.

—— (2005a): 'Linguistic politeness research: Quo vadis?' In R. J. Watts, S. Ide and K. Ehlich (eds), pp. xi–xlvii.

—— (2005b): 'Linguistic politeness and politic verbal behaviour: Reconsidering claims for universality.' In R. J. Watts, S. Ide and K. Ehlich (eds), pp. 43–70.

——, S. Ide, and K. Ehlich (eds) (2005): *Politeness in Language: Studies in its History, Theory and Practice* (2nd edition). Berlin: Mouton de Gruyter.

Wierzbicka, A. (1985): 'Different cultures, different languages, different speech acts.' *Journal of Pragmatics* 9, pp. 145–198.

—— (1991): *Cross-Cultural Pragmatics: The Semantics of Human Interaction.* Berlin: Mouton de Gruyter.

Wildner-Bassett, M. (1984): *Improving Pragmatic Aspects of Learners' Interlanguage.* Tubingen: Narr.

Williams, J. (2005): 'Writing centre interaction: institutional discourse and the role of peer tutors.' In K. Bardovi-Harlig and B. S. Hartford (eds), pp. 37–66.

Wolfson, N. (1983): 'Rules of speaking.' In J. C. Richards and R. Schmidt (eds), *Language and Communication*, pp. 61–89. New York: Longman.

—— (1988): 'The bulge: a theory of speech behaviour and social distance.' In J. Fine (ed), *Second Language Discourse: A Textbook of Current Research*, pp. 21–38. Norwood, N.J: Ablex Publishing.

—— L. D'Amico-Reisner, and L. Huber (1983): 'How to arrange for social commitments in American English: The invitation.' In N. Wolfson and E. Judd (eds), *Sociolinguistics and Language Acquisition*. Rowley, Mass: Newbury House.

Wood, L. A. and R. O. Kroger (1991): 'Politeness and forms of address.' *Journal of Language and Social Psychology* 10 (3), pp. 145–168.

Yamashita, S. (1996): *Comparing Six Cross-Cultural Pragmatics Measures*. Unpublished Ed.D dissertation, Temple University.

Yates, L (2005): 'Negotiating an institutional identity: individual differences in NS and NNS teacher directives.' In K. Bardovi-Harlig and B. Hartford (eds), pp. 67–97.

Yeung, L. N. T. (1997): 'Polite requests in English and Chinese business correspondence in Hong Kong.' *Journal of Pragmatics* 27, pp. 505–522.

Yoshida, T. (1994): 'Interpersonal versus non-interpersonal realities: an effective tool individualists can use to better understand collectivists.' In R. W. Brislin and T. Yoshida (eds), *Improving Intercultural Interactions: Modules for Cross-Cultural Training Programmes*, pp. 243–267. Thousand Oaks: Sage.

Yoshimi, D. R. (2001): 'Explicit instruction and JFL learners' use of interactional discourse markers.' In K. R. Rose and G. Kasper (eds), pp. 223–244.

Yu, M. (1999): 'Universalistic and culture-specific perspectives on variation in the acquisition of pragmatic competence in a second language.' *Pragmatics* 9 (2), pp. 281–312.

Yule, G. (1996): *Pragmatics*. Oxford: Oxford University Press.

Appendix 1

Judgment Task

Situation 1: Shortland Street

Shortland Street is a show about people who work in a hospital. Nick and Angela are lovers. In this scene they are talking about their friend Donna. They are living with Donna, but Angela isn't happy. She thinks Donna does not like her.

Angela:	I just get this vibe (iya na kanji) from her.
Nick:	Vibe? What kind of vibe?
Angela:	Like she really doesn't like me. Like I get on her nerves. (kanojo no ki ni sawaru)
Nick:	No, Donna's not like that. She's great.

Situation 2: Shortland Street

Sophie and Kate are talking to another woman. They don't know her very well. The woman is staying with them in their house. Sophie does not trust the woman because she will not tell them about herself. Sophie is talking to the woman about the woman's lover, who has hurt the woman. But the woman does not want to talk.

Woman:	Look, do we have to talk about him? It's over, I'm out of there, it's okay.
Sophie:	Except you still have his car. And you can't let him get away with abuse (boryoku o furuu), you should inform the police.

Situation 3: Shortland Street

Luke is a school student. He works in a coffee shop. Albert is living with Luke's family and helping in the coffee shop. In this scene, Albert's wallet is missing. He is very worried, and he thinks Luke stole the wallet.

Albert:	Hand it over (kaeshite kure)!
Luke:	Well, I haven't got it.
Albert:	Well someone has. (shouts to everyone in the coffee shop) Which one of you has robbed me, eh?

Situation 4: Shortland Street

The doctor is dating the woman. She has just told him that she is married. But she still wants to date him. He is very unhappy about dating a married woman. In this scene she has asked him to go to London with her. He doesn't want to go.

Woman:	I've got a buying trip (kaigai shutcho) coming up, and I want you to come too.
Doctor:	That's out of the question (muri da).

Situation 5: Shortland Street

Two doctors are talking. They are a similar age and they know each other, but one is a new doctor, and the other is an experienced doctor who is in charge of other doctors. They are talking about a formal dinner. The junior doctor is looking forward to the dinner, but the senior doctor is not.

Junior doctor: Hey, who knows? Dress us up and get us out of this work environment, we might even enjoy each other's company (issho ni ite tanoshimu).
Senior doctor: Maybe.
Junior doctor: Hey, might turn out to be a fun evening.
Senior doctor: Having attended more of these suit functions (seishiki na shoku-ji-kai) than I choose to remember, I seriously doubt it.

Situation 6: Holmes

Holmes is a news show. A few months ago in a New Zealand prison, two prisoners were beaten by prison guards. The two men in this programme are arguing about whether the prisoners should get money from the government because of what was done to them. One of the men is a political leader called Richard Prebble. The other man is a lawyer called Peter Williams.

Willams: You must agree that these people are entitled to compensation (bai-shokin o ukeru kenri ga aru), you agree with that?
Prebble: No, I do not agree with that.

Situation 7: Holmes

In this scene, Richard Prebble the political leader and Peter Williams the lawyer are still talking about the two prisoners who were beaten by their guards.

Willams: And remember, these are people who are in custody (keimusho ni iru), they have difficulties with communication (hito to hanasu koto), they can't run away, they were in cells (roya).
Prebble: (shakes head)
Williams: And not only were they shocked (shokku o uketa), they were shocked by the way the warders, the prison officers (keimusho no kanshi-in) lied.

275

Situation 8: Shortland Street

Nick is in the hospital, talking to a doctor. The doctor is treating his lover, Angela, who is very ill. Nick works at the hospital, so he knows the doctor.

Nick: (shouting) Angela doesn't know what she wants. You can't listen to her. You've got to ring (denwa o kakeru) me.

Doctor: Okay, we will from now on.

Situation 9: Street Legal

Two men are talking to a policeman. One man is a lawyer called David, and the other man is his friend. They are looking at a piece of paper. Someone has written on the paper in a foreign language.

Policeman: What's this?

David: That's his tag (shome), the rest is Swahili (Swahili-go).

Friend: Ah, actually (jitsu wa)…it's Greek.

Situation 10: Shortland Street

A doctor is talking to a female patient. Her head has been hurt, and her face does not look very good. The doctor and the patient do not know each other.

Patient: Can I have a mirror now?

Doctor: I don't think that's a very good idea. Your face is still very swollen (fukurande iru).

Situation 11: Holmes

A woman from the Holmes show is talking to the Prime Minister of New Zealand. They are talking about a recent meeting between people from businesses and people from the government. The Prime Minister is talking about the meeting on the Holmes show because she wants people to hear the ideas from the meeting. The Prime Minister and the woman do not know each other very well.

Prime Minister: The important thing, firstly, is that the dialogue (taiwa) happened and that many people came. Everyone who could come did come. Secondly, I think there was a huge desire...

Woman: No no no no no no no. Some people weren't invited.

Situation 12: You've Gotta Have It

Two women are in a fashion shop. One woman, called Nicky, knows a lot about fashion, and she is working on the TV programme. She is choosing clothes for the other woman, Shelly. Shelly is a singer looking for clothes that will make her look nicer when she is performing. Shelly and Nicky have not met each other before.

Shelly: (trying on white leather belt) Aw, yeah!
Nicky: Screams 80s (80-nen-dai rashii). Oh, that's scary (shumi ga warui)!
Shelly: (singing) I'm your Venus...
Nicky: Um, I think no.
Shelly: You don't?
Nicky: I mean, it's up to you (anata shidai desu) of course.

277

Situation 13: Street Legal

In this scene, a male lawyer called David and a female lawyer called Joanie are talking. They kissed each other recently, but they are not married or in a relationship. Also, they work for the same company, so they have to work together. Joanie is telling David that the kiss was not important to her.

Joanie:	I mean it was, um, a supportive hug (dakishimeru).
David:	(looks away from Joanie, at the ground)
Joanie:	Between friends (tomodachi doshi)
David:	Yeah, Joanie. If you say so. That's all it was.

Situation 14: Street Legal

A woman called Adriana is in a hotel. She wants to speak to a woman who is staying at the hotel. But the hotel worker cannot find the woman's name on the computer. Adriana and the hotel worker do not know each other.

Adriana:	Look, could I leave a message in case you've made a…in case she calls in?
Hotel worker:	Certainly.
Adriana:	Can you tell her that Adriana Saunders called?
Hotel worker:	Excuse me?
Adriana:	Adriana. A-D-R…
Hotel worker:	Yes, Ma'am. I can spell the name.

Situation 15: Shortland Street

Two friends, Shelly and Bianca, are in Shelly's bedroom. Bianca likes one of Shelly's shirts. She wants to borrow it. But Shelly doesn't want to lend it to her.

Bianca: Can I borrow it please?
Shelly: Er, no.
Bianca: Why not?
Shelly: It's new. I've only worn it once.

Situation 16: Shortland Street

A senior (experienced) nurse is talking to a senior doctor. They have been talking to a junior (new) doctor who has done something wrong. The junior doctor has just left and the senior nurse and the senior doctor are talking together. They have only known each other for a few days.

Senior doctor: I'll speak to the other doctors, they won't pull a stunt (baka na koto o suru) like this again.
Senior nurse: If they did, you'd be the last to know.
Senior doctor: Sorry?

Situation 17: Shortland Street

A woman is talking to a doctor. They know each other well, but the woman is not a doctor. She thinks that another doctor, called Victor, stole some money from the hospital. The doctor does not think so. He tells her the problem is over.

Woman: You doctors are all the same. What's he done, promised you a percentage (wakemae) next time?
Doctor: You know, for your information, Victor didn't pocket (nusumu) that money.
Woman: Yeah, right.

Situation 18: Street Legal

David is a lawyer. He is speaking to a policeman. David believes that some people tried to kill David's brother because they thought his brother was hiding stolen car parts with a man called Kimble. But the policeman does not think so. He wants David to go away. The policeman and David know each other quite well, because they have worked together many times before.

Policeman: Those stolen car parts (nusumareta kuruma no buhin) have got nothing to do with Kimble and whatever problems he's got.
David: That's a lie (uso).

Appendix 2

Discourse Completion Task

Situation 1

You are driving your car out of the car park at the Polytechnic. Another car is driving close behind you. Suddenly a cat runs in front of your car! You stop the car quickly. BANG! The car behind you (ushiro ni) hits the back of your car. You are both okay, but the other car has a broken light. The driver is a 50-year-old teacher, but you don't know his name. You know the accident (jiko) isn't your fault, but the teacher thinks it is, and he may want you to pay for his car. You have no money! The teacher says: 'Look what you've done to my car! Why did you stop like that? This is your fault.'

You say:

_____

_____

_____

How serious is this situation for you (not the teacher)? Circle one:
         1: Not very serious
         2: Quite serious
         3: Very serious

Situation 2

You are in a coffee shop. You are talking to two people from Polytechnic, Tom and Rick. Tom is a friend, but you have never met Rick before. Your friend Tom says that he wants to take a writing class because he is not very good at writing essays (sakubun). Rick laughs at Tom and says: 'Only stupid people need to do those classes.' (He turns to you) 'Don't you think so?' You have heard that the class is very good.

You say (to Rick):

_____

_____

_____

How serious is this situation for you (not Rick or Tom)? Circle one:
        1: Not very serious
        2: Quite serious
        3: Very serious

Situation 3

You are in the computer room at the Polytechnic. You are using a computer to design a poster (posuta). You have to give the poster to your teacher by 5pm today. You are very late! A technician (gijutsu-sha) is helping you. She works with all the computers in the room, and she knows a lot about them. You know the technician well, and you are friendly with her. You say you want to print the poster in colour. But she says 'No, we can't print in colour. We can only print in black and white.' You know that you CAN print in colour, because you have done it before - three or four times! But you can't remember how to do it, and you need her help.

You say:

_____

_____

_____

How serious is this situation for you (not the technician)? Circle one:
    1: Not very serious
    2: Quite serious
    3: Very serious

Situation 4

You are in town with your friend, who is a student. You walk past a shop that sells second-hand (chuko) furniture. Your friend sees a big, purple and pink sofa (nagaisu) in the window. 'Oh, that's nice,' she says. You look at the sofa. You do not like it at all. If you tell her you don't like it, she may be a little upset that you disagree with her opinion. Your friend says: 'Pink and purple are good colours. Don't you think it's beautiful?'

You say:

_____

_____

_____

How serious is this situation for you (not your friend)? Circle one:
    1: Not very serious
    2: Quite serious
    3: Very serious

Situation 5

You are in a car with the head teacher (gakubucho) of the English school. He is driving to the airport to meet another student. You don't know the head teacher very well, because he is new at his job. He doesn't know Christchurch very well. As you drive up to a traffic light (shingo) he says, 'I think we should turn right here.' You know where the airport is. You know that he should turn left, not right. If he turns right, you will be five minutes late meeting the student.

You say:

_____

_____

_____

How serious is this situation for you (not the head teacher or the other student)? Circle one:
         1: Not very serious
         2: Quite serious
         3: Very serious

Situation 6

You are walking along a footpath (hodo), carrying a small computer in a bag. The footpath is for people walking and people on bicycles. A young woman is cycling toward you on the footpath. You have never seen her before. You step aside to get out of her way, but the woman's bicycle handle catches your computer bag. You drop your computer, and it breaks. You need your computer and you don't have any money to get it fixed. But the young woman says: 'That's your own fault. You know there are bicycles on this path. You should have got out of the way!'

You say:

_____

_____

_____

How serious is this situation for you (not the young woman)? Circle
one:
        1: Not very serious
        2: Quite serious
        3: Very serious

Situation 7

You have a meeting at 4pm with your teacher. You have known him
for a long time and you are friendly with him. You know the meeting
was at 4pm because he sent you a note. The note said 'Let's meet at 4
o'clock at my office'. So, at 4 o'clock you go to his office. But when
you arrive your teacher looks a little angry. He says: 'You're late. I
told you to come here at 3 o'clock.' He probably won't be angry for a
long time. But he made the mistake, not you!

You say:

_____

_____

_____

How serious is this situation for you (not the teacher)? Circle one:
        1: Not very serious
        2: Quite serious
        3: Very serious

Situation 8:

You are living in a flat (apato) with your New Zealand friend. You and your friend are making a chocolate cake for a big party at your flat tonight. Your friend says to you 'I think you should put some brandy (sweet alcohol) in the cake mix.' You think brandy will make the cake taste bad. Also, some people might not like alcohol in their food!

You say:

_____

_____

_____

How serious is this situation for you (not your friend)? Circle one:
       1: Not very serious
       2: Quite serious
       3: Very serious

Appendix 3

Role Play Scenarios

Role Play 1:

Native Speaker of English:
You are an English teacher. The other person is a Japanese student from your school. You do not know him/her very well. You are riding on a bus together. You are both going to a party in Riccarton. You are not sure where you should get off the bus! You reach the shopping centre at Riccarton. You think the party is near here. You tell the student that you want to get off the bus.

Japanese Learner of English:
You are a Japanese student of English. The other person is an English teacher from your school. You do not know him very well. You are both going to a party. You are riding on the bus together. You know where the party is. It takes about five minutes on the bus to get there after you pass the shopping centre at Riccarton. The teacher wants to get off the bus at the shopping centre. You want to stay on the bus for five more minutes.

Role-Play 2:

Native Speaker of English:
You are the mother/father of a New Zealand family. The other person is a young Japanese student is who staying at your house for a year. You know him/her well. Right now you are in a department store with the student. You are buying curtains for his/her room. You want to buy dark green curtains, because the walls in his/her room are also a dark colour.

Japanese Learner of English:
You are a Japanese student, staying with a New Zealand family for one year. The other person is your New Zealand host father/mother. You know him/her well. Right now you are in a department store with your host father/mother. S/he is buying curtains for your room. Your room has a lot of dark colours in it, so you want light, coloured curtains to make the room look bright. But your host father/mother wants dark, dull, boring colours! What can you say?

Role-Play 3:

Native Speaker of English:
You are a New Zealand university student. The other person is a Japanese student of English. You don't know him/her at all. You are a member of the international students' club. You are making a big paper poster with the other student, and you plan to hang it outside to advertise your club. You have a good photo for the poster, and you show it to the other student. You tell him/her that you think it will look good on the poster.

Japanese Learner of English:
You are a Japanese student, studying English at university. The other person is a New Zealand university student. You don't know him/her at all. You are in the international students' club at university. You are making a big paper poster (posuta) with the other student, to advertise your club. Your partner shows you a photo. S/he wants to put it on the poster. You do not like it, because it's very dark and there are not many colours. You don't want to put it on the poster.

Role-Play 4:

Native Speaker of English:
You are a New Zealand university student. The other person is a Japanese student of English who is living at your flat. You are good friends. Right now it is winter, and the flat is cold. You are going out together for the evening. You want to have the heater on in the flat so that it will be warm when you come back.

Japanese Learner of English:
You are a Japanese person living in New Zealand and studying English. The other person is a New Zealand university student. You live in the same flat (apato) together. You are good friends. It's winter now, and your flat is cold. You are going out together for the evening. Your friend wants to have the heater on so that the flat will be warm when you come back. But you want to turn the heater off - it's a waste of money to have it on when the flat is empty. It's dangerous too.

Role-Play 5:

Native Speaker of English:
You are a worker in a coffee shop. The other person is a Japanese customer. You do not know him/her. The person comes to your cash register with coffee and a cake. You tell him/her that the coffee and cake are $4.50. The person gives you some money, and you put it in the register. You give him/her 50 cents in change. Then s/he says that s/he gave you ten dollars, so you should give him/her more change. You think s/he only gave you five dollars.

Japanese learner of English:
You are a Japanese student in New Zealand. You are in a coffee shop. The other person is a New Zealander who is working at the cash register (reji). You do not know him/her. You buy coffee and a cake. The person at the cash register says the coffee and cake cost $4.50. You give the person ten dollars. S/he should give you $5.50 in change. But s/he only gives you fifty cents! S/he thinks you only gave him/her five dollars! So you tell him/her that you gave ten dollars, and s/he should give you more change (o-tsuri).

Role-Play 6:

Native speaker of English:
You are a student at Polytechnic. The other person is a Japanese person studying English in New Zealand. You are friends. You are at your home with your friend. You are listening to a music CD. The CD is from a band called Smash. You like this music very much. You tell your friend how much you like Smash.

Japanese learner of English:
You are a Japanese person studying English in New Zealand. The other person is a New Zealand student, studying at Polytechnic. You are friends. You are at your friend's home. You are both listening to a CD of a band called Smash. You don't like the music at all. You think it is loud and boring. You like classical music much more. But your friend really likes Smash! What will you say?

Appendix 4

Personal Information Form

1. What is your nationality? _____
2. What is your first language? _____
3. How old are you? (please circle)
       17–22 23–27 28–35 36–50 51+
4. Are you male or female? (please circle)
       Male Female
5. What is your occupation? _____
6. How long have you studied English? _____
7. Have you ever studied any other languages? If so, what languages have you studied? _____
8. Have you ever spent time in a country (apart from New Zealand) where English is the main language?
       Yes No

If you answered 'yes', please answer questions a, b, c and d. If you answered 'no', please go on to question 9.

    a) Which country were you in? _____
    b) How long were you there? _____
    c) Did you live with a host family?
    Yes No
    If not, who did you live with? _____
    d) Did you attend an English language school?
    Yes No

9. Have you studied in New Zealand before?
       Yes No

If so, how long were you in New Zealand? _____
10. How long have you been studying in New Zealand this time?

_____

11. Please circle what you think your English ability is.
Elementary   Lower-intermediate   Intermediate
Upper-intermediate   Advanced
12. If you have scores from English language tests (such as TOEIC, TOEFL, IELTS etc), please write them here. _____

Index

295

297

CONTEMPORARY STUDIES IN DESCRIPTIVE LINGUISTICS

Edited by

DR GRAEME DAVIS, lecturer in the History of the English Language at the Open University, UK, and

KARL A. BERNHARDT, English Language Consultant with Trinity College London and for the London Chamber of Commerce and Industry International Qualification.

This series provides an outlet for academic monographs which offer a recent and original contribution to linguistics and which are within the descriptive tradition.

While the monographs demonstrate their debt to contemporary linguistic thought, the series does not impose limitations in terms of methodology or genre, and does not support a particular linguistic school. Rather the series welcomes new and innovative research that contributes to furthering the understanding of the description of language.

The topics of the monographs are scholarly and represent the cutting edge for their particular fields, but are also accessible to researchers outside the specific disciplines.

Vol. 1   Mark Garner: Language: An Ecological View.
          260 pages, 2004.
          ISBN 3-03910-054-8 / US-ISBN 0-8204-6295-0

Vol. 2   T. Nyan: Meanings at the Text Level: A Co-Evolutionary Approach.
          194 pages, 2004.
          ISBN 3-03910-250-8 / US-ISBN 0-8204-7179-8

Vol. 24   Ian Walkinshaw: Learning Politeness: Disagreement in a
        Second Language.
        297 pages, 2009.
        ISBN 978-3-03911-527-3